THE SUNNY HOURS

Rosemarie Dalheim

Pen Press

First published in Great Britain by Indepenpress

All paper used in the printing of this book has been made from
wood grown in managed, sustainable forests.

ISBN13: 978-1-78003-123-1

Printed and bound in the UK

Indepenpress Publishing Limited
25 Eastern Place
Brighton
BN2 1GJ

A catalogue record of this book is available from
the British Library

Cover design by Jacqueline Abromeit

May memory, like the sundial,

mark naught but sunny hours

CONTENTS

1. FOREIGNER

Outside, the hot sun shone on the houses and pavement opposite the little private school in Marlborough Avenue in the Yorkshire city of Hull. Inside, it was cool and shady in the upstairs classroom where the end of term exams were in progress. My desk stood by the window, and as usual, my eyes were more on the outside world than on my work. A clatter from the desk across the aisle diverted my attention. Betty, my best friend, had dropped her ruler. It sounded like a thunderclap in the quiet room. Exams were always conducted in a hushed, awe-inspiring silence, broken only by the scratching of pens and the rustling of paper. Trust Betty! I looked at her as she bent to pick up the offending article, her face scarlet, blue eyes twinkling, corn-coloured hair falling about her face. Betty was bold and daring, cheeky and loveable, the exact opposite of me. My hair was dark and straight, my eyes brown, my face pale and my character timid and retiring. Before she straightened up, Betty grimaced comically at me. I smiled back and felt a terrible urge to giggle, all the more because of the fearful silence around us. "Rosemarie, get on with your work!" Miss Winifred's voice cut icily into the silence. I looked up and saw her eyes fixed disapprovingly on the pair of us. Now it was my turn to blush. It was always like that, I thought. Betty got off scot free and I was the one who was blamed.

I stared at the exam paper pretending to be thinking hard. Surreptitiously, I glanced at my watch - only half an hour to go. I'd better finish the exam. It was Geography and, being a favourite lesson, presented no problems. 'What are the Capital cities of the following countries?' the question read. That was easy; London was England's, Paris for France and Berlin was the capital of Germany. Off I was again, in the land of daydreams - Berlin, where I'd been lots of times. It was where Tante Agnes, Tante Hanny and my cousin Konrad lived. I thought of them all, the fun we had with Konrad, the spoiling and indulging from Tante Hanny. Dear lovely Berlin! I felt Miss Winifred's eyes on me again and hastily looked at the next question. A small sketch-map of the British Isles was depicted on the paper - name the islands on the above map. Another easy one! That was the Isle of Wight at the bottom near the white cliffs of Dover. Up there were the Orkneys and Shetlands, but which were which? I guessed. That little one on its own was the Fair Isle, where they made fancy jumpers, Anglesey was near Wales, and that little shape in the sea between England and Ireland was the Isle of Man. They had cats without tails. Funny name for an island, didn't they have women there? That was the last question. I blotted my paper, read it through and put down my pen. Miss Winifred was tidying up her desk. Betty was still frantically scratching away. Outside, shrill voices borne on the summer air announced the fact that the younger children, who didn't do exams, were already leaving. I saw them spill into the street in their fresh green blazers and cream Panama hats with dark green hat-bands proclaiming the school motto 'Esse Quam Videre.'

"Put down your pens" commanded Miss Winifred, and those who hadn't already finished did so, promptly.

"Pass your papers to the front." It was only a small class of a dozen or so pupils and the papers were soon collected by the monitor and placed on Miss Winifred's desk.

"You may go now," said Miss Winifred. Released from the silent room, we collected our blazers and hats from the little cloakroom and clattered down the stairs. The big kindergarten room opened off to the right of the stairs. This was presided over by the kind, motherly Miss Freeman, whom everyone loved. I ran in, while Betty waited in the hallway, and there was my young sister, Anita, sitting on a small chair, patiently waiting to be collected. She jumped up, called out a shrill "Good morning Miss, Freeman" and

2

together we joined Betty and ran thankfully out into the tree-lined avenue. Free at last!

There was no need to hurry home as it was only a short walk down the local shopping street and, taking off our blazers, we dawdled home as was our wont. The sun was hotter than ever - we wore our summer uniforms of green cotton tunics and short-sleeved white cotton blouses. I was thinking of the little toy shop we were soon to pass, one of the highlights of the daily journeys to and from school.

"Wasn't the exam crude?" said Betty, breaking into my thoughts of toy dogs and painting books. 'Crude' was Betty's latest word, she used it indiscriminately to describe anything and everything.

"Mmm yes," I said. It wouldn't have been fair to say it had been easy or boast that I had finished it early while Betty was still struggling with the answers. It just wasn't done.

"Could you do the one about capitals?" Betty went on.

"I bet I got them all wrong," I said modestly.

"I only knew London," said Betty, "what's the capital of Germany anyway?"

Immediately I felt on the defensive, for some reason the mention of Germany always made me feel guilty.

"Berlin I think," I murmured, trying to sound doubtful and unsure.

"Oo, heck, so it is," said Betty, "I put Oslo." I tried not to look smug and self-satisfied, but Betty hadn't finished with me yet!

"Anyway," she said, "you're German." Crushed, I subsided; there was no answer to that one. It was Betty's trump card, to be flung down victoriously whenever she felt I had got the better of her. Betty so triumphantly English and I so shamefully German! Although we were best friends she never allowed me to forget my true nationality.

"Train!" shrieked Anita and everything was forgotten - exams, nationalities, and toy shops - as we raced towards the level crossing. Anita had heard the bell preceding the closing of the gates before we had. In those days the trains to the seaside used to come puffing down the small branch line, holding up traffic at regular intervals - a pleasant and welcome diversion on our daily walks to school. We chased Anita to the crossing, the gates of which had already clanged shut. Our favourite policeman, named by Betty 'Bobby Beetroot,' because of his highly coloured face, was on point duty and waiting to see us across the road. No time for more than a quick "Hello," as we rushed past him, hell-bent for leather, and up onto the little bridge that spanned the railway line. It was intended for pedestrians, but cyclists carrying their machines easily and expertly used it too. Our aim however, was not to get to the other side. We didn't live there We were only interested in gaining the centre where we could stand and watch the train passing beneath us, dramatically engulfing us in a cloud of black, delicious, choking smoke. We made it in time and gazed down ecstatically. The train stopped at the little station, Botanic Gardens, and picked up a handful of passengers who, we were convinced, were going to the seaside. How we envied them.

"I wish I could go," said Betty wistfully. "Think how nice it would be to go paddling today." We agreed, and turned to go back down the steps. Since that time, they have taken the line up to the sea; the little station with its tiny booking office and the small waiting room has gone now. So too has that little bridge. Nowadays people go to the sea by car, or take the bus. It can never recapture the magic of our little station, and the train coming round the curve and under the bridge. But the days of progress and economies on the railways were still far away in those sunny, pre-war days. The little train would still go puffing merrily to the sea for a further quarter of a century. Such things never entered our heads; everything around us was permanent and safe.

We ran back down the steps. The gates had opened again and Bobby Beetroot was too busy directing three streams of traffic to even glance our way. Not far to go home now, left down a short tree-lined avenue, across the road and turn right. There we were in Sunny Bank, a long row of large Edwardian houses basking serenely in the sunshine, and opposite them the lovely, overgrown, wooded grounds of Hymers College, our favourite playground.

Our house, number ten, was one of the first, and distinguishable only from the others by a porch with stained glass windows. Betty didn't have a porch – to me it was a small status symbol! Because of the heat of the day, the front door stood wide open with a glimpse of the cool hall inside. We still had iron railings around the front gardens in those days and our gate was lovely to swing on. Talking to Betty and swinging on the gate, I was suddenly aware of a movement in the hall. 'Oh no,' I prayed silently, 'not Marta,' then, 'don't let her come to the door.' Hastily I jumped down and ran towards the house. Too late! Marta, our German maid, was already in the porch and a stream of German words floated out into the quiet, midday English air. Horrified, I hurried in, hoping Betty hadn't heard, or at least was out of earshot. But, at the door I turned and saw Betty standing at the gate, her eyes round and staring.

"Ooo," she said, grinning hugely, "how crude," then skipped off to her home further down the road.

Once inside the house though, it didn't matter anymore about being German; this was where I belonged. Marta urged us to wash our hands and put on our pinafores, as lunch was waiting to be served. Anita flung her Panama hat onto the newel post where it sat rakishly over the featureless mahogany face. All the year round this newel wore the appropriate seasonal headgear; straw hats or Panamas in summer, woolly caps or velour hats in autumn or winter. Sometimes, even a scarf would be draped round it for good measure. Anita having beaten me to the newel post, I hung my hat and blazer more decorously on the oak hallstand where a Grammar School blazer and cap proclaimed the fact that our brother, Eberhard, was already home.

Marta bustled off into the kitchen, which lay in the back regions, telling us off for being late. We rummaged in the drawer that held our pinafores and cheekily answered her back in German. Marta had not been in England long and her knowledge of English was fearfully limited. She had been taught to say, "Nothing today, thank you," when she answered the door to anyone who wasn't the milkman, the window cleaner, the postman or other legitimate caller. She had simplified this to "Nozzingzanksay," which caused us much embarrassed amusement as we listened, giggling, from the top of the stairs, or the dark recess of the so called gas cupboard. Now, hands washed, and school uniforms covered by pinnies (mine green with coloured embroidery and Anita's white on blue) we went into the dining room.

Mama, Papa, and Eberhard were already seated at the large table. The room faced north and even on sunny days was cool and dark. The French windows stood open onto an equally shady small courtyard fringed with ferns and London Pride. Beyond lay the garden with its neat borders, shrubs and lawn, hot, sunny and inviting.

There would be time to go and play there before afternoon school. We climbed onto our chairs and Mama rang an electric bell which sounded in the back regions, where, in a glass-fronted, wall-mounted box, a little flag waved frantically. It announced 'dining room', and Marta, who had been awaiting this signal, entered bearing large tureens which she set on the table. A waft came out of one of them – oh no, I thought, not sauerkraut! But sauerkraut it was and there was no getting away from it. Betty, I thought, will be eating nice normal food, like meat, potatoes, and peas. It was a good thing she couldn't see the stuff we had to eat. She would definitely have called it "Crude!" So, while Eberhard and Anita tucked into their sauerkraut like good little Germans, I picked at mine and pushed it around on my plate. Papa, seeing me struggling with my plateful, made the remark he made without fail, whenever we didn't like a particular food set before us. "Be glad that there isn't a war on and you were interned. Then you'd be so hungry you'd eat anything and it would not be even half as nice as this." I

6

sighed; I knew all about being interned. Papa had been interned in the 1914-1918 war. It was something that happened to German men who lived in England. Papa was wont to say with a kind of proud finality, "If ever there is another war, I shall be interned immediately." It made him sound different, and rather important.

"Tell the story of the maggots," I begged. I had heard it a hundred times already, but now, though hardly a mealtime topic, it would be a diversion and take my mind off the sauerkraut. So the story was repeated and we all listened raptly.

Apparently, one day the internees, who were then in the Alexandra Palace in London (what they were doing in a palace I couldn't imagine), were served salt herrings which were crawling with maggots. At first the men had refused to eat them and the Commandant had been called, who in turn called the Medical Officer. The M.O. had viewed the offending livestock and then pronounced them as 'Not injurious to the health,' whereupon, according to Papa, the hungry men had eagerly and gratefully eaten the lot.

"I hope," said Papa at the conclusion of his little anecdote, "that you never have to live through a war as we did."

"I hope so too," said Mama, and she repeated another equally well known tale also concerning the war and herrings. During the war, her mother had been queuing up for a ration of half a herring per person. While waiting for this meagre allotment, she was drawn into conversation with the woman beside her.

"My husband," the woman informed her, "already starts to tremble at the mere sight of a herring." Mama and Papa laughed heartily at this old story. Funny, I thought peevishly, why do Germans make such a fuss about herrings with all those horrible little bones. Mama rang the bell for the second course. I had finished my sauerkraut, and there was fruit and custard for dessert. Wars were things in history books, and children weren't interned anyway. Why should I worry about herrings, with or without maggots? I took off my pinny,

7

folded it and put it away, then off I ran into the garden to play, until Betty called for me for afternoon school. I was just a child playing in the sun, and for a while, forgot I was German.

2. THE DALHEIMS

There was really no doubt about it. Our family were German through and through. Papa used to say that the Dalheims had originally gone to Germany from Sweden, but on the whole Papa was very vague about his family. He claimed he had a bad memory! Mama said a bad memory made life easy. She was the one who remembered birthdays and anniversaries, and sent cards, letters, and presents to all Papa's relations in Germany and America. Thanks to her, the links were kept until we were old enough to take over.

It was from Tante Hanny, Papa's younger sister, that we heard tales of their childhood and origin. For generations the Dalheims had been farmers in the province of Brandenburg, East Germany. Papa's grandparents had a farm in the village of Trebbin, and one thing Papa did remember was his visits to their farm. There were orchards where he used to play with his brother, and the bed that he slept in was set so high in the wall that a small ladder was provided to climb into it. Papa's father, however, was not a farmer; he was a master tailor who had a thriving business in the garrison town of Brandenburg making uniforms for the officers of the various regiments stationed there. He married a pretty girl from Alsace, and they reared a family of two boys and two girls. The first born was Agnes, who took after her mother in looks with dark eyes and hair. The second, born in 1882, was a boy, Gustav, our Papa. He favoured his father, with lighter colouring, tending to auburn. Then came another boy, Max, who was dark like Agnes. The youngest, Hanny, was an afterthought, being born when Agnes was already fifteen years old. Hanny was the family beauty with blonde hair and blue eyes. Before Hanny there had been another boy, Arthur, who, according to Hanny, was the most beautiful child ever seen. "Like an angel," she would say, "with his blonde curls and his deep blue eyes." Sadly, this little boy had died at the early age of three. His death devastated his mother. After the funeral she would take flowers to the tiny grave daily. She would sit there for hours on end, grieving and weeping, neglecting her household, husband, and remaining children.

Grandfather Dalheim was, by all accounts, a kindly and tolerant man who also grieved for his small son. But after a while he took a firm stand and delivered an ultimatum. He told his wife that she must restrict her cemetery visits to one a week and care for the remaining children and himself again, or he would leave her. In those days such a threat, coming from a man like grandfather, must have been a startling one. At any rate it had the desired effect, and family life once more resumed its accustomed routine. The family lived in a large comfortable apartment, and were well off. There were servants to do the work, nursemaids for the younger children, and all grandmother had to do was to ensure that things ran smoothly.

The little family grew to maturity. The two boys, after attending the local school, went on to a business college where they showed an aptitude for commerce. The girls were both local beauties, and as Agnes was so much the older, she took charge of the young Hanny and more or less brought her up. In spite of her strict Prussian upbringing Hanny had a wonderful, flighty, frivolous girlhood. She was much sought after by the young officers in the town and attended balls, receptions and other entertainments, encouraged by her indulgent parents and older sister. She had no end of pretty clothes and handsome admirers by the score. In later years Tante Hanny would reminisce fondly over her youthful days.

"I could have married anyone I wanted," she would sigh, "I could have married into the nobility – I could have had riches, position, anything at all," and her eyes would grow misty as she lost herself in daydreams of what might have been. As it turned out she married a police inspector, and according to Tante Agnes, it was a catastrophe.

Those were the days when one's place in society, especially in Germany, was very important. It didn't matter what you were, but who you were. The Dalheims had apparently at one time been of the nobility, and had been the 'Von' Dalheims. There was even a family crest to prove it. So the Dalheims held their heads high. True, they were only a good middle class family, but their predecessors had been noblemen, and they let nobody forget it!

It was Max, the younger son, who first left the nest. At the age of nineteen not only did he leave Brandenburg, but, surprisingly, he also left Germany and went to London. There he worked hard as a representative for a German firm and finally, at a very early age, acquired his own small factory, which made leather goods. He was even more adventurous – he married an Irish girl called Beatrice, bought a large house in New Barnet, and settled down to the life of an English gentleman. He wrote home such glowing reports of the opportunities awaiting business men in England that Gustav decided to go too.

3. ROSE

In 1909, at the age of twenty six, Gustav left Germany and set foot for the first time on British soil. In later years he was to say that coming to England was the best thing he ever did in his life. After the narrow, provincial atmosphere of Brandenburg, the cosmopolitan, free and easy life of London in those pre-war days of 1909 greatly appealed to Gustav.

He was invited to stay with Max in his roomy New Barnet house, until he found suitable, more permanent accommodation Determined to become as successful as Max, Gustav soon found a position with the Herald Yeast Company, and before long he was courting an English girl, Rose Andrews. She was an attractive girl with soft brown eyes and dark hair, and before long Gustav decided to follow Max's example to marry and settle in England. We still have an old postcard, written in spidery Gothic script that Gustav's mother had sent in reply to his news – Max has married an English girl and it seems to be working out. So, with his parents' and sisters' blessing, Gustav married Rose, and on their honeymoon he proudly took her to Brandenburg to be introduced to the family. In the meantime, Gustav had been given the northern region by his firm, so he and his new bride settled down happily in a rented house in Arnold Street, in the city of Hull. In 1911 a son was born, whom they called Lionel.

The little family was blissfully happy, as Gustav's business was thriving thanks to his hard and conscientious work, the child was healthy, and they hadn't a care in the world. Rose and Gustav lovingly furnished their house, and there was a feeling of permanence and peace. For a present at Christmas 1913, Gustav gave Rose a 1914 diary, and she started it off enthusiastically, fully intending to keep it up all the year. The homely little diary makes fascinating reading.

It is an insight into the typical life of a young wife in those days. She wrote down a recipe for cow's heel brawn, and then for several days searched for a cow's heel. At last she wrote triumphantly, 'Got a cow's heel – hurrah!' At the back of the book she kept her weekly accounts and under wages she entered 'Four shillings.' This presumably was for the servant girl Mary, for she figures in the diary too.

Next, the young family acquired a larger house in Coltman Street, and before moving in, Mary was recorded as going to clean it. Then came details of a new carpet bought for the drawing room. Finally came the day of the move and two days later the entry in the diary states – 'Mary ran away, Mrs White helped out.' Apparently the move had been too much for Mary. Servants, however, were easily replaced, even at four shillings a week! Rose noted in her diary after only a couple of days 'Got a new maid called Florence,' and life settled down peacefully again. Peacefully, that is, until mid-summer when the war which had been threatening Europe finally broke out, on August 4th. Rose had not kept her diary for a while, but on that date, she wrote 'War between England and Germany declared. Awful. Came back with Papa.' (her name for Gustav). Presumably, they had been on holiday.

So, their happy life began to change, slowly but surely. On the 8th she recorded Papa had to go to the Police Station for being a GERMAN. Expect him any minute. The next day she wrote, 'Just heard that Papa will not be released, taken on filthy ship with hundreds of others. This was to be Papa's first experience of internment. Rose made frantic efforts for his release, but to no avail. On the 13th she visited him, and wrote that she was 'Awfully worried.' There followed more miserable days, but suddenly, on the 17th, Papa was released and Rose was ecstatic. Alas, her joy was short lived, for two and a half weeks later, on September 4th, the police called at the house, and once more took Papa to the police station. The next day he was taken to York, 'What shall I do?' a distraught Rose wrote in her diary. On September 7th, she herself had to report to the police and then on, weekly 'For being married to a German.' Every day she wrote in her diary how lonely she was, and how she longed for Papa's release. She took up knitting to pass the time. She made herself ill with worry, and had to 'Get up and go and report myself – feel very bad. Went to Mr W. Hate Mr J.' (Whoever they were, presumably police officers). On September 29th came the last entry – 'Do hope Papa will be released tomorrow,' but he wasn't, and a discouraged Rose, wrote no more in her diary. The war dragged on miserably to its close. The happy, carefree, pre-war existence of Gustav and Rose was never to return. Because of his command of the English language and his trustworthiness, Gustav obtained a post in the Commandant's Office in the Alexandra Palace Internment Camp.

The Commandant used to say, "You write it Dalheim, and I'll sign it!"

It helped to pass the days, if nothing else. As the weeks turned to months and the months to years, the inferior food, the cramped close quarters, and the lack of clean fresh air took their toll on Gustav's health. He contracted T.B., and because of this, was eligible for early repatriation. He returned to his parent's home in Brandenburg, where Rose and Lionel joined him as soon as possible. There was a short, blissful period spent in the clean air and beautiful countryside of the Black Forest where Gustav and Lionel spent hours rowing on the calm waters of the Titisee, while Rose watched contentedly from the bank, a picnic basket beside her. Soon, she planned happily, we will go back to England and start life all over again.

Gustav was pronounced cured and it seemed that all their troubles were over. They returned to Brandenburg to make plans for the future. Sadly, all came to naught, for Rose, never the strongest of girls, became ill. The war with its separations, worry, and inadequate nourishment had put a great strain on her. The doctor said that all she needed was rest, good food and plenty of fresh air, but in spite of all the loving care the family could give her, she went rapidly downhill. The doctor took Gustav aside and told him he suspected that Rose had cancer and there was nothing more he could do. She was only thirty two years old when she died, on July 19th 1919, leaving behind a shattered Gustav, and young Lionel. Her parents obtained permission to visit occupied Germany for her funeral. Grief-stricken, they begged Gustav to allow them to take Lionel back with them. It would be a comfort for them, and besides that, the boy had missed much of his education. Reluctantly, looking at their sad, old faces, Gustav agreed. He would, he promised, return to England as soon as was humanly possible. So, Lionel returned to England. He went to live with his Aunt Nellie (Rose's sister), Uncle Oswald and cousin Audrey. A few years later the family emigrated to the U.S.A and Lionel went with them. There were tearful farewells and Gustav returned to his parents home, alone once more.

Before long he had obtained a position in the overseas department of the great Continental Rubber Concern in the city of Hannover. He left Brandenburg and its sad memories behind him. He flung himself into his new job. Every day was like another, the work was routine and fairly dull, but what did it matter, it was an occupation and paid a reasonable salary.

One day Gustav went to collect some papers from another department. His colleagues had been talking about the new girl who worked there, and how attractive she was. Gustav decided to go and see for himself. As he entered the room, he saw a dark haired girl seated at the desk. She had her back to him, and his breath caught in his throat. Something about the way she held her head reminded him suddenly of Rose. The girl turned and smiled at him briefly, like Rose, her eyes were brown, but there the likeness ended. His business concluded, Gustav returned to his office in a daze. That glimpse of a smiling young girl's face remained with him for the rest of the day.

Her name, he found out, was Marianne Schmidt, and he was determined to get to know her better. For Gustav the dark days were over at last, the sun had suddenly come out in all its brightness for him again. For he was to marry this girl and their life together would be a long and happy one. So it came about that our Papa met our Mama.

4. "ONE AND HALF A DOZEN"

Mama's family, too, were country people. An ancestor on my mother's side, so the story went, had been French and a General in Napoleon's army. He was wounded in some war or other, and in recognition of his services was given a farmhouse and land in the village of Marienau, in the Province of Hannover. He changed his French name of Deaus around a little and spelt it Daues instead, It sounded more German. He settled down quite happily in his new country. My great-grandfather Daues married a girl from a neighbouring village, whose name was Luise Bertram. An old photograph shows him as rather a stern looking man, whereas his wife, with her dark hair fluffed about her face, had an elfin prettiness. Great-grandfather however, must have had a sense of humour, for when anyone asked him how many children he had, he would reply, "One and a half dozen." On seeing the look of surprise as the enquirer worked that out to be eighteen, he would laugh and say "Yes, one son and six daughters." The boy's name was Wilhelm, after his father and the girls were Charlotte, Anna, Sophie, Luise, Marie and Lina. Marie, the second youngest daughter was our Mama's mother and our beloved 'Oma.'

From an early age the children had their tasks about the farm and house. They fed the chickens and pigs, helped with the harvest, picked fruit, and helped bottle and preserve it. It was a hard life, but a happy one. When the youngest child, Lina, was only eighteen months old, their mother died at the early age of forty two. The eldest daughter Charlotte, barely out of childhood herself, took over the task of running the large household. It was expected of her and she did it competently, aided by the three sisters next to her in age. Life, however, was not all work and no play. As they grew older they were courted by the local men and one by one they married.

Living in the neighbouring village of Rott was a schoolmaster, Schmidt. His family was the reverse of the Daues, with one daughter and six sons. One of the sons, also Wilhelm, married Anna Daues, and his brother Eduard became engaged to Marie.

By now all were married in the Daues family, with the exception of Wilhelm and Marie. Wilhelm ran the farm and Marie the house. Wilhelm too was engaged, his bride-to-be a local girl. Marie promised to postpone her own wedding and stay on after her brother's wedding, to help the young bride with the running of the household. Wilhelm was determined to have the farmhouse in perfect condition before he married, so he had a new wing added to the old house, with large and beautiful rooms. It was almost completed and the roof going up, when he went to inspect the work for himself; alas, no one had told him that part of the floor was only temporary. He went crashing down to the hard ground below, broke his neck, and died instantly. Marie found him – it was a terrible tragedy. The sisters gathered together for the funeral and later discussed what was to become of the farm. There was no male heir, it belonged to the six girls.

"We must sell it," said Marie, "Eduard's career is in the city. I'm over thirty. I've waited long enough and I'm getting married as soon as possible. Your husbands are all settled in their own careers and none of them has an interest in farming. Selling is the only answer."

The sisters were horrified. Sell the farm, that had been in the family for generations! Never! The only solution was, that Marie must break off her engagement immediately. She must marry a farmer, a younger son from a neighbouring farm – it was her duty, she had no choice. They discussed among themselves the most suitable match. Marie took no interest in the merits of the various eligible men suggested by her sisters. She sat silent and stubborn; her mind was quite made up. The farm, which she now hated, with its tragic memories, MUST be sold. The sisters scolded and pleaded, but she was adamant. Besides, she pointed out, if the farm were sold all would share in the not, inconsiderable proceeds. Somewhat mollified by the carrot thus dangled before their eyes, the sisters finally, if grudgingly, gave their consent.

Actually, they never really forgave her for giving up the family heritage. As for Marie, she married quietly soon after, still dressed in mourning for her brother, and she never set foot in the old family home again.

Marie and Eduard set up home in a large apartment in the Pfundstrasse, in Hannover. It must have been so different from her previous rural existence, but sister Anna who lived in the same street, took her under her wing, and initiated her to the city way of life. Then there were always visits to the other sisters, who still lived in the country.

They were a close knit family, who always gathered together on special occasions – birthdays, christenings, confirmations, weddings, and funerals. Marie and Eduard had three children, the firstborn, a boy, was born on St. Valentine's day 1895, and as was customary, was named Eduard, after his father. As a baby, he could not get his tongue round his given name, and instead called himself "Ete," a name which stuck for the rest of his life. Next, Marie had a girl, born on the 1st January, 1897. This child she named after herself and Anna. Anna had insisted on the child being her Godchild, so the name chosen was 'Marianne.' This was to be our Mama. Marie thought her family was complete with two children, then surprised everyone, including herself, by having another baby when she was forty-one years of age. It was another girl, given the name Amalie, after Eduard's mother.

5. EDUARD

If Papa was, on the whole, reticent about his past, Mama, on the other hand, always had a host of lively memories that she shared with us. Not only would she regale us with tales of her own childhood and girlhood, but also put us in the picture with all her numerous relatives. We got the impression that life in the 'olden days,' was far more exciting than our own. There were endless family gatherings, outings to the countryside, holidays by the sea, school trips and nonstop girlish fun. Brother Ete was wonderful at gymnastics and a brilliant scholar too. Little sister Amalie, always called Mane, was a pretty, forward child. The youngest of sixteen cousins, she was indulged and made much of by her parents, aunts, uncles, and older cousins. She was much in demand for reciting poems at parties and anniversaries, and she performed with great aplomb and composure.

The family lived well, in their large city apartment, now in the Boedekerstrasse, close to the extensive Eilenriede woods, which are such a feature of Hannover city. The young Mane kept her roller skates in the entrance hall, and little tearaway that she was, spent every spare minute skating endlessly up and down the woodland paths. At home there were the usual maids, washer women and dressmakers, employed to keep the household running smoothly. The two girls could follow their own pursuits and hobbies without being burdened by household chores.

The years passed happily. Ete decided on a medical career, and was accepted by a university, to start in the Autumn of 1914. Mama persuaded her father to let her stay on at school and prepare herself for college. So much for youthful aspirations. The 1914-1918 war was by now looming over Europe, and young men of eighteen and upwards were being called up for military training. Young Ete, discussing the situation with an older cousin, was told he had a choice – either he could complete his studies and then do his military service, or he could do his military service first and defer his university education for a year. The cousin recommended the second option, and said Ete could devote himself to his studies and go into practice immediately afterwards. Tragically, as it turned out, Ete took his cousin's advice and signed up without delay; he joined a regiment for training. He had not been in the Army many weeks, when the war broke out, and his regiment was immediately sent to the Belgian front. Young, untrained, inexperienced as they were, could they have possibly even guessed at the horror that was awaiting them?

Back home in Hannover, the family, having had no word for a while, worried and waited. Then came the devastating news. Almost the entire regiment had perished on the 6th August, in one of the first battles of the war. Ete was one of the unlucky ones; a young life, so full of promise, cut short by an enemy bullet. The little family was shattered and for a time clung to the futile hope that maybe it wasn't true – maybe it was a mistake. Eduard Schmidt was a common name, maybe it wasn't true – maybe it was someone of the same name. Perhaps he had been wounded, perhaps taken prisoner, perhaps, perhaps, perhaps. But soon they had to accept what they had known in their heart of hearts all along – nineteen year old Ete was dead, buried in a war grave in Belgium. Never would laughing, teasing Ete come home again. However, life had to go on.

The family picked up the threads, and slowly, sadly, life for the remaining ones continued as before. Well not quite as before, one thing had changed. From then on, the great, glittering, candlelit fir tree that used to grace the drawing room from Christmas Eve until Ete's birthday party on February 14th, was missing. It would never return. Mane was eighty when she told me of this sad little aftermath, and even then, almost seventy years on, her voice still shook with all the hurt and bitter resentment of the twelve year old from whom the war had taken not only her adored big brother, but her Christmas tree as well.

21

6. SAD TIMES

Mama continued with her chosen career; she went to college, and at the age of twenty emerged as a fully qualified teacher. The year was 1917. The family had moved to a smaller apartment the year before and now lived in the Simrockstrasse, on the fashionable south side of Hannover. When Mama left college the war was in its third year, and in the cities food was becoming scarce. The college tutors advised the girls to try for teaching positions in the country, where food was still plentiful. Not only would they benefit, but they would help their families too. So it came about that Mama became governess to three girls who lived at Rebberlah, a large estate on the Luneburg Heath. The eldest girl, Lotte, was only eight years younger than Mama, and they immediately became friends for life. The younger girls, Elisabeth and Ursula also took to their new teacher and for Mama an idyllic new way of life began.

As at all schools in Germany, there were lessons only in the morning. Lunch was followed by a nap and after that walks, whatever the weather. Mama was ecstatic about her new position. She grew to love the Heath, with its wide skies, its pine forests and ever changing colours. The girls took her to their favourite haunts, she learned to drive the pony and trap, she visited the girls' relations and friends on the neighbouring estates – in fact she became more or less one of the family. She got on well with her employers and this friendship was to span more than half a century. Occasionally, apart from the usual holidays, Mama would have a weekend off. Then she would come home laden with butter, eggs and other delicacies, as much as she could carry, for her kind employers were more than generous.

The war dragged on to its weary close. Mama's family was not the only one to suffer bereavement. Several cousins were killed, and their families accepted it bravely; hardly a family was spared. For Mama's Tante Anna fate had a harder blow in store. Her first baby boy she had lost in infancy, so when a second son was born, he too was named Wilhelm, after his father. Judging by the old photographs, he was a very handsome fellow. According to Mama he was the wittiest of all her cousins, the apple of his parents' eye. He became a schoolmaster, and when the war broke out he joined the cavalry. We have a photograph of him taken with his beautiful horse 'Nil', which he worshipped. When he came home on leave, he would talk endlessly of its beauty and intelligence, so much so that the family would tease him about it. Wilhelm survived the war and apart from an arm wound was more or less unscathed.

"What happened to his horse?" I used to ask Mama, but she didn't know.

"It belonged to the cavalry and probably stayed there," she said. However, Wilhelm's arm wound was worse than anticipated and refused to heal. Treatment failed and Wilhelm, once the jolliest of men, became more and more depressed and morose. His mother, now widowed, did all she could to make life pleasant for him again but nothing helped. One day she heard the sound of a shot from his room, and rushed to see what had happened, but the door was locked. She summoned help and the lock was forced. They found Wilhelm dead with a bullet in his heart. They told Anna that it was an accident, that he hadn't known it was loaded. Whether or not Anna believed it, the sisters never knew. They kept up the myth, but everyone in their heart of hearts knew that Wilhelm just couldn't face life anymore – he too was a war casualty.

All the Daues sisters had their share of sorrow, for those who had not lost their sons as a result of the war had other family tragedies. Sophie, who had three girls, Sophie, Trudchen and Aenne, lost her husband, who was a builder, in a tragic accident. Her daughter, Trudchen, at the age of seventeen, after an unhappy love affair with a married man, took her own life by jumping into the river Wester. It was several days before she was found, and her mother, in those terrible days when she was missing, would spend night after night driving up and down the deserted roads in her pony cart, calling, "Trudchen, Trudchen!"

Her youngest daughter, Aenne, even in her eighties, would still tell the tale, with tears in her eyes. Aenne herself lost a leg a few days after her fiftieth birthday, during the second world war, but she came from good, tough Daues stock, and I never heard her complain or indulge in self-pity. Lina, the youngest of the Daues sisters, outlived all the others, and reached the great age of ninety-two. She was an enchanting old lady, but sadly, although her two sons survived the war, her only daughter and son-in-law were killed in a road accident when Lina was in her eighties.

7. WEDDED BLISS

As the 1914-1918 war neared its end and the girls at Rebberlah were growing up, the two eldest were going to school in the neighbouring town of Celle, and Mama only had little Ursula to teach, and supervise the older girls homework in the afternoons. At last Ursula too joined her sisters at school and Mama went back to Hannover, promising to visit her ex-pupils in holiday times, or whenever she could. In Hannover, jobs were scarce and Mama was offered a temporary position at a boarding school on the Danish border. This job completed, Mama was again at a loose end, whereupon her father suggested she have six months at home, just pleasing herself. He was, after all, fairly well off, and could support two daughters at home. It was not to be, for Mama's tutor called one day and asked if she could fill a gap in a local school, which again was a temporary position, but could become permanent. So off Mama went eagerly to her first real teaching post in a city school. It was certainly a big change for her – the classes were large and the classrooms cold, for fuel was scarce, and everyone kept their coats on. Mama soon settled in. There were other young members of staff and it seems to have been a very happy time.

Gradually, life in Germany settled down to an uneasy peace – food, especially in the cities, was still scarce, money was tight and jobs hard to find. The returning soldiers and prisoners of war found a changed country and their prospects were bleak. Returning schoolmasters were applying for posts that didn't exist, and the authorities decided that instead of turning away breadwinners on whom families were dependent, it was the young, newly qualified women teachers who would have to go. Mama and several of her young colleagues were told that their services would no longer be required. Of course, they all understood the position, and neither could not, nor would not, keep places from men who had fought so gallantly for their country. It was still a big blow for a young girl eagerly starting her new career, but in those days there was no women's equality. They were still dismissed automatically on marriage, and such a rule was never queried.

Mama's father, whose salary had never suffered, was still earning more than enough to keep his family, but Mama was now used to being independent. She and a young teacher friend discussed the future, and her friend said that she had heard that there were openings for women in commercial colleges. All they had to do was to take a course in shorthand and typing, do a year or so practical work and after that it was plain sailing. Besides, they could be earning money during the day and take their course in the evenings. This they did and also enrolled in foreign language classes.

Finding a secretarial job with no real qualifications was no easy task. Mama applied to several firms, including one in South America, but at last was asked to attend an interview at the giant Continental Rubber factory. She went, and because she was fluent in English and French, and also had a working knowledge of Spanish, she got a job in the overseas department. As she returned home, elated, to tell her family the good news, little did she know that this step forward was to change her life.

Mama found her job at the Continental works lively and interesting. She sat at a large table, with her back to the door, facing a large map of the world; on either side of her sat two male clerks, and between them there was much joking and teasing. Those who needed translations or typing doing would come in behind her and place the work beside her. Usually Mama was so busy that she would only acknowledge this with a brief nod, and a word of thanks, without even looking up to see who had come in. After a time, her two companions noticed that one man seemed to come in more often than anyone else, and they used to tease Mama, and say, "Here he comes again!" "Who?" Mama said. "Why, the fellow who's looking for a wife!" they would laugh. Mama blushingly said "Nonsense," but she sneaked a glance at her frequent visitor. It, was, of course, Papa. One day, instead of giving her a translation to type, he slipped a little note to her, asking her to accompany him on a walk in the Tiergarten, in their lunch hour. Mama accepted with alacrity; she liked this man with the gentle voice and kind eyes, and wished to get to know him better.

Mama used to tell us about her first walk with Papa in the Tiergarten. There had been a heavy hoarfrost, and trees, grass, fences, everything was thickly encrusted in glittering frost. It was a beautiful sight. One walk led to more, and soon they were courting regularly, even talking of marriage. When Mama told her parents however, they were decidedly cool. "Never marry a businessman," they said, "it's too uncertain, marry someone in a profession." Besides, they pointed out, they knew nothing about his background or family, and in those days, this was still very important. But Mama came from a new generation; she wouldn't marry anyone else, she informed her parents. She loved her Gustav, and knew he was absolutely right for her. So her father, as she found out later, wrote to the Burgermeister of Brandenburg and asked about Gustav's family. Back came a glowing report of the respectability and good connections of the Dalheims. That settled it; although Mama had already decided that come what may, she would marry her Gustav, to have her parent's blessing made her very happy.

On 27th May, 1922, they became engaged, and planned to marry within the year. Mama gave up her job, and together with an ex-school friend, Elfriede, who too was engaged, went to learn the art of cooking, in the kitchens of an exclusive restaurant. This was quite common in those days; the girls were unpaid and helped the chef, who in return taught them the tricks of his trade. Certainly, Mama became a wonderful cook. The cooking course over, she began to prepare for her wedding.

Inflation had hit the country hard, and there were shortages of everything. Accommodation was scarce, but in spite of all this, the young couple decided to marry on September 16th, and not wait any longer. Elfriede, now married to a school teacher, found them an apartment in the village where her husband taught. This was Kaltenweide, several miles outside Hannover, and Mama and her mother went to inspect it. It turned out to be the ground floor of an extremely large house.

This house had originally been built as an inn, but the man who had built it so hopefully was refused the licence to use it as he had intended. There were already two inns in this tiny village, and in fairness to these two established ones, the authorities deemed it was enough. So the house was rented off for private accommodation. A family lived upstairs, but downstairs, with its enormous public rooms and verandas, was vacant.

It was summer when Mama saw it, and it looked spacious and beautiful, with the large garden round about it. The village was quaint and picturesque. When Gustav saw it, he was equally delighted – like Mama, he too loved the country life. He said he could easily cycle daily to Langenhagen, the next village, and from there get the train to Hannover. It was all settled and Gustav wrote to Hull, to the store where his furniture was, and asked them to send it on.

In those days of scarcity, Mama was delighted to have a completely furnished home provided, and she looked forward to the day when the furniture would be delivered. Happily, they arranged it about the huge rooms, and once the carpets were down and the curtains and pictures up, it was as nice a home as anyone could wish for. A young girl from the village, called Anna, was engaged to come in daily as maid of all work, and now Mama could concentrate her thoughts on her wedding. She and her mother searched the shops for suitable material for a wedding dress, and finally ran to earth a length of cream shantung. Luckily the fashion was for shortish, straight dresses, and the dressmaker made up the material into a very pretty dress. It was trimmed with expensive Brussels lace, which had been hoarded for years, and now came in very useful.

The wedding was celebrated in Hannover, as planned, on September 16th 1922. In spite of shortages, the wedding breakfast was lavish and plentiful, a turkey and other luxuries having been sent from Rebberlah. There was no honeymoon; the young couple went straight to their new home, where the next day the entire family of aunts, cousins, and various other relatives, descended on them for afternoon coffee and pastries, and to inspect the accommodation.

Both Papa and Mama enjoyed village life, and settled down happily. Elfriede and her husband introduced them to various people with similar tastes and backgrounds, and they enjoyed an active social life. Once the warm autumn days had passed, the large rooms lost their cosiness and the winter winds entered through every nook and cranny. Mama and Anna, the maid, wrestled with the large stoves in the kitchen and living room, but usually their efforts were rewarded with lots of choking smoke and little heat.

Then an old school friend gave Mama a dog.

"You'll need a dog in the country," she said, as she brought a prettily marked brown and white terrier, "she's six months old and house trained, her name is Hexe."

Mama always said that Hexe was a real "little lady," brought up in the city, she was obedient and charming. Mama and Papa taught her tricks and loved her as much as she loved them.

The first winter in Kaltenweide passed, and spring returned to the little village, with it the warmth, blossoming trees and flowers. There was no hope yet of finding anywhere suitable to live in Hannover. Having survived the winter, Mama said she didn't mind living there as long as Papa didn't mind cycling to the train at Lagenhagen every day. Papa said he enjoyed his cycle rides down the quiet country lanes, even in bad weather. It was relaxing and gave him a chance to unwind. In June, their first child, a boy, was born. They called him Eberhard. Mama chose the name because it was similar to Eduard, in memory of her brother.

8. KALTENWEIDE

Mama and Papa were to live in Kaltenweide for over four years. They became used to the large inconvenient rooms, the temperamental stoves, the enormous kitchen, and the terrible cold winters. But the summers more than made up for that. Mama used to say that during the summer months, Kaltenweide was simply idyllic – there was no other way to describe it. The little picturesque village, with its timbered Niedersachsen houses, dozed peacefully in the warm weather, the gardens ablaze with colourful flowers. The rutted lanes, so muddy and impassable in the winter, became dusty tracks in the summer, and led out of the village and into the smiling countryside, with its golden cornfields, little woods, and further out, the tracts of purple heather that Mama loved so much. It was an ideal place to bring up, children.

I was born on November 1st, 1924, in a nursing home in Hannover, and the name chosen for me was Rosemarie – Rose after Papa's first wife, and Marie after Mama. It was typical of Mama, that she should choose this name for me. It was to keep green forever the memory of Rose, who had died too young, but because she had died, a new little family had come into being. It was only right that the first little girl should be named after her. If she hadn't died, there would have been no me! Papa once wrote to Mama later commenting on our names, 'Eberhard – may he be as hard and as strong as the 'Eber' (wild boar) and Rosemarie – whose name combines the past and present and for whom I predict a golden future.'

I was christened along with about a dozen other screaming infants at the hospital chapel, not because I was delicate, and there was any doubt that I would survive, but because it just happened to be more convenient. Tante Mane, who was one of my godmothers, held me in her arms, she recalled that we were at the end of the line, and by the time it came to my turn to be sprinkled with the Holy Water, the Pastor had none left. He therefore tipped the bowl over my head and a couple of tiny drops dripped onto my screwed up, loudly protesting, red face!

When I was just a few weeks old, Mama contracted diphtheria. In those days it was still a killer, so Eberhard was packed off to stay with Mama's parents, (now our Oma and Opa) and Mane. I, being so young, was allowed to stay. There followed some anxious days, but with the help of a good doctor, who called daily, Mama pulled through, and was little the worse for her illness.

Eberhard came back from Hannover in time for Christmas, and once again the winter came with all its attendant disadvantages, and Mama and Papa made serious attempts to move back into town. Before they found anywhere suitable, the spring and summer returned and all thought of moving was once more abandoned.

Papa still cycled to Langenhagen and back every day. His work at the Continental was fairly monotonous, and gave little scope for individual enterprise. Cycling back and forth along the country lanes, Papa had plenty of time for quiet thought. Over and again he thought about the future. Was this what he really wanted? Surely there must be more for him than this fairly dead-end job? He longed to be independent, and to have his own business. Truth be told, what he really missed was England, and the English way of life.

He had lived too long in England to feel one hundred percent German anymore. Although he would always love Germany, certain things and attitudes irritated and annoyed him. Deep down in his heart he knew that his future no longer lay in Germany, but in England. Instead of seeing the tree-lined lanes he cycled down, he saw the streets of Hull, homely and ordinary perhaps, but full of warmth and friendliness. He pictured the bright coal fires that burned in the kitchen grates, inside the houses. The eternal kettle on the hob, the endless cups of tea, the genuine friendship and hospitality of the people who lived there. For Hull's citizens are truly among the friendliest folk in England.

He began to make plans, first by himself, and later with Mama, who was soon enthusiastically fired with the same desire to go and live in England. The country that had so recently been Germany's great enemy was even now not kindly disposed towards Germans. But she knew as well as Papa, that wars are planned by Governments, and not by the ordinary people. The more Papa told her of life in England, the more she liked the sound of it. After all, she had an adventurous streak in her; had she not once applied for a job in South America? England was nearer, and not such a big step, and one could always come back.

Having been in the yeast trade previously, it was the obvious choice for Papa's line of business. He still remembered the customers he had visited before the war. He knew that German yeast was the best for baking and small bakeries. His mind was made up. He approached the big North German firm of Gebrüder Asmussen and asked if they would be interested in selling their products in England. It turned out that they were very interested, and Papa set off to see them and lay his plans before them.

In England one or two large distilleries had the yeast monopoly, and all small bakers had no choice but to buy their yeast from them. The German yeast would be offered at a competitive price, so Papa knew that the 'little men' would be only too pleased to buy from him. He could almost guarantee instant success. Asmussens decided to give it a try, and a delighted Papa returned to Kaltenweide to tell Mama the good news.

It was decided that he would go alone first and start the business rolling before the family joined him. He wrote to the Home Office and asked for permission to return to England. Back came the reply; he was granted a stay of six months after which the position would be reviewed.

"Six months is all I need," said Papa, "by then I will have a good business going and the future will take care of itself."

He handed in his notice at the Continental, and on a September day in 1926 set off for England, with high hopes and the good wishes of relations and friends. Papa always called himself an optimist, and because of this he knew he was going to succeed.

Arriving in Hull on the boat train from Harwich, he wondered where he could stay the night. He asked a railway official if he could recommend a place. He could not have picked a better person to ask.

"Why, Sir," said the man, "my missus takes in lodgers and she just happens to have a spare room. Have a cup of tea in the waiting-room, I'm off duty in a few minutes, and I'll take you." Papa found the waiting room, and drank a brew of strong tea, while he waited for his new friend to appear. In no time the man was back.

"Tom Burton," he introduced himself, "are you ready, Sir?" Papa, Mr Burton, and the luggage piled into a taxi, and Mr Burton gave the address, "10 Crystal Street," and off they went.

Having arrived at Tom Burton's house, Mrs Burton took charge. She showed Papa to a spotlessly clean front bedroom, brought a jug of hot water, and informed him that tea would be served in the front parlour as soon as the gentleman was ready. Washed, changed and ravenously hungry, Papa soon descended to the front parlour. A fire burned brightly in the grate, the furniture was old fashioned but good, and a table with a starched, snowy-white cloth was laid for one. After an excellent and generous Yorkshire high tea, Papa settled in one of the rather stiff armchairs by the fire, lit a cigar and prepared to enjoy his first evening back in England. So far, so good. When Mrs Burton came in to clear the table, he complimented her on the meal and asked if she would consider him as a long-term paying guest. She told him she would be delighted, and so began an association of two families that was to last a lifetime.

The Burtons already had one lodger, who occupied a back bedroom and had his meals in the kitchen along with the family, which also included two teenage children, Ivy and Fred. Papa was told he could have the front parlour entirely for his own use.

"What I really need is a room as an office as well," said Papa. Mrs Burton proved even more accommodating.

"You can have the back room," she said, "but if you don't mind, there's a man who comes in and sleeps on the sofa every night, but he won't bother you."

Papa said he didn't mind a bit, a price was agreed on, and Papa wrote to Mama there and then, that he was already most comfortably settled in and happy.

He soon worked out a routine of travelling about the area, seeking out his former customers, slowly but surely building up a good business, On days when he wasn't travelling, he wrote letters in his office, banging away on an old typewriter and in between, he wrote long letters to Mama, telling her how he was getting on. Orders were coming in thick and fast and the baskets of yeast began arriving from Germany. It was all highly satisfactory, and Papa was sending money to Mama. Before long his income far exceeded his salary with the Continental. All his old customers had been glad to see him back, and dealt with him in preference to the large firms.

Back home in Kaltenweide, the winter was approaching. Mama's father had suffered a stroke, and it was a worrying time for all. By Christmas he was a little better, and when Papa came home for a few days for the Christmas festivities, he and Mama began to talk of the family joining him in Hull, as soon as possible. Papa once more wrote to the Home Office in good time, asking for his permission to stay to be lengthened, and for permission for his family to join him.

January brought icy cold weather, deep snow, and something even more alarming to Kaltenweide. There was a prowler around the village, and instead of going home at night, Anna now stayed and slept on the living room sofa. She was of little comfort, as she was as frightened as Mama, as they fearfully locked and bolted the large apartment before going to bed. A cousin lent Mama his army revolver, which she kept in the drawer of her bedside table. She had no idea how to use it, but its presence gave her a certain amount of bravado and comfort. I shudder to think of a loaded revolver lying in a drawer, easily accessible to two small children, but obviously Mama was more worried about the prowler then the possibility of us finding it!

One morning Anna looked out of the kitchen window and saw the imprints of two great feet, in the snow outside. The prowler must have been in the night and tried to gain access! Mama sent for the police, whereupon the village policeman came, examined the footprints, and said thoughtfully.

"Hm, a big, heavy man, if they're anything to go by."

Seeing Mama's terrified face, he suggested that perhaps it would be better if she and the children would spend the night with friends until the police caught their man So, every night, Mama packed up a little bag of necessities and we all set off to the Gosewitsch's farm, as they had kindly offered to take us in. Anna went back to her mother, and Hexe, brave little dog that she was, stayed behind to guard the house!

9. HEXE

In England, Papa worried about Mama, alone in Kaltenweide, and he redoubled his efforts to get the family across. In the New Year of 1927 came good news at last! The family was allowed to join him, albeit only for six months. Papa was jubilant, his efforts had paid off. Better still, Mrs Burton had offered to put up the entire family until we could find more suitable accommodation. Letters crossed and recrossed the North Sea, until at last, it was all settled.

We were to leave Germany at the end of March, the furniture was to be stored until it would be required again, the landlady was given notice and Anna had found another job. Mama, Eberhard and I would stay in Hannover until the day of departure. There was only one problem left to solve - Hexe. What on earth would happen to her? There was no question of taking her to England with us. There were strict quarantine regulations, six months isolation in kennels. After that, who knew if we would be staying in England, let alone have a suitable home of our own. Mama was genuinely fond of Hexe, and wanted the best for her, so looked around for a new home for her. It was not easy. Hexe had one fault - she chased hens. That meant, a farm was out of the question, private houses already had a dog, or didn't want one. Anna too, asked around; then one day, a farmer called to say that he would take Hexe. His first question was, did she chase hens? Mama reluctantly said she did, but the farmer was delighted. That was the dog he wanted, as his wife was a keen gardener and complained constantly about the hens ruining her garden! Hexe was the perfect answer. He took her, there and then, and would keep her tied up until we left the village. Mama watched Hexe being dragged away on the end of a rope, and wondered if she was doing the right thing. Hexe had never been tied up in her life – how would she take it?

The farmer seemed all right, and Hexe was only five, young enough to adapt to a new home. In a few days we would be gone and she would have her freedom again. She would probably come straight back and look for us, but in time, she would stop looking and settle down. So Mama consoled herself, and besides she told herself, if things didn't work out in England, we would be back and Hexe would be ours again.

It was many years later that we found out what really happened to Hexe. When we were children, Mama used to tell us about Hexe and the funny little ways she had. There were photographs of her, and as a dog-crazy girl, I would gaze at them and wish Hexe was still ours. I knew all the reasons why she had been left behind, but to me they were just hollow excuses. Then, when I was about nine years old and on a visit to Germany in the summer holidays, Mama took us back to Kaltenweide again. We were going to visit Anna, who was now married and had her own home in the village.

"We will go and look at our old house," said Mama, "you probably won't recognise it at all."

The house didn't interest me much, only one thing about Kaltenweide was uppermost in my mind.

"Can we go and see Hexe?" I asked.

"Yes, if she's still alive," said Mama.

"Alive?" I was horrified, "why shouldn't she be?"

"Dogs don't live as long as people," explained Mama, "don't forget, Hexe is older than you – she'll be about twelve, and that's quite old for a dog."

"Of course she'll be alive, she must be," I insisted.

"I'll ask Anna about her first," promised Mama, "she's sure to know."

We duly arrived at Kaltenweide's tiny, flower bedecked station, and were met by Anna. I endured the remarks and comments on how Eberhard and I had grown and changed beyond all recognition, and how delighted Anna was to meet our little sister, Anita. We passed the house where we used to live, it looked very nice, I thought. Mama and Anna were deep in the past, laughing, remembering. At last we reached Anna's house and settled round the table in her small sitting room, Anna bustled about with coffee and cake. I tugged Mama's sleeve, "Ask about Hexe," I hissed, "you said you would"

"In a minute," said Mama. We tucked into 'Zuckerkuchen' and drank milky coffee and I had a happy little daydream. We would go and see Hexe, and she would remember us and come to England with us. I would carry her wrapped in a blanket and tell her to be still and pretend to be a toy, then there wouldn't have to be any silly quarantine. I woke out of my reverie – Mama still hadn't asked, she and Anna were still talking about boring people.

I nudged Mama, "Ask," I whispered.

"Oh, yes," said Mama "Anna, do you know what became of Hexe?"

"Hexe," replied Anna, "she's dead!"

It is strange how certain scenes in one's life remain fixed in the memory forever. To this day, I can see the room where we sat around the table with its dainty embroidered cloth and pretty china – Anna in a navy blue dress holding the, coffee pot, and saying quite calmly that Hexe, our Hexe, was dead! I can still feel the shock going through my body, my heart seemed to drop in my stomach, my throat closed, and I nearly choked on the dry zuckerkuchen. Dead! Hexe dead! My little dream of the happy reunion faded and shrivelled, as dead as Hexe. Mama and Anna were still talking, as my numbed mind followed the conversation.

"Well, of course, she would be old," said Mama, "we thought we might have visited her."

"She's been dead a long time," went on Anna," "the farmer had to shoot her."

My heart did a second somersault, my throat was so tight I couldn't speak or swallow.

"Shoot her!" said Mama, shocked, "but why?"

"She started killing hens," went on Anna relentlessly, "you can't have a dog that kills hens."

'Oh, Hexe,' I sobbed inside myself, 'why did we ever leave you?' I was not a child who interrupted adult conversation, but I had to know more, I had to hear all the details. I forced myself to speak over the great lump in my throat.

"How did he shoot her?" I croaked. Anna looked at me, she was not unkind, but she'd been brought up in the country, where killing and shooting animals is commonplace. She was totally matter of fact about the whole thing.

"I suppose he put down a dish of food for her, and while she was eating it he shot her," she said with brutal candour, not sparing my feelings.

The reality would, I realise now, have been far worse than Anna's version. No farmer would waste food on a dog he was about to shoot. He would simply have tied her up, and while her brown, bewildered eyes gazed up at him apprehensively, he would have callously taken aim. I hope that, for Hexe's sake, he was a good shot.

"What a shame," said Mama, "I'm really sorry about that."

She and Anna went on to talk of other things, but my fertile imagination was off on another track. I saw a small, trusting, brown and white terrier happily eating her very last meal. I heard the traitorous shot and saw the little dog fall on its side, red blood welling from an enormous wound, staining the white, silky coat and running on to the grass. It was too horrible to think about; perhaps, I comforted myself, she hadn't really died, just pretended to. Then, when the farmer wasn't looking, she got up and ran away, ran to Hamburg, boarded a ship and came to Hull, then she would run to our house, and live with us forever. Even as I made up this improbable story I knew it couldn't possibly come true. It was just too far-fetched!

Sensing my distress, Mama suggested we three go out and play in Anna's garden. Anna went into the kitchen and came back with a bowl of scraps.

"You can feed my hens," she said, "they're in a run at the back of the garden." Obediently, we children left the room and went out into the sunny garden, but I had momentarily gone off hens. While the others threw the food to the squawking birds and laughed at their antics, I walked gloomily round the garden, my thoughts full of revenge. I would find out where that horrible farmer lived. I would creep in and find his gun, then I would shoot him! The thought of him lying, covered in his own blood, cheered me up. Serve him right! Again, it was a totally improbable childish dream.

The visit over, we walked back to the railway station down the summer-scented village street.

"Where does he live?" I asked Mama.

"Who?" she said mystified.

"The farmer who shot Hexe."

"Oh, the other side of the village, we don't pass his house this way."

I was disappointed – another little plan of mine had come to naught.

"I hope he's dead," I said viciously.

"I shouldn't think so," said Mama, "he wasn't that old, hurry up now or we'll miss the train."

Poor Hexe, she was only a small terrier, but I shall always think of her with regret. We had been her family, and she had been a loving, faithful little creature, and it just didn't seem fair that she was abandoned to such a cruel fate. She deserved better than that.

10. A FOREIGN LAND

Our last days in Germany were tinged with sadness, for Mama's father had recently suffered another stroke, and the doctor held out no hope for his recovery. He had lapsed into a coma, and it was only a matter of time now before the end came. Oma urged Mama not to put off her departure date, there was nothing to be gained she said. Mama, Eberhard and I therefore stayed with Tante Anna, for there was no place for two tiny, lively children in a house where a man lay dying. When the time came for goodbyes to be said, Mama, with a last look at her unconscious father, took leave of Oma. Brave little Oma, she was losing her husband, and a daughter was going overseas, but all her life she had coped with difficult situations.

"Don't worry about a thing," she said to Mama, "go and start your new life in England and come back and see us as soon, and as often as you can." Mane went to the station with the three of us, and arranged us and our luggage on the Hook of Holland boat train. A school friend of Mama's was there too, and looked at Eberhard and me clad in our velveteen smocks, Eberhard's green and mine a rich purple.

"How sweet they look," she exclaimed, "like a violet in the field." It was a remark Mama quoted many times. Although all the heavy luggage had been sent on in advance and Mama had only a couple of travelling bags, two small children are always a handful on a train journey. Mama was grateful to the gentleman who shared our carriage. When at last they reached their destination, he carried a sleepy Eberhard, while Mama followed on to the ship, carrying me. A stewardess showed us into our reserved cabin and helped Mama put us to bed, then Mama herself subsided gratefully on to her own bunk for her long-earned rest.

So, we left Germany and our life there, and in future would only return for holiday visits. It was a milestone in all our lives. Mama lay on her bunk listening to the throb of the engines, worrying in case it was going to be a bad crossing. Pessimistic friends had informed her that this was the time of spring tides, and the sea could be very rough. Tired out, Mama eventually slept, and over the dark waters the ship carried us safely to the port of Harwich, where we docked, early on the morning of 23rd March, 1927.

Mama woke early, and peered eagerly out of the porthole for her first glimpse of England. She barely had time for more than a glimpse of docks and warehouses, when there was a knock at the cabin door.

"There's a gentleman come for you!" announced the stewardess brightly, and close behind her was Papa, with his reassuring presence. Papa immediately took charge, and while Mama dressed the two of us, he packed the overnight bag, made sure that nothing was left behind, and escorted us on deck. The immigration and customs formalities were quickly dealt with, and in no time at all, we were sitting in the train bound for Hull. Breakfast had been partaken of in the dining car, and now we were all together again, at last, in a carriage to ourselves. Mama allowed herself to relax in her seat, the worst part of the journey was now thankfully over, and she could sit back and watch the unknown English countryside unfold before her eyes.

It was a blustery day, the wind chasing fluffy, white clouds across a dazzling blue sky, there was a promise of spring in the air. While she and Papa discussed the scenery and the obvious differences in the villages, farms and towns that passed, Eberhard and I sat with our noses pressed to the window, gazing raptly at objects that seemed to whizz past our eyes. Cows and horses in the fields were greeted with cries of delight. What did we really care that we were in a foreign country for the first time in our lives? Cows and horses are the same the world over! What mattered was that we had Mama and Papa together again, and our little world was secure.

We did not realise, of course, that this was our first sight of the country that was to become our permanent home, that we would come to love and feel at home in, more than we ever would in Germany. The land of our birth would be to us the foreign land, where even as children we would at times feel alien and strange. But these thoughts were far from the mind of the solemn-faced, dark haired, little girl, who sat on her father's knee, shouting out in German at everything that took her fancy. She probably wondered why Papa kept telling her other names for the familiar objects she saw. "Kuh ist cow, Pferd ist horse." My very first lesson in English was in progress, but I didn't know or care. At last we reached our destination, Hull. Sleepy by now, and no doubt fractious after the long journey, we were carried to the taxi rank for the final stage of our journey.

Of course, I remember nothing of my first sight of Hull, the city that was to become *my* city; the city I was to love fiercely forever! I have found out since that in Hull, there are two types of inhabitants; those who love Hull, and those who hate it. The latter leave as soon as they get the chance, but the former remain loyal forever. We were to belong to the former group. On the short taxi ride to 10 Crystal Street, Mama looked out at the very ordinary streets, with their small shops and drab houses that compared so unfavourably with the elegance of Hannover, and the rural prettiness of Kaltenweide. But a feeling of contentment and warmth crept over Mama, she couldn't explain it; she used to say that she felt that this was where she belonged. She would be happy here – she had come home.

At 10 Crystal Street, the taxi stopped and we alighted, the luggage was seen to, and the driver paid off. Papa flung open the door with a flourish, "Welcome," he said, and we entered the dark, narrow hallway. From the back regions, the motherly figure of Mrs Burton approached, volubly hospitable. She shook hands formally with Mama, and took polite little Eberhard's outstretched hands in hers.

"What a beautiful child," she exclaimed, "never have I seen a handsomer one." She looked at me, but the sight of this large lady descending on us, saying things that I couldn't understand proved too much for me, and if she said anything about me, it was drowned by howls, as I hid behind the safety of Mama.

The house in Crystal Street was to be our house for the next ten weeks. Mrs Burton cooked, cleaned and washed for us, and for half a crown a week, the young daughter, Ivy, took Eberhard and me to the park every afternoon, while Mama had a rest. After a month of this existence, Mama began to get restless, she longed for her own kitchen, for a garden for us to play in, for a bathroom – in other words, for her own home. Mrs Burton was an excellent cook, a real Yorkshire cook, but Mama was ready for her own brand of German cooking, her own way of seasoning meat and vegetables, good honest rye bread, instead of the everlasting "white pap," as she called it. The bread problem was soon solved, Papa heard of a Jewish baker in the vicinity, whose bread was all that could be desired, strong, dark rye. From that day on, we had a regular order.

Finding a house took a little more time, but at last their efforts were rewarded. A house in Louis Street, just across the main road, Spring Bank, was for rent. Papa paid the rent in advance, and came home proudly bearing the key! Mama hadn't even seen the house, but Papa assured her it was just what she wanted.

11. 7 LOUIS STREET

The house in Louis Street was typically late Victorian, rather pretentiously called 'Ardwick Villa, a small front garden and a privet hedge behind iron railings, separated it from the pavement. Papa unlocked the front door with ceremony and he and Mama went in to inspect the accommodation. It was quite roomy, and if not perfect, at least it was better than just renting a few rooms in someone's house. Downstairs were two large reception rooms, a big kitchen, a wash house, and the usual offices. The back garden was pleasant, with lawns, flower borders and beautiful stone urns, filled with geraniums, a small rustic shed stood at the back. Behind the boundary wall at the end of the garden was the platform of the small local railway station 'Botanic Gardens.' Upstairs were four bedrooms and a large bathroom. Mama went round allocating rooms.

"This will be our bedroom," she said, standing in the big empty room, which faced the street, "the smaller adjoining room will do for the children, the back bedroom will make a nice day nursery, and the room right at the back overlooking the garden will be your office." Papa approved, it all fitted in very nicely.

"Just one thing," he said, "if we're going to get a maid to live in, where is she going to sleep?" Mama considered the problem, and solved it immediately.

"In the bathroom," she said, "there's plenty of room for a bed and a chest of drawers, with the hot water tank in the corner it will be warm and cosy, besides, she will only be in it during the night, so we can still use it the rest of the time." A strange arrangement, but as time proved, amazingly it seemed to work very well!

In no time, everything was arranged and the furniture, once again, crossed the North Sea. Mama asked Mrs

Burton's assistance in finding a suitable maid. The Burtons belonged to the Salvation Army, and Mrs Burton asked around. She came up with a plump, cosy, Yorkshire girl, called Dolly, who came to see us and promised Mama she would help get the house ready before we moved in. In her previous job, she had worked for an elderly couple who owned a small shop; living space above the shop was very limited, and there was no place for Dolly to sleep, so she had a mattress under the shop counter! The bathroom was certainly an improvement on that and she was really quite grateful. Dolly was a happy, contented girl, and her wants were few; all she asked for was Sunday afternoon off to go to her meetings, where she would go, dressed in her uniform and bonnet, greatly admired by us.

Once the family was established in 7 Louis Street, Mama began to feel more settled. At first, the ringing of the front doorbell would cause some alarm and consternation, and she would call for Papa or Dolly to answer it, but as her confidence in the English language grew, that hurdle was soon overcome. Our new neighbours proved to be pleasant and helpful. On one side lived two kindly, elderly sisters, who, soon after we had moved in, gave me, to my great delight, a doll's tea-set. On the other side lived a couple called Robinson. Mrs Robinson, who was older than Mama, promptly took charge. She invited Mama round to tea and introduced her to a modest social life. She took her to concerts, theatre matinees, shopping trips in town, and so on. She corrected Mama if she slipped up in her English pronunciation or grammar. Mama, having picked up a lot of local and Yorkshire expressions from Mrs Burton and Dolly, would come out with sayings like "I'll wait while Thursday."

"You must never say while Thursday, dear," Mrs Robinson would chide gently, "the correct thing to say is, until Thursday."

Papa liked his new office overlooking the garden. Mr Burton, now retired, helped him, Fred became the office boy, and a pretty girl called Muriel Ellis became his secretary. She was a pleasant, friendly person, and was to stay with us for many years, indeed, she became one of the family. We children couldn't pronounce Muriel, instead we called her a strange, half German name, Morgel. This was adopted by Mama and Papa too, and Morgel she was to us forever. As we grew older, and became more English, we discarded the baby talk and called her instead Miss Ellis, but to Mama and Papa, she was always Morgel.

The office was a place where we were always welcome, we would be given pencils and scraps of paper and spend hours scribbling and drawing strange shapes. Every so often Morgel would shout "Moocoorovan," and we would rush to the window where we had a good view of the railway lines which passed the bottom of the garden. Morgel's strange call meant that the cattle trucks were passing. The poor beasts gazed bewilderedly out of the vans, their large, gentle eyes viewing for the last time, the world they were soon to leave. Poor creatures, they were on their way to the abattoir. We, luckily, didn't know that; we just thought they were having a ride on the train!

At the back of the garden, Papa constructed a large sand pit for us, and our first summer in England passed happily. As the autumn drew on and we spent more time indoors, Mama, who by now was expecting another baby, decided she needed more help. A young girl called Marjorie was engaged to look after Eberhard and me. She came every day, took us for walks (if it was fine), and amused us in the nursery, where a fire burned cosily in the grate, when the weather was cold.

On January 26th the baby was born, a little girl, she took the other half of Mama's name, Anne, but Mama decided to call her the Spanish diminutive of Anna, 'Anita.' Having a baby in those days for women like Mama, was a very leisurely affair. Anita was born at home. I remember going in to see her with Eberhard, when she was only a couple of hours old. The midwife was bathing a small, red, shrieking, creature! "This is your new little sister," Papa said proudly, while Mama sat up in bed and smiled happily at us. For a whole month Mama took life easy. Mrs Burton came to run the household, and helped by Dolly, everything ran smoothly. All Mama had to do was to nurse the baby and get her own strength back.

Soon, our first year in England had passed. How our lives had changed in such a comparatively short time. We were now a family of five living in a pleasant house. Papa's business was flourishing – he had no problems lengthening his permit to stay in England. He was, after all, giving full time employment to five people, and as such, was an entirely 'desirable alien!' Mama and Papa's small circle of friends had widened. There were still the Robinsons, Truswells and Websters, and besides these, there was a German pork butcher and his family, the Wagners, and a young couple called Clark. He was English, and his wife was a German from Cologne – they too had three children.

When Anita was five months old and was due to be christened, Mama decided that as we did not belong to a church in England, the baby would be christened at the family church, the Nazarethkirch in Hannover. Once more we were all together again in Germany, staying with Oma and Tante Mane. Relations came from far and near to attend the christening, and also to partake of Oma's delicious cakes. I missed most of the ceremony in the church, as I started to become restless and irritable. Mane took me out into the warm sunshine. She didn't mind at all – her Italian admirer lived in the house next door to the church. She said that in my tantrum I had kicked off my shoe, which had flown into the shrubbery, whereupon she and her boyfriend spent the entire length of the service looking for it! Knowing Mane, she probably flung the shoe in herself and looking for it was of secondary importance once she and her handsome Italian were together in the shrubbery.

While over in Germany, Mama advertised for a maid to come back with us. Dolly had left us to go back to the little shop where she had originally helped. The old man's wife had died, and he had begged Dolly to return, which kind-hearted Dolly did. We had not seen the last of her however, for she returned to us later for a short while to help out between German maids. The new baby having been duly christened and admired by all the relations, we came back to Hull, bringing with us the new maid, Agnes. Papa had left a couple of weeks before, and when we returned home a surprise awaited us; a pretty terrier puppy. His name was Boy.

The next three years passed happily, Oma and Tante Mane came to visit us several times, and we would go across to see them for weeks at a time. Eberhard by now was five years old, and therefore school age in England. This caused quite a problem! In Germany, children started school after their sixth birthday, so when the school attendance officer called, Mama put her foot down firmly.

"Five years old is far too young," she informed him, "in my country the children start at six, it's quite soon enough. Besides, his English is not good enough for school yet." So she argued and remarkably managed to postpone the day for a whole year. She was, after all, a qualified teacher herself, and Eberhard could already add, subtract, and do most things that children of that age learn at school. As for reading, Mama said that that would follow naturally once he'd mastered the language. As it was, we could both understand English, but were strangely reluctant to speak it. Marjorie, Dolly and Morgel had done their best, but we stubbornly refused to say anything but "Yes" and "No."

After Eberhard's sixth birthday, in June, Mama began looking round for a suitable school for her beloved little first born. It was not an easy task. These were the days when private schools flourished, some large, some small, some just a handful of children in someone's front room; there was a bewildering choice. At the end of Louis Street a passage led to a large Council school, which couldn't have been nearer to us. It had been the suggestion of the school board man, but it was not even considered. Mama discussed schools with our

Newsagents wife, who had a small boy the same age as Eberhard.

"Robert goes to Miss Sawden's in Duesbury Street," said Mrs Butterwick, helpfully.

"It's a good little school and there are no roads to cross. Come with me when I collect Robert this morning and have a word with Miss Sawden."

Mama set off at the appointed time, taking both of us with her. Miss Ada Sawden, a tall gracious lady, her white hair elegantly piled on her head, received us kindly. Yes, she would be delighted to take us both next term.

"Oh, no," said Mama, "only the boy will be starting, the little girl is not even five yet." Miss Sawden looked at the two of us, holding hands, shy and tongue-tied, she sensed a problem.

"Wouldn't it be better for both of them if they started together?" she suggested, "after all, if they can't speak English yet, they won't feel so alone if they have each other." Mama opened her mouth to say that there was no question of me starting yet, that she didn't believe in children starting school before they were six, when she suddenly changed her mind. She saw me, tightly holding Eberhard's hand. She knew I was a dependable little soul, I wouldn't scream and cry and carry on, it wasn't my way. I would be a reassuring and comforting little presence, an anchor in the storm for my brother who was a much more highly strung, nervous child than I was.

She had been worried about Eberhard, alone in a strange foreign school. We had always done everything together, and we would share this big event in our lives too.

"Very well," she said, "she is only four, but why not? It's a very good idea." So the German custom of starting school at six was conveniently waived in my case, and we were duly enrolled as pupils at Miss Sawden's school, or, to give it its official name, 'The Fish Street Memorial School for Girls and Preparatory for Boys,' as the notice at the gate proclaimed. The cost for tuition was two guineas each per term, stationery and books extra. Miss Sawden smiled down at the two of us benignly.

"Goodbye children," she said, "we will see you again in September."

12. THE MISSES SAWDEN

The first day of the autumn term and our first school day was a bright and sunny one. We set off rather anxiously, one on either side of Mama, down Princes Avenue. We each carried a small new attaché case, containing a mid-morning snack. This first term was to be mornings only, to break us in gently. The little school was housed in two large upstairs rooms behind the Fish Street Memorial Church, in Princes Avenue, the school entrance was in Duesbury Street. Mama gave us into the care of a young teacher, who led us to a cloakroom halfway up the stairs, and so started an entirely new phase in both our lives.

Up to now we had had little contact with other children, having played only in our own garden, chattering away to each other in German. Now, suddenly, there seemed to be children everywhere and all speaking English! The young teacher, who was called Miss Herrick and assisted with the younger ones, helped us remove our coats and find our pegs. Then she took us to our classroom and introduced us to our teacher, who rejoiced in the somewhat intimidating name of Miss Bull. She was in charge of the younger end of the school, while Miss Sawden herself coped with the older children. There were actually two Miss Sawdens, Miss Ada and Miss Emily, but Miss Emily only came twice a week to take singing with the older girls.

Both classrooms had single wood and iron desks for about twenty children, and apart from a large map of the world on Miss Sawden's room, and one or two religious pictures, the walls were completely bare. However, each room possessed a large fireplace, where, on cold days a fire burned brightly and cosily. The teacher's desks were strategically placed close by.

I remember our first school day perfectly well; we were seated at the front of the class and given tracing books. I traced a camel and Eberhard a horse. We were then provided with slates, a squeaky slate pencil and a small damp sponge in a tin. We copied letters from cards placed before us, but more than that I don't recall. Opposite me on the wall over the fireplace hung a large picture of Jesus, carrying a lantern, and proclaiming 'I am the light of the world.' I was terrified of Miss Bull, and I don't think I spoke a single word to her for the first few weeks at school. Discipline was of the strictest, and we accepted it quite happily, after all, this was what school was all about.

Nowadays, children start school in bright, joyful classrooms, toys are spread about, there are colourful pictures on the walls, and admission teachers are jolly and understanding. Halfway through the sessions there are playtimes in the fresh air. How different from Miss Sawden's little school! Yet when I look back it is with great nostalgia. The four years I spent there were perfectly happy ones, and I do not remember ever not wanting to go. We soon settled in and made friends with the other children, and with this, our English became fluent quite naturally, although talking in lesson time was firmly discouraged. Silence, in Miss Bull's eyes, was golden, and no talking of any kind was permitted, except in answer to Miss Bull's questions.

Playtime, if such it could be called, was the only time she relented. For about ten minutes every morning we were allowed to leave our seats, eat our lunch, talk to each other in whispers and generally relax. There was no playground to run about in and let off steam, but we managed without. The boy's toilet was downstairs and permanently unlocked, but the girl's was off the cloakroom, and locked. Miss Bull kept the key, and it had to be asked for in a discreet whisper! All the years I was there, I never once set foot in that toilet. Nothing would have induced me to ask Miss Bull for the key. Such a thing was far too personal. However, Miss Bull must have been aware that small children occasionally need exercise, so every so often we had drill. We stood in rows at the back of the classroom and did arm movements, or marched around to music. If Miss Bull was feeling benevolent we played, The Mulberry Bush, In And Out The Windows, The Farmer's In His Den, and Nuts In May. Apart from these slightly frivolous moments, we remained in our desks, learning to read, write and reckon. The windows were too high to see much else beside the sky, in its various changing moods, so there were no distractions. Nowadays, children paint or crayon freely with glorious colours, they are encouraged to express themselves, and their natural talents are fostered. We had bur tracing books first, and later on coloured pastel crayons and small black pastel paper books into which we meticulously copied picture cards of exquisite, detailed wild and garden flowers. I still have the books, and looking at them now, it seems incredible that a small girl could execute such exquisite, neat and painstaking copies, but as I had a great love of drawing combined with a natural talent, small wonder that I enjoyed this activity. However, it gave no incentive to any imagination or initiative on my part.

Indeed, praise and encouragement were very thin on the ground, mistakes and untidiness were pounced upon, but good work was expected and therefore not remarked on, at least not in Miss Bull's class. Miss Sawden graciously acknowledged one's efforts by a little system of her own. After marking a piece of work which pleased her, she would put the capital letter G at the bottom, this stood for good; a really good effort would receive V.G. – very good, but the highest accolade, and therefore comparatively rare, was V.G.I. – very good indeed. Nowadays, children in the admission classes are encouraged by little shrieks and trills of delight by the teacher. The most untidy hieroglyphics and messy drawings are treated like masterpieces. Children are told what clever little beings they are, how hard they are trying, and so on. I know, I was an admissions teacher myself! I often wonder what Miss Bull would have thought of today's teaching methods. I think she would have strongly disapproved. Her strict regime produced excellent results – there is certainly no doubt about that!

According to the school reports written in Miss Sawden's flowing script, I was a diligent child, who learnt to read very quickly. Indeed, I don't remember learning at all, it just came to me and at once all my lovely story books were open to me. All that were in English, that is. The German ones from Oma, nearly all in that strange Gothic print, were still a mystery to me. I was, however, determined to read them, and struggled with the funny letters, until I finally mastered them, and could read the lovely gruesome tales of the Brothers Grimm by myself. To give Miss Bull time to do her marking and clearing up at the end of the day, we had a totally silent lesson, called 'learning.' We each had before us a pile of books, open at the appropriate place. We read a chapter of scripture from our small New Testament books, a hymn from the Hymn Book, then a row of words from the spelling book. We did not learn phonetics, we spelt as everyone else did, by using the names of the letters. Miss Bull would hear our spelling the next day, and woe betide any child that didn't know its lesson – but at least we learnt to spell correctly.

Tables were also learnt, and these were chanted in class together, with Miss Bull pouncing on individuals to make sure they knew them, and were not riding on the backs of others. The bottom book of the book pile was the reading or story book, according to one's ability. It was always my aim to get to it as quickly as possible, but if one reached it too soon Miss Bull would become suspicious in case one had skipped the more essential work! I used to sit staring at the other books until I felt a decent interval had elapsed and I could devote myself wholly to my story book. The teaching of sums was entirely mechanical and therefore easy. It was not until years later that I discovered what 'tens' and 'units' really were! We simply wrote T and U over columns of numbers, and later, as one progressed to three figures, H.T.U. We multiplied, divided, added, and took away. We borrowed numbers and left others on the 'doorstep.' I have never had a mathematical brain, but we must have been well taught, for at my next school I was ahead of the others in sums, and it was only at High School that I took my rightful place, at the bottom of the class!

Apart from drawing, our other light relief was needlework. While the boys modelled in Plasticine, we girls embroidered ready-traced tray cloths or tea cosy covers. All my efforts were sent to Oma, who was delighted with them. We did keep one cloth, and I still have it, a pattern of lazy daisies and French knots, of which I was very proud.

As we sat and stitched away, Miss Bull would read to us, children's classics and other stories. She would always stop at the most exciting place so that we couldn't wait for the next lesson. Sometimes, when Miss Bull was in a benign mood, between lessons, or if we had done our work satisfactorily, she would play a game with us. This strange game, one of her own invention, was our greatest treat and we could never get enough of it. It was called 'Hearing the Pin Drop.' We would sit with our eyes tightly closed, while Miss Bull, with her hands behind her back, holding a pin, stood facing us. Suddenly, she would drop the pin. If you heard it, you could put up your hand and open your eyes. The last one to put up their hand was out, the game went on until all were eliminated, except one child, when we all applauded with hand clapping. Too eager children, whose hand shot up before the pin dropped, were also eliminated, as were those who peeped! It sounds a very tame game, but it was tremendous fun, and a red letter day whenever we played it.

Promotion in Miss Bull's class followed a simple system. As one became older, one moved backwards, so to speak, until one reached the last row of desks. Once established in the back row, we knew that we would soon be in Miss Sawden's class. This advent was regarded with some awe and trepidation. The only contact we had had with Miss Sawden so far was at the morning assembly, when Miss Bull's class would file into the top class, two by two, and row up in front of the desks. Then we sang a hymn and said the

Lord's Prayer. We sang all the favourite hymns of childhood, Jesus Bids Us Shine, Onward Christian Soldiers, and There Is A Green Hill Far Away. Miss Sawden and Miss Bull faced us, watching eagle-eyed for any recalcitrant child that dared to open its eyes during prayers. I always had a fearful urge to peep, but on the rare occasions I succumbed to the temptation, it would be to find Miss Bull's glassy eye fixing me. She used to tell us that she had eyes in the back of her head, and for a long time I believed her. Miss Bull, with her horn-rimmed glasses and dark cropped hair, was practically a God in that little class, how could we possibly disbelieve her!

Eberhard went up into Miss Sawden's class before I did, and began to learn History, Geography, and French. It all sounded terribly grown up. At the age of eight, he sat for the entrance exam for the Grammar School, as did all the other boys of his age. They must have all passed, for they left Miss Sawden's and started their new school the following September.

I, and the rest of my group, went up into Miss Sawden's. We were back on the front row again, and behind us sat the 'big' girls, who, if they didn't pass the High School exam, could stay until they were fourteen. All boys had to leave when they were eight anyway. It was our turn to do History, Geography, and French. We had a large book called *Highroads of History*, lavishly illustrated with coloured, and black and white pictures, depicting historical events through the ages. There was King Alfred, burning the cakes, Robert the Bruce and his spider, a copy of the painting 'When did you last see your father', and so on. It was a delightful way to learn History, and much more fun than the wars and dates at High School later on. At the end of the book was a portrait of Edward VII and one of Queen Alexandra, and that was where History ended for us. There was also a portrait of Queen Victoria, who to my mind was the image of Miss Sawden.

Both the Miss Sawdens wore their clothes discreetly ankle length. One memorable occasion, Miss Emily fainted during a singing lesson, slipping sideways off her chair with a little sigh, whereupon, Miss Bull, in whose room the singing lesson always took place, rushed up and put a screen round the recumbent figure. She shooed us off into the other room, but not before my shocked eyes had seen the long black boots, with dozens of little black buttons, that Miss Emily's rucked up skirts revealed! I felt that I had intruded upon something very personal and private. We were convinced that she was dead, but Miss Bull's and Miss Sawden's ministrations must have fully restored her, for later in the week, she was back for lessons. She was her smiling, gentle, old self, and let us sing all our favourite songs.

Our Geography lessons were based on a prettily illustrated little book, called *Children of Other Lands*, and the large map of the world, which decorated one wall. We learned of the strange customs of foreign children, and Miss Sawden would point out on her map where their often, equally odd abodes, like igloos and wigwams, were located. The little German girl and boy depicted wearing traditional dress, playing on a hillside with a goat, in front of a pretty Black Forest house, seemed as foreign to me as the Chinese children, with their coolie hats and rickshaws!

French, being an essential part of one's education, Miss Sawden tackled valiantly. Her pronunciation was appalling, as I found out later, nevertheless we painstakingly learned vocabulary and grammar from a small book called *French Without Tears*; again there were plenty of pictures to help sustain our interest. In later years, this foundation in French, stood me in good stead.

There was no drill in Miss Sawden's class; instead we used to do country dancing occasionally, Sir Roger de Coverley and We'll Catch A Fox, being our favourites. Apart from this, there was no form of exercise whatsoever. We still carried on with our needlework and crayoning, but there was no more 'Hearing the Pin Drop.' For our entertainment, Miss Sawden cut out the children's strip from her daily newspaper, and every morning it would repose on a small table beside her desk. As we came into the room in the mornings, before we took our seats, we were allowed to study the pictures and follow the adventures of Japhet and Happy of the Arkubs. By the end of term Miss Sawden had collected a large pile of these strips, and in the general relaxation of the rules, on the last days of term, we would happily colour the little pictures.

As Christmas drew near, both Miss Sawden and Miss Bull unbent sufficiently to hang up a few brightly coloured paper garlands, which were enough to send us into subdued ecstasies of anticipation of the joys in store. Once, in the Christmas term, Miss Sawden showed us a little decoration she had made. It consisted of a cotton reel covered in silver paper and tied round with purple ribbon.

"Who has a Christmas tree at home?" she asked, and everyone's hand shot up. "Well," said Miss Sawden, "if one of you could please break off a small twig from your own tree, we'll push it into this reel and it will look just like a tiny Christmas tree, won't it?"

"Yes, Miss Sawden," we chorused.

"In fact," went on Miss Sawden, carried away by her idea, "why don't you all make one at home – we could put them on the window sills. They would look so pretty, especially if the ribbons were all different colours." Although we were all enthusiastic, nobody took up her suggestion, and the little ornament waited in vain for its bit of twig. It was relegated to the window sill behind Miss Sawden's desk, where it remained, sad and lonely, waiting for the companions that never came. Its hopeful loneliness saddened me, but there was nothing I could do about it. The 'Weihnachtsmann' brought our tree only on Christmas Eve, and that would have been too late.

There was always a party on the last morning of every term. Not for us, the cakes, jellies, ice-creams, and sandwiches of today's school parties! We would all troop into Miss Bull's classroom, where the desks had all been pushed against the walls for the occasion. Then we played Oranges and Lemons, Hunt the Thimble, Musical Chairs, and all our favourite games, with Miss Sawden presiding regally, Miss Emily playing the piano, and Miss Bull becoming almost human, gaily organising everything. At eleven o'clock, with cries of "Good morning, Miss Sawden, good morning Miss Bull!" we all trooped home, clutching our reports, and for a while, forgot all about school.

13. "A ROUGH NIGHT"

Starting school did not curtail our long annual holiday in Germany. Private schools in those days, had eight whole weeks in the Summer, with a month at Easter and Christmas. Half-term holidays however, were one day only. We always knew when our German holiday drew near; the large cabin trunk would emerge from the box room, and Mama would start to pack several days in advance. We wore our oldest clothes, the best being stowed in the trunk as soon as they had been laundered. All was bustle and excitement.

Anita and I each packed our own small suitcase, into which went our two favourite dolls, Peggy and David, complete with their clothes and bedding. Peggy and David went on every holiday with us, they were part of the family. We had numerous dolls, but these two were special. Peggy was a celluloid doll, a present from Oma for my sixth birthday, and David arrived the following January for Anita's third. David had a celluloid head and cloth body stuffed with straw. At that time our German maid Elfriede, was always singing a song about 'Jung Siegfried'. Anita fancied the name, and called her new doll Jung Siegfried. That Easter however, while we were on holiday in Scarborough, our landlady, Mrs Scott, asked Anita what her dolly was called.

"Jung-Siegfried," chirped Anita. "What, dear?" asked a puzzled Mrs Scott. "Jung Siegfried," repeated Anita patiently.

Mrs Scott was still mystified," That's a funny name," she said, "why don't you call him something nice, like David?" "All right, I will," said the accommodating little Anita, "I'll call him David."

We now always crossed the North Sea on ships that sailed directly from Hull, either going to Rotterdam, with the

British A.H.L. line, or going to Hamburg with the German Argo Line. We children preferred the Argo ships, as they carried fewer passengers, and Emil, the steward on one of them was a great pal of ours. Moreover, the Hamburg route took thirty six hours, which meant two nights on board and one whole lovely day at sea.

Mama, who was a bad sailor, preferred the shorter crossing to Rotterdam. Whichever ship we were on the procedure for us was always the same.

"Once we're out of the river," Mama would say, "it will get rough, and we must all lie down." This rule was rigorously adhered to, even on calm crossings. When we sat down to our evening meal on board, we would be told, "Eat something, so that you have something to be sick on!" Delightful thought.

Immediately after our meal, we would repair to our cabins. We children in a four berth cabin, with Eberhard in a top bunk and Anita and me in the lower ones. Once settled, Mama would rummage in the locker and produce the most revolting tin receptacles, rusty, stained, unappetising. These would hook over a bar provided at the head end of the bunk.

"Here are your Kotznapps," she would say, "all ready for when you need them." The horrid word suited the hateful things – why Mama didn't use a more refined word I don't know, I suppose being sea-sick is too basic a function to be even remotely elegant! "Oh, Gott," Mama would say, "I can feel it rocking already, we're in for a rough night! If I don't lie down soon I'll be sick in here!" and with this cheerful attitude she would totter off to her own cabin. Papa, on the other hand, was an excellent sailor, he boasted that he had never been sick in his life and the best place was up on deck, in the fresh air.

Now, prepared for all emergencies, we lay in our narrow bunks, too excited to sleep. The little steamer clanked and creaked, the water carafes tinkled musically in their holders, and the tiny curtains at the porthole swung to and fro. Halfway through the night a pallid and swaying Mama, clad in her dressing gown, would appear in our cabin. In a faint voice she would say: "everybody all right, anybody been sick yet? I've been sick lots of times. Oh Gott! What a night!" and retching horribly, she would depart to her cabin for another session with her Kotznapp. It's a miracle we didn't all turn out to be terrible sailors, with all the encouragement we got! Sometimes we obliged by being a little sick – probably purely psychological, for I have never been sea-sick since those days.

Worse was still to come, when Mama discovered a ghastly anti sea-sick sweet, called 'Hamibon'. She bought them in Germany, and because they were German, it followed that they were good! Now, as soon as we were out of the river, she passed these square monstrosities around.

"Don't chew them," she'd say, "let them dissolve slowly in your mouth." Dissolve slowly they did, they filled our entire mouths, and took at least an hour to go. The taste was revolting, like machine oil, and it settled heavily in our stomachs, guaranteed to make us sick before the night was over. Once the ship reached the Elbe or Maas, or on homeward trips, the Humber, all was well again. Even Mama was miraculously restored to rosy-cheeked health!

Our German holidays always followed the same pattern. First, we stayed in Hannover with Oma and Mane, then we would go to some little resort in the Hartz Mountains, or other hilly area, or to the Baltic coast, with Oma and Mane joining us. Then we would visit the Berlin relations. Papa used to leave before we did, or join us later; after all, he couldn't leave his business to run itself for eight weeks, and besides, he was often in Germany on business and could visit Hannover and Berlin then. Arriving in Hannover, everything seemed to join up with the year before. There was Mane meeting us at the railway station, there was the taxi into which we all piled, chattering nineteen to the dozen, and there at last was the Simrockstrasse, and waiting to welcome us, unchanging, adorable, our very own, dear, sweet, little, Oma.

14. OMA

The only grandparent I remember was Oma, Mama's mother. Dear Oma, how lucky we were to have her. She was small, spry, determined, good-humoured, kind, and totally loveable. In those days, elderly widows always wore black, and Oma was no exception. She dressed in black from head to toe, and that to my mind was the way all Omas looked. Her clothes reached nearly to the ground, revealing black stockings and shoes. I used to wonder how she could tell one garment from another, for they all looked alike to me. When we went out visiting, or elsewhere, she changed from black blouse and skirt, into a black dress; to my mind she still looked the same, so why bother? She had a collection of high, flower pot sort of hats, that we used to try on secretly. The only bit of relief she allowed herself was in the pinafores she wore in the mornings, they were black printed with tiny white or grey flowers. After a few years of widowhood, women were allowed to go into lilac or purple, but Oma cared for neither and black was her colour for the rest of her life. Once, however, she splashed out on a tea-gown that had a jabot, edged with gold braid, and was reprimanded by her elder sister, Anna, who considered it to be too frivolous!

Oma was a wonderful companion, and her fund of stories was inexhaustible. Having grown up in the country she knew lots of myths and superstitions. Those that fascinated me the most were of thunderstorms. I would listen in delighted horror as Oma told true tales of what had happened to friends of hers in the old Marienau days.

How the lightning had come into the room at a celebration meal, and danced over the knives and forks, and how once it had even raced over a piano keyboard, and played a ghostly tune; how it had struck houses and people in the fields, or sheltering under trees. "Don't laugh when the lightning is about," she would warn us, if we laughed defiantly from the safety of indoors. So we sat in silent awe as the fierce storms that German summers abound in, crashed and flashed about us. Sometimes Oma would fold her hands and say a little prayer for our protection, which we would fearfully repeat after her, the terrifying words – "Den Schlafenden lass ruhen, den Fresser den schlag tot," "Let the sleeper rest, strike dead the glutton!"

She also used to recite a particularly gruesome little poem, about a grandmother, a great-grandmother, a mother, and child, who were together in a room while a storm raged outside. The gist of it was that each person talked about their plans, the child of tomorrow's play, the mother and grandmother of what they could do in the future, and the great-grandmother asked only that the Lord have mercy on her soul. The ghastly end of the poem was a thunderbolt striking the house, killing all four. The moral was that one should always be prepared for one's end, at whatever time of life. How I loved that poem! I couldn't get enough of it, with its wonderful, hateful end.

If Oma was sewing near a window when a storm broke out, she would always put away her scissors, and cease work. Then we would all move away to the furthest end of the room. The inevitable, though unintentional result of all this has left me with a deep-seated fear of thunderstorms, especially in the open. The first clap of thunder sends me scurrying to the nearest building as fast as my wobbly legs can carry me. I can't really blame Oma for this, as I was an avid listener, and shamelessly encouraged her. I wouldn't have it otherwise, those tales of Oma's were an important part of my childhood. Besides these tales, Oma would, of course, tell us all the old German folk tales. We knew them all by heart, but Oma would tell them in all their gruesome detail, as they had originally been told, before modern editions cut out the gory bits, and gave happy endings. In Oma's versions, blood flowed, heads were cut off, bodies slit open and children swallowed whole. The lot! The one which appealed to me most was the part where Rumpelstiltskin stamped his foot into the ground in rage, and then took hold of his other leg and pulled himself in half! To go to market with Oma was another delight. She would never buy any fruit without first sampling it. I used to go with her from stall to stall, enviously watching, as she tasted and rejected fruit until she found the perfect choice.

"Why can't I taste?" I would ask, and she would reply "Because children aren't allowed to."

Children were allowed to do very little in Germany, we soon found out. We were not allowed to do this or that, and led a very restricted life on our visits. If we played out in the street outside Oma's house, we couldn't come running in and out, the way we did at home. Out was out, until we were called in. We couldn't do anything at all that made a noise between two and four o'clock in the afternoons, when it seemed as if all Hannover settled down for its afternoon nap! We would tiptoe about the apartment, whispering and hissing at each other, painting in our books on the balcony, or looking at the old-fashioned books in the bookcase. Then at last we would hear Oma moving about in her kitchen, and the glorious aroma of fresh coffee would fill the air. Then suddenly, all was noise and bustle, the table would be set with delicious cakes, and maybe even cream, and our favourite meal of all, afternoon coffee, would be served.

Oma's apartment was on the third floor of number 24 Simrockstrasse. Shallow steps led up to the large front door. Once inside the spacious entrance hall, it was cool and dim, and a flight of steps led toward a huge stained glass window on the first half-landing. How I loved that window – the other stair windows were plain glass and one could see over the gardens to the other houses, but the great stained glass window was magical and beautiful. Five more short flights of stairs and we were on the third floor, where two large wood and glass entrances, placed diagonally on the landing, led to two apartments. Oma's was on the right. A highly polished brass plaque on the side of the door bore the name, 'E.

Schmidt', in elaborate, Gothic print. The front door opened into an extremely large entrance hall, the rear of which, in the daytime, was permanently shrouded in gloom. Opening off this were six rooms, the doors of which had a top panel of glass, which lightened the gloom a little. On the left, were three rooms, Mane's bedroom, the dining room, and the drawing room. The two reception rooms were enormous, and connected by large wood and glass sliding doors, which were usually thrown open in the summer. The furniture was equally grand, with much carving and decoration. Each room had a large tiled stove in one corner. The high windows, with their heavy lace curtains, looked out across the street, and the dining room had a corner window, which enabled one to see even further.

The drawing room was always called the 'salon', and contained, besides heavy green plush furniture, the ornate piano. We were allowed to practise on it, its back was decorated with dainty fretwork panels, behind which was stretched a piece of pale green silk. When not in use, the keyboard was covered by a long strip of green felt, embroidered with lilies of the valley. I felt it was all wrong to play my silly finger exercises on this elegant piano. It needed to be played properly, or not at all. Besides, I was on holiday, and the last thing I intended to do was practise. Eberhard, on the other hand, was a much better pianist, and played often, the little tinkling tunes sounded pretty and professional. One in particular, called 'The Gypsy's Tent', will always remind me of Oma's salon. Papa, with his bold, confident touch, really brought the piano to life, and Oma was always asking him to play – she said that it was good for the piano.

The piece of furniture which was my favourite, was a tall slim kind of cupboard, that Oma called her "Vertico." With a name like that, it just had to be special! It was fashioned in a dark, almost black, wood, and was ornately carved, full of small shelves and a mirror at the back. The doors opened to reveal Oma's treasures. I would always ask if I could look into it, and first I would always look to see if my things were still there, and they would be! The little tray cloths and the embroidered tea cosy, mounted on blue velvet, that looked so elegant and grand. I would gaze at it, proudly stroking the velvet, and admiring my handiwork, which really consisted only of a few blue and orange lazy daisies! The Vertico also housed Oma's very best china, the thinnest, daintiest china I had ever seen. This was only used, so Oma said, on very special occasions, christenings, birthdays, confirmations, funerals, and such like. Each piece was worth a fortune, and was white and gold, delicately sprigged with violets.

"When you are grown up," Oma would tell me, "it will be yours." I could not believe my luck! I had visions of myself, elegant and grown up, dispensing tea or coffee to other equally elegant adults, proudly passing round the dainty cups and saucers, and serving delicious cream cakes on the pretty plates. Alas, it was never to be, for Oma's house, during the bombing of Hannover, received a direct hit and everything was destroyed with it, the Vertico, the tea set, and the cosy. So many lives were lost in those terrible air raids, and indeed in the whole stupid war. It seems trite to mourn the loss of a tea set and a tea cosy, but the set was Oma's pride and joy, and the cosy had been embroidered with so much love for a beloved grandmother, by small sticky, six-year old fingers. However, that day was still far off and as long as Oma lived, her treasures were safe.

The other rooms in the apartment consisted of Oma's bedroom, the bathroom and the kitchen. Oma's bedroom, true to tradition, had two great beds, a couple of enormous wardrobes, chests and wash stand, with a pair of ewers and bowls. It was austere and rather bleak, but off it was a balcony, and for us this was the best room of all. For it was really just like a room, enclosed as it was on three sides, furnished with table and chairs, and even a carpet. The fourth side was open and overlooked the gardens, and on this side Oma had her balcony boxes crammed with glowing geraniums, they were constantly in bloom, and to this day, whenever I smell the strong scent of geraniums, I am, in spirit, back on Oma's balcony. While the grown-ups were discussing, to our ears, boring topics, in the salon or dining room, we children played on the balcony. It was our special place, and I always wished we had a balcony at home.

The bathroom was like most bathrooms. It had a great copper water heater, heated by gas, which sprang into action with much clanking, bubbling and hissing, at bath time. There was always much excitement and a hint of panic in case it got too hot, and blew up! I was always thankful when bath time was over, and I could escape from the room and the temperamental monster that lived there.

Oma's kitchen was her very special domain, which had an aroma all of its own, of spices, herbs, cooking, and coffee. Oma spent most of her time in the kitchen, her small black figure, bustling between cooker, sink, table and pantry, busy cooking, baking, stirring and mixing. I loved to follow her around and help if allowed to, which I usually was. The kitchen furniture was all painted white, and what intrigued me most were the furniture legs. For practical reasons all the legs were painted black, six inches up from where they rested on the floor. They reminded me of white ponies, with black hooves.

"When I am dead," Oma used to say, "you can have the kitchen furniture." I didn't want Oma to die, but I looked forward to owning the furniture! The kitchen too was blown to smithereens, and I am so glad that Oma died before the outbreak of war, and did not live to see her little world shattered about her ears.

It must have been quite formidable when our family of five invaded Oma's fairly small domain, but we were all snugly and comfortably bedded down in our appointed places. Mama and Papa had Oma's bedroom, Eberhard slept on the sofa in the salon, Oma on the dining room sofa, and Anita and I shared Mane's room with her. This was a long, narrow room and contained two single beds and a chaise-longue. Always referred to as a 'Shezzalong', it was years before I learned how it was really spelt! Mane and I each had a bed, but to poor little Anita fell the honour of sleeping on the red plush Shezzalong. Luckily, she was small and thin, for it was very narrow and to stop her featherbed from slipping off, a chair was pushed against it, so that Anita lay in a semi-cage. When we were settled in our beds, Oma would come and say goodnight. This was always a special time – if we were lucky this was the time she would regale us with stories. I always remember a night that stands out, when Oma came in and sat at the side of my bed. When she had told us a story, she said to me, "Now say your prayers, and go to sleep." I stared at her, slightly embarrassed. "Don't you say your prayers before you go to sleep?" asked Oma.

"No", I said, "we say our prayers at church and at school."

"I always say a little prayer before I go to sleep," said Oma gently, "let's say one together." She folded her soft, old, work-worn hands over my chubby ones, closed her eyes and spoke a sweet, simple prayer. I closed my eyes too, but opened them to peep at Oma's serious old face, so absorbed in what she was saying. Dear, kind Oma, that incident made such an impression on me, that I resolved to please her, and be good like her. After that, I never missed out on my nightly prayer.

We would only visit Oma a few weeks every year, but the times we spent together were special and wonderful. Looking back over half a century, there is so much I still remember. Once I accompanied Oma to the cemetery and helped her water and tend the plants on the family grave. Later on at home I said to her, to the delight of the rest of the family.

"Oma, when you are dead, and in the grave, I'll come and water you, but I won't use water – I'll use wine." I called her "Kleine krümelige Oma," for once, helping her make the beds I noticed crumbs in her bed. I had heard that old things crumbled away! Shocked and horrified, I told Mama, Oma was so old, she was crumbling away! Mama reassured me that they were only biscuit crumbs, for Oma liked a little munch before she went to sleep.

Oma was deaf in one ear and also had trouble with one eye. One had to be sure one walked on the good side! On country walks, we would look for eyebright flowers for Oma's eye. Down the sunlit lanes of childhood memories I see them go – the little old lady clad in black, and trotting by her side, a small, sturdy child, in a light cotton dress. I see them walking hand in hand through the peaceful countryside, the child stopping now and then to pick the pretty, healing, eyebright flowers, and presenting them to the old lady. I see Oma holding the eyebright to her eye and me asking anxiously.

"Is it getting better Oma?" and Oma replying reassuringly. "Yes, my child, it helps my eye wonderfully." Dear Oma, she and I had a very special bond.

15. SUNNY BANK

During the third year of the tenancy of the house in Louis Street, the landlord approached Papa. He asked Papa if he would be interested in buying the house; the price would be eight hundred and fifty pounds. Mama and Papa took stock of the situation. The house and garden were pleasant, the position practical for trams, trains, shops and schools, and yet there were certain disadvantages. There was no maid's bedroom and the master bedroom could only be reached by going through the children's bedroom.

"If we're going to buy a house," said Mama, "I'd want something bigger than this."

So Papa and Mama went house hunting.

There was plenty of choice, the so called Avenues area that lay on the other side of the level crossing had a wide choice of large family houses. Mama and Papa were in no great hurry, and it became a pleasant occupation that summer, going round empty houses. Sometimes they took us children along too. I remember one house in particular, for it had a dog kennel in the garden. I begged them to buy it, we didn't have a dog at the time, and I was longing for another. I thought a dog kennel automatically had a dog to go with it!

Later, after we were settled in our new home we would go walking through the park or down the Avenues, and Mama would point out the houses we nearly bought. They all seemed nicer than ours, but Mama told us they were either too dear, or they had other disadvantages.

One such house was the one next door to Amy Johnson's parents house. She had just made her historic flight and we knew all about how she'd flown over a great sea, full of dreaded sharks that would have torn her to pieces had she ditched into the sea! We used to play a game called Shark

Ships, huddling on the sofa pretending the floor was the sea, full of sharks ready to eat us if we so much as put a toe on the ground. It would have been nice to live next door to such famous people. It had a tremendously long garden full of fruit trees.

"Why didn't you buy it?" we'd ask.

"The kitchens were horribly gloomy," Mama would reply, "and besides it cost thirteen hundred pounds."

On fine sunny days, when Mama took Anita out in her pram, she would walk over the level crossing and down a pleasant road, named Sunny Bank. It was quiet and peaceful, and there were houses only on the sunny side of the street, opposite were the beautiful grounds of the former Botanical Gardens, now the property of the school, Hymers College. As Mama only walked there on fine days, she had the impression of permanent sunshine. She thought it was well named Sunny Bank, and the houses were well built and comfortable looking.

"I would like to live in Sunny Bank," she told Papa, but there were never any houses for sale there. Papa had an idea, "Let's put an advert in the paper," he suggested. So into the local paper went an advert asking for a house in Sunny Bank. To Mama's delight there was actually a reply, from a Mrs Josselin De Jong, who lived at number ten. She was selling her house, she wrote, for £1,100, and if Papa was interested would he please make an appointment to view.

In spite of Papa saying the price was too high, his ceiling price being £950, and not a penny more, Mama phoned immediately and arranged to view the house that very day. There was no harm in looking, she said, and maybe the price could be negotiated. That afternoon she and Papa walked to Sunny Bank, and rang the bell at number ten. The house had a porch with stained glass windows, which appealed to Mama straight away.

"We won't be living in the porch," Papa said, "nice though it is. Let's see the rest of the house first." A trim maid, neatly dressed in her afternoon uniform answered the doorbell.

"Mr and Mrs Dalheim?" she asked politely, and then she admitted them into the hall, with its dark panelling.

Like people, houses have a character, a soul, whatever you like to call it. Entering a house, one can feel if one is the right sort of person, for the personality of the house immediately. Some houses repel instantly, others are indifferent, and some welcome you with warmth and happiness. Number ten Sunny Bank was of the third category, and the minute Mama set foot in it, the house welcomed her. She knew from the first moment that this was to be her home, happiness was soaked into its very bricks.

Over sixty years later the house still retains a wonderful atmosphere, frequently remarked on by friends and visitors. On the other hand numbers eight and twelve on either side, are both unhappy houses, their tenants coming and going. Twelve, especially, seemed doomed, its occupants divorcing with monotonous regularity!

Now combined with number fourteen, into a small hotel, its jinx seems to have been lifted – in effect, twelve has ceased to exist.

But I digress.

The maid ushered Mama and Papa into the front room. It was large, light and elegantly panelled in white and pale blue. Mrs De Jong rose to greet them, and dispatched the maid for tea and cakes.

"What a beautiful room!" exclaimed Mama.

"Yes," said Mrs De Jong, "I've just had all this panelling done, the porch too is new, it cost £200, I will show you the receipts later. That is why I am asking £1,100."

"This is my house," thought Mama happily, accepting a cup of tea from Mrs De Jong. "In this room I too shall serve tea, in my best china cups.

The refreshment partaken, Mrs De Jong rose.

"Shall we see the rest of the house?" she asked. Eagerly Mama followed her, while Papa came more reluctantly, he could tell that Mama had set her heart on the house, without even seeing the remaining rooms. Mama went delightedly from room to room. The north facing dining room, though somewhat gloomy, would be cosy in winter. The morning room, with its blue tiled fireplace, would do as a sitting room for the maid in the evenings. The kitchen, though smaller than in Louis Street, overlooked a very pleasant garden.

"There are two apple trees, a lilac, a laburnum, and a red may tree out there," said Mrs De Jong, "they are beautiful in spring."

Upstairs were five more rooms, and two attic rooms, and a box room at the top of the house.

"It's perfect," said Mama, "absolutely right for us."

Papa kept quiet, it was a nice house, there was no doubt about it. The tour of inspection over, Mrs De Jong led the way back into the drawing room.

"I'll just get the receipts," she said diplomatically, and off she went.

Left alone, Mama and Papa looked at each other. "Just what we want," said Mama, "try and get the price down."

It's no use," said Papa, "she keeps telling us how much she's spent on it."

"Try," urged Mama.

Mrs De Jong came back with a sheaf of papers, and handed them over, Papa studied them. "Yes, I can see you have spent a lot," he said, "It's a very pleasant house, but a little more than we intended to spend. You wouldn't think of coming down in price a little?"

Mrs De Jong was firm, "I'm sorry," she said, "but that's my price."

"Can we have time to think about it?" asked Mama, "we really do like the house."

"Of course you can," said Mrs De Jong, "I am not in a desperate hurry to sell, and I can see you like it."

It did not take Mama very long to bring Papa round to her way of thinking, and in no time at all a mortgage was arranged, and all the machinery of house purchase set in motion.

Happily, Mama allocated the rooms. The big front bedroom overlooking Hymers' grounds, would be the master bedroom. The small front one, Eberhard's, the back bedroom Anita's and mine. The two rooms in the wing for Papa, the large one overlooking the garden, the office for the staff, and the smaller one a private room for Papa. On the second floor, the front attic, which stretched the entire width of the house, would make the perfect playroom. The attic would be the maid's bedroom, so at last our maid could have her own room, and not have to sleep in the bathroom!

16. 'ALL FOUND'

In the years before the war, housemaids were easy to come by. Their wages were low, their privileges few, and their demands modest. We had a succession of maids, German and English, and each one played a part in our childhood memories.

The back attic was sparsely, but adequately furnished. An iron bedstead, a wardrobe, chest of drawers, wash stand, and plain wooden chair. Cold lino on the floor was relieved by a small bedside rug. The tiny, bleak skylight had a lace curtain draped over it. There was no form of heating whatsoever, and the bed was provided with blankets and an eiderdown to keep out the chill, but lacked the luxurious feather beds the family cuddled under.

Even now, when I go into the back attic in winter and the chill of the room envelopes me, I spare a thought for the brave young girls, whose abode it was. Did they feel any resentment, I wonder, as they climbed out of their bed into the icy darkness of a winter morning, and went downstairs past the bedrooms, where we still snored blissfully under soft, downy, feathers! I console myself with the thought that even our bedrooms were not heated, and our floors too were only lino with bedside rugs. Hot water bottles were our sole comfort, together with flannel nighties or pyjamas.

Only in rare cases of illness did the little paraffin stove, that made such a pretty pattern of light on the ceiling, appear in our bedrooms. The cosiness of lying in the dark, with the only light being the soft radiance of the illuminated flower like design above one, and the little glowing red window at the side of the stove, took away much of the misery of being ill.

Apart from this, Mama was a firm believer in cold sleeping quarters – many a time she told us how they used to break the ice in their ewers, on those cold Hannover mornings of her childhood.

Yet the maids were young and healthy, and most of them quite happy with their attic. For many of them, it was the first time they had had their own room. One of them even commented on the bedside rug, she hadn't had one at her previous place, and this to her, was a touch of luxury!

The procedure of employing a new maid was always the same. Mama would sit at the table in the front room, with a note pad and pen before her. The hopeful girl would arrive at the appointed time, armed with her references. Mama would read them through, tell her the duties to be performed in our house, ask the girl if she had any questions of her own, and, if she was suitable, engage her on the spot. If not, she would tell the girl she would let her know, and in due course send her a letter, politely regretting that the post had been filled by a more suitable applicant.

The fortunate girl who had been accepted, would then be taken on a tour of the house, which culminated in a visit to the back attic. If the girl was then willing to take on the job, further details were discussed.

Uniform was provided. In the morning the girls wore blue or green cotton overalls, over which they wore large, nurse like aprons for serving meals and answering the door. For the dirty work, a kind of grey sackcloth apron was provided. Their heads were adorned with a large white semi-starched type of mob-cap. For afternoons and evenings the girls provided their own dark blue or black dress, and Mama provided the dainty broderie anglaise head band, slotted with black velvet ribbon, and an equally dainty tea apron to match.

Times off were Sunday afternoons, a weekday afternoon, and one evening a week. With wages Mama was generous; if the girl had been earning ten shillings a week at her previous place, Mama offered twelve shillings and sixpence, which, if the girl gave satisfaction, would rise to fifteen shillings, and that was usually the maximum. Everything else went by the curious expression 'all found'. That meant really all meals and laundry provided. Mama realised that hard work required good wholesome food, and was generous in that respect.

Mama had a strange system for the midday meal and high tea. As soon as the tureens with the food were on the table, she would fill a plate for the maid, this was placed on a corner of the sideboard, and then Mama rang the bell in the wall and a little flag would be set dancing in a glass box on the morning room wall. The maid would then collect her meal. Anything left in the tureens was hers too if she was still hungry.

Teatime was the same. Mama would butter large slices of rye bread and cover them with various kinds of sausage from our German pork butcher, and cheese, and always a piece of cake to finish up with. The maid had her own small pot of tea in the morning room. If we children liked the maid, and we usually did, we were allowed to take tea out and join her at the big square table. Tea with the maids was always great fun. They would tell us about their families, their boy friends, their love letters, and so on.

One maid, a skinny red haired girl, with glasses, whose name was Janet, had had an operation, for what I don't know. She would tell us gleefully how they'd cut her open, taken everything out, put it back and stitched her up again. Because of this, I presume, she couldn't eat the strong rye bread, sausage and cheese that Mama provided. She had to eat white bread and Golden Syrup instead. She had her own loaf and pot of syrup. We watched enviously as she spooned the golden, sticky stuff on to soft, white bread and butter, while we chomped our way through hard rye bread crusts, and sausage.

Then there was a maid called Violet, who brought her afternoon uniform of dark green dress and coloured apron and cap. We thought her very elegant and superior, but when we got to know her, she was great fun.

Maids left for various reasons, to better themselves, to get married, and so on. One stole a bottle of perfume from

Mama's dressing table, and was found out. She didn't come back, and her mother returned the perfume. Sometimes, an unsatisfactory maid would have to be given notice, and here Mama's courage deserted her. This was always Papa's job. The time for this terrible business was usually after tea, when the maid was washing up. Our tea would be eaten, for the most part, in silence – for once we children would eat in the dining room, and not in the morning room with the maid.

Papa and Mama would be rehearsing what to say, then after the table was cleared and the washing up in progress, Papa would clear his throat and with a firm, if reluctant step, head towards the kitchen, with Mama a few paces behind. We children would sit fearfully, holding our breath waiting for their return. It would all be over in a few minutes. Mama and Papa would return with set faces, and outside in the kitchen, the louder reckless clattering of the pots showed how the maid had taken the news. Either she was defiant, or upset. We children would steer clear of the kitchen out of sheer embarrassment, and the next few days, while the hapless girl worked out her notice, would be days of silence and constraint.

Sometimes, we had German maids, Mama would consider them harder workers, and besides, she would say, they understood German cooking. I preferred the English girls, they were, in my opinion, far easier to have about the place. Once they were used to our strange German ways, the fact that we had wooden platters to eat from at breakfast and tea, instead of normal plates, that we slept under great white feather beds, ate funny bread, and spoke German about the house, life went on without problems. They could gossip with the neighbour's maids, take us to the playground in the park, and answer the front door with confidence.

A German maid, on the other hand, was a hazard all the way. I would cringe inwardly every time she answered the doorbell. Keeping out of sight in case I should be spotted and called upon to act as interpreter, yet close at hand in case it should be Betty or another friend calling for me – in which case I could fly to the door before the maid had time to utter a word. When German maids called us in from our games of Hopscotch, Eggie, or Block, they would command instant obedience. The first guttural shout sullying the pure English air of Sunny Bank, and we would rush into the house, to stop any further utterances, nearly knocking the poor girl over in our rush to get her safely back indoors, where she belonged.

English maids, calling to us in their homely, Northern accents, "Cum on in fer yer tea!" could safely be ignored for a minute or two and we could at least finish our game.

To be avoided at all costs, was an excursion to the park with a German maid. This was sheer purgatory! We would try to steer her away from our favourite places, the playground, the aviary and the conservatory, to the less populated parts of the park, where there was no-one to overhear their chattering in German! The girls, however, were adamant and we were forced to go where the crowds were. Answering their questions in muttered German, so as not to be overheard by other children. This made the maids shout even louder, "Wie bitte?" and "Was sagst Du? Sprich doch deutlich!" and scarlet-faced with mortification one would repeat the answer hurriedly.

But there was one hurdle that had to be overcome by us, with both German and English maids, this was, in our opinion, our strange underwear. As the autumn progressed and the winter grew colder, Mama would start her winter routine for the protection against our catching colds. First, there was cod liver oil and malt extract, taken daily, then small cubes of strong smelling camphor placed in a tiny, drawstring muslin bag would be hung round our necks, then came the terrible and much hated 'Leibchen'. These were garments worn over our vests, and under our dresses or jumpers. We loathed them, they were broad bands knitted in garter stitch, which reached from armpit to waist, fastened with rubber buttons, and had wide straps over the shoulders. Worse still, they were knitted in a very dark grey wool, we called it black, and even the fact that the wool had originally come from Oma's farm in Marienau, made little difference. They were, in our opinion, hideous, hateful garments. There was no English translation, so we made our own, we called them Lippchens, which really didn't even sound very English!

How I longed for the soft, white, fleecy lined liberty bodices, that English children wore. I would show Mama the advertisements for these desirable garments in magazines, but all my hints fell on stony ground.

With every new maid there had to be the dreadful moment of truth, when the Lippchens were revealed for the first time. In winter we undressed by the fire, our night clothes warming on the fender. This was all very nice and cosy until Mama and Papa were out for the evening, and the new maid was in charge.

"Come along, she'd say, "hurry up, time for bed. Get those clothes off."

We'd say feebly, "In a minute," and, "I'm just finishing this," until tired of our delaying tactics, she would lose patience, and yank our clothes off herself. , We would stand there red faced and ashamed as the Lippchens would be revealed, in all their horrid glory! Perhaps we overdid the sensitivity bit, for no maid ever passed a comment.

As we grew older, we grew out of our black ones and Mama's supply of Oma's wool ran out and she knitted us white ones instead. Then finally, when I was at High School, and almost too old for such childish garments, we at last achieved the longed for liberty bodices!

Of all the maids we had, one stands out far ahead of all the rest. This was Elsie. We adored her. She was, by her own admission, ginger haired and freckled. Her face was permanently friendly and beaming, her plump shape round and cuddly. When she left us to look after a sick relative, we were desolate. Then, one day, Mama told us that Elsie was coming back. We couldn't wait for the day of her return, and when it came, we hurried home from school and rushed straight into the kitchen. There stood the dear familiar figure, busy at the sink. Suddenly we were tongue-tied and shy, until she hugged us tightly and we took up our happy relationship where we had left off.

Mama, too, liked Elsie; she was a hard worker and unbelievably cheerful. Then one day Elsie confided in us that she had a boyfriend, called Bill, and they were 'courting.'

"What's he like?" we wanted to know.

Elsie rolled her eyes heavenward, "Ooo," she said," tall, dark and handsome."

We gazed at her in awe. Our Elsie courted by a tall, dark and handsome; man. It was indeed a miracle. He used to write to her, and Elsie would sit by the fire in the evenings, reading his letters, with much giggling and eye-rolling. We longed to get hold of them, but Elsie, when she had read them, would push them down the front of her dress – "To keep it warm," she would tell us.

Elsie and Bill would go dancing and I would picture her with her good looking escort, whirling and twirling, under great crystal chandeliers. Then one day Elsie informed us that she was having a new dance dress made, and it was to be backless! She would let us see it when it was finished. In the meantime, she showed us a snippet of the material. I had expected frothy net, or organza, or pastel satin, so was rather disappointed when she showed us a piece of ordinary fine cotton material in a dusty pink, with a pattern of navy and red spots.

"D'you like it then?" she asked.

"Why don't you have silk, or something posh?" I asked.

"Oo, I can't afford that," said Elsie, "I can always cut this short and wear it in the summer."

At last the dress was completed, and Elsie proudly unwrapped it and hung it on a coat hanger on a knob on the morning room cupboard.

"There," she said, standing back admiringly, "what d' you think of it?"

I thought it was quite terrible – after all the anticipation the real thing was nowhere near my expectations. It hung there limply, a skimpy, high necked, long sleeved, ankle length dress, in a cheap cotton print. I couldn't hurt Elsie's feelings. I loved her too much.

"It's very nice," I said, with unconvincing enthusiasm.

"You said it was backless," accused Anita.

"Oo, yes, so it is," said Elsie, "look!" and she showed us. The back was slit from waist to neck.

"That's not backless," said Anita, "it's just not fastened up!"

"It's backless enough for me," said Elsie.

"Your vest will show," said the practical Anita.

"I won't be wearing no vest luv," said Elsie.

"Then you'll catch cold!" threatened Anita.

"My love will keep me warm," giggled Elsie daringly, "A vest would only get in the way!"

"In the way of what?" asked the irrepressible Anita.

"Never you mind," said Elsie, rolling her eyes heavenward with a cheeky grin.

We saw Elsie several times, setting off in her dance dress. Over it she would wear her ordinary coat. My vision of Elsie, under the crystal chandeliers went out of the window, it just wasn't in keeping with the reality!

After a while, Elsie became engaged, and one day Anita and I actually met the paragon Bill! It was Elsie's day off, and she was getting ready.

"Go and see if Bill, is waiting for me at the end of the passage," she said, "and tell him I won't be long."

"How will we know it's Bill?" I asked.

"Oo," said Elsie, "tall, dark and handsome, of course, and wearing brown suede shoes."

We rushed out to see the apparition. Standing near our back entrance stood a nice ordinary looking man. He was wearing brown suede shoes. Anita was bolder than I was.

"Elsie won't be long!" she shouted. He looked at us and smiled.

"Thank you," he said politely.

We raced back into the house, where Elsie was peering into the small scullery mirror, putting on her lipstick. "We've seen him!" we gasped breathlessly.

"I told him you wouldn't be long," said Anita.

"Well what did you think of him?" asked Elsie.

"He's all right," I said simply.

"Yes, he is," added Anita loyally

"Oo," said Elsie, gazing upwards," "he's more than just all right for me!" and she rushed out of the door in a cloud of 'Evening in Paris', to join her Bill.

Soon Elsie and Bill had fixed their wedding date. Bill was out of work, and they were having a Registry Office wedding. We were very disappointed.

"Aren't you wearing a white dress?" queried Anita.

"Can't afford one," said Elsie, "I'm wearing a suit, green, to match my eyes!"

"Will you still have to say 'I will'?" I asked – that was the only part of the wedding service I knew about.

"Of course," said Elsie, "and Bill will too."

"What if Bill says 'I won't'?" said Anita cheekily.

"Gerraway, don't be daft!" cried Elsie, laughing happily.

So Elsie left us, and went to live with Bill, in a small rented house. Mama and Papa gave them a green basket bedroom table and chair to match.

We didn't quite lose touch. One Christmas, Mama and I went to see her. We took a Christmas present for her, an elaborate, silky, quilted tea cosy, for Sundays, explained Mama. We didn't reach her house, we met her in the street, pushing her first born, a little girl, in the pram. Elsie thanked Mama for the present, and put it on the pram, she told Mama that times were hard, and that Bill was out of work again. She smiled and joked, as she always did, but Mama saw the heartache behind the brave front. She took some money out of her purse, and put it into the baby's tiny, cold fingers.

"There," she said, "buy her some gloves with that."

When we got home, Mama told Papa about it. She was still upset.

"If only I hadn't given her a silly, useless tea cosy," she reproached herself over and over again. "I didn't know things were so bad. I should have given her something useful. That baby had such cold hands."

As the years went by, Elsie had two more children, both sons, and I believe times were never as bad as they had been. Years later, we met her with her daughter and little grandson. She was still the same jolly, joking Elsie we had always known.

"Oo," she said, "D'you remember how I used to make you clean your teeth every night, even when you didn't want to?"

Yes Elsie, I remember, and so much more. Much more than that!

17. CHRISTMAS MAGIC

We finally moved into Sunny Bank on 27th November, 1930. I remember sitting in an empty tea chest in the morning room, while Mama and the maid sorted out china on the table. Mama and the maid were discussing the move.

"Nothing broken," said Mama, "Really everything went very well, and by Christmas we will be completely settled."

In my little tea chest house, I heard the word Christmas, and hugged myself happily, thinking of the joyful time soon to be upon us.

Christmas in our family was by far and away the greatest festival of the year. It outshone holidays, birthdays and Easter. This was an occasion which involved the whole family, and Mama and Papa, remembering their own happy childhood Christmases, were determined to make our celebration as happy as theirs had been. Something to look back on with sweet, nostalgic pleasure, they certainly succeeded. Our Christmas was so special, so different, nothing will ever erase it from my memory.

As soon as the Calendar announced the fact that it was December, an indefinable something crept into the air, Mama called it Advent. From Oma came our yearly Advent Calendar, in a large envelope. This was a colourful picture, usually of a Christmas tree, on which the numbered ornaments and baubles lifted out, one each day to reveal the small picture of a toy or similar Christmassy object. The Calendar didn't start functioning until the 6th December, St. Nicholas' Day. On that day, we regularly had a small family ceremony to mark the occasion. It was unbelievably simple, and yet, for us children, it was a great exciting event, a milestone on the glorious road that led to Christmas.

Papa would place three small wooden candle holders on the mantelpiece, one belonged to each of us. Eberhard's was Santa Claus, while Anita and I had angels, mine in a green dress and Anita's in blue. Each figure held a tiny candle aloft. Papa would light them with a great flourish, the lights would be put out, and sitting there in the light of the tiny flickering candles and the firelight, Mama and Papa would sing the simple Advent carol, 'Alle Jahre Wieder', with us joining in when we remembered the words. When the candles had burned low and were blown out and the ceiling lights switched on once more, Mama would pass round a dish of small honey 'Lebkuchen' that had been sent by Oma. We were allowed one each, and the taste of the little cakes combined with the lingering smell of the extinguished candles would fill me with an excitement, almost too great to bear. The next time the little candles would be lit would be on Christmas Eve – an unbearably happy thought!

We firmly believed in Father Christmas, and even when we found out that he was just a myth, we went on pretending to believe, for the sake of the younger members of the family. Secretly, I was quite delighted to find out that our presents came from Mama and Papa! One had far more chance of getting what one desired. Hints would be dropped, and when out shopping with Mama she could be steered into the toy departments and shown what I would like Father Christmas to bring me. A harmless little deception that fooled nobody, but nine times out of ten paid handsome dividends. As the dark December days drew on, and the cut outs to be removed on the advent Calendar diminished in number, so the feeling inside me grew like a great bubble which would finally burst on Christmas Eve.

We went about on our best behaviour to avoid finding the dreaded birch under the Christmas tree. We knew full well this awful object would never find its way into our house, but it was as well to take precautions!

From the kitchen, wonderful smells would emanate. There would be trays of delicious biscuits and small cakes, and Mama would let us eat the crooked and over-baked ones. The rest were put away until Christmas. Would the time never come?

Nowadays, Christmas is upon us before we are ready for it, all is bustle and rush. In childhood days, the time crept on leaden feet, but then inevitably, the great day would draw near. We sang carols at school and as the last day of term was upon us, now it wouldn't be long. At home, the big front room would now be kept locked, with all parcels brought by the postman kept there, and only Mama and Papa allowed to go in. Christmas cards gathered in increasing numbers on the dining room mantelpiece.

We never saw our tree until Christmas Eve, but even though it was smuggled into the front room when we were not around, we could always tell as soon as it was in the house. That glorious smell of resin and pine needles would infiltrate every corner of the house, informing us that the TREE was here!

Then at last, at long last, the 24th December would dawn, and the last cut-out taken off the calendar − it always revealed a tiny picture of the Holy Family. All we had to do now was wait for the evening.

Papa would disappear into the front room all day, only emerging for meals. He was 'helping Father Christmas', we knew. When I was small, I was firmly convinced that that benign, red-coated, white-bearded, gentleman was in our very own front room getting everything ready just for us. It never occurred to self-centred little me, that millions of other children were waiting for him too!

The midday meal over, another unusual event took place. We children had to have a rest to prepare us for the late night we were about to have. Eberhard had his own room, but Anita and I were tucked up in Mama's bed. In the room below us we could hear the soft murmur of voices, and incredibly, in spite of the surging excitement within us, we would actually drop off to sleep.

We would wake to Mama's voice calling us, and the pink shaded lamp over the bed switched on. Outside, it was already dark, and sleepily we would put on our Sunday clothes and go downstairs for tea. Mama and Papa too, wore their best clothes, and indulgently answered all our questions. Was Father Christmas finished, had Papa seen anything he'd left, and so on. Then the meal was over, the table cleared, and the maid hurried off to finish her kitchen work, for she had the evening off.

Mama and Papa would both disappear into the front room, while we three sat in the dining room, on tenterhooks, our ears straining for any sound announcing Mama's return. For that was the signal. Mama would then come in, saying, "Father Christmas is nearly ready – listen for the bell."

Into the hushed, waiting silence came at last the long awaited sound – the tinkling of a little goat bell. We would sit savouring the moment, to give Father Christmas time to get out of the front room window, and then Mama would say, "Come on, now it's time." Bunched around Mama, we would take the few steps out of the dining room and into the hall, and then the front room door was flung open to reveal the glory within! What indescribable glory it was too!

In the bay window, stretching from floor to ceiling was the tree, enormous, spreading, dominating the whole room. On its scented branches were fixed hundreds (or so it seemed) of flickering candles, that lit up the entire room. Hanging off the branches were the coloured and shiny silver and gold ornaments that we knew and loved, for they appeared year after year. On the mantelpiece stood the three little wooden Advent figures, with new candles, adding their brave little glow to that of the splendid apparition in the window.

The scent from the tree, the candles, the plates of Christmas honey cakes and the perfume that Mama wore, all combined into the unforgettable scent of Christmas. It really was Christmas at last! Already my eyes would be straying round the room, trying to locate my own pile of presents. There were piles of presents all over the room, some on armchairs, some on small tables, but we had to wait until we were shown which was our own particular pile.

"Look at the tree first!" Mama would say, thinking of the hours of hard work Papa had put in, decorating it. Papa would stand, beaming, beside it, and Mama would always say it was the most beautiful tree we had ever had, or the biggest or the best decorated. The tree duly admired, Mama would then show us which were our presents. Though we were not spoilt with pocket money or presents the rest of the year, when Christmas came, we were showered with gifts. Of course added to those from Mama and Papa, were those sent by Oma and Mane, and the Berlin relations. Beautiful German toys even more magnificent and complicated than any to be had in England.

We would fall upon everything with shrieks of joy. Here were all the things we had desired and many, many more we hadn't even thought of. Mama and Papa would sit on the sofa, enjoying our pleasure. They had their own presents too, but I'm sure their best Christmas present was the sight of their children enjoying with such gusto the great and happy occasion that had been planned with so much love and forethought.

So many Christmases have come and gone since those happy, childhood ones, but still the magic remains, and will forever, thanks to Mama and Papa. The first excitement of the presents over, Papa would go to the piano and play all the lovely German Christmas songs, starting with our favourite one. 'Am Weihnachtsbaum', a lovely tune and lovely words, about two angels coming down from heaven to bless the family round the Christmas tree. I was always convinced I could see two shadowy, white robed figures standing by our tree, with their arms raised in blessing. Imagination? Perhaps, but small children see things that grown-ups have forgotten how to. Then Papa would play 'Stille Nacht' and

'O, Du Fröhliche', and many more from our special Christmas song book. By now, the candles would be guttering to an end, and they would be extinguished one by one, until only their smell remained. Then the electric lights would be switched on, and we could examine our presents once more.

The ringing of the front door bell would announce the arrival of Morgel. More presents! She would stay a while, drinking a glass of wine with Mama and Papa and admiring our new toys. After Morgel had gone, it was our bedtime, and we would go happily upstairs, looking forward to getting up next day.

Christmas Day had an atmosphere all its own. To come downstairs into the Christmas room, with the pale December morning light filtering through the tree branches, was like being in a forest. The toys were all still there in the soft, green gloom, and last night's scents still lingered in the air. But it was different. Where the night before all had been magic and spun gold, now it was tangible and real.

Eberhard's model train, which acquired new pieces every Christmas, would fill most of the floor space, the lines running in and out of the tables and chairs. The little train, chugging round the room, past its tiny signals and level crossing and other delights, was as much part of the scene as the glittering tree in the window.

Traditionally, Fred with his wife and small daughter, would visit on Christmas morning, and again gifts would be exchanged and admired. We would spend the rest of the day happily immersed in our new toys, emerging only for meals, which again were full of special treats.

English children have their great day at Christmas, and no doubt for them the occasion is as happy as ours; but even as a child, when it came to Christmas, I was glad we were German, and followed the lovely tradition of Christmas Eve – Holy Eve as it is referred to over there.

Were we children aware of the religious significance of Christmas? Yes, we knew and loved the story of the baby in a manger, but probably we didn't see much connection between that and Father Christmas, and indeed there is none. It is only with maturity that one truly celebrates Christmas, with the present-giving being a pleasant traditional addition.

18. EASTER FUN

After Christmas and Mama's and Anita's birthdays in January, the next milestone of our year was Easter.

"Soon the Osterhase will be coming," said Mama, and a feeling of excitement at the imminent arrival of the little hare that brought us Easter eggs would rise within us.

Not the ecstatic pre-Christmas feeling, nor even that purely selfish anticipation of one's very own birthday, but a pleasant looking forward all the same. Our Easter weekend started with Good Friday.

"This is the holiest day in all the year," Papa would say.

It began like a Sunday, with a fire in the drawing room, and us children wearing best clothes, but there the similarity ended. For when we were young, Good Friday was a day for being quiet, it was the day Jesus had died on the cross.

"When I was a little girl," Mama used to say, "we were not allowed to laugh, sing or play the piano on Good Friday," and because she and Papa had been brought up this way, it was carried on in their own family.

We were quiet, we almost spoke in whispers, and nothing could bring home the message of Good Friday more clearly than that one quiet day in our lives. With the passing of years Good Friday gradually changed for us. One laughed and sang as on a normal day.

The first time Papa played the piano on Good Friday, I was shocked.

"You mustn't play," I warned Papa, "It's Good Friday!"

"It's all right," Papa reassured me, "I'm playing a Hymn."

Now for most people, Good Friday is just an ordinary weekday, the shops are open, one goes about one's business. The majority of people don't even go to church. But for me the very words Good Friday conjure the quiet, the feeling of sadness that was always there on this holiest of days.

Easter Saturday was just like any other Saturday. We wore our play clothes, and could romp about the house and garden as we pleased.

Then came Easter Sunday. The sun always seemed to be shining on Easter Sunday. Even the dining room, the gloomiest room in the house, was filled with a golden light. There were vases of bright daffodils and narcissi on the sideboard and table. The soft buttercup yellow tablecloth, reserved for special occasions, would grace the table. There would be boiled eggs, a special treat, and hot cross buns, even more special, for breakfast.

Breakfast over, Mama would say, "Let's see if the Osterhase has been." We would run into the front room, carrying small baskets, and the search for Easter eggs would begin. We knew all the places to look, under cushions, behind flower pots, and so on. When they were all collected in our baskets, came the grand sharing out, to make sure we all had the same quantity and sizes. Sometimes a particular one was missing, and we would search frantically. On warm days the egg search was carried out in the garden. This was more fun and took a lot longer, inevitably there were eggs missing and Mama and Papa had to join in the search, until at last all were gathered in. Once shared out, we made our eggs last as long as possible, eating a small piece daily, and invariably leaving till last the silver paper-wrapped rabbits and ducklings that Oma had sent.

The sunny Easters of our childhood seemed to us the foretaste of warm sunny days to come. We had four weeks off school, and it was time for our first going away holiday of the year.

As far as holidays were concerned we were certainly fortunate, as we always went away twice a year. To set us up after a winter of coughs, colds and other childhood ailments, Mama believed in good, fresh, sea air. Living in Hull, we had a splendid choice of East coast resorts close at hand.

Sometimes we would rent a furnished house for a few weeks at Hornsea or Bridlington. There would be a general exodus from Hull, with the maid coming too. We would spend happy days on the beach, whatever the weather.

Once, we even went as far as Bournemouth, where we stayed in a guest house and the weather was like summer all the time. My very favourite place however, was Scarborough. Not because of the town or beach, but because we stayed at the house of a Mrs Scott. Mrs Scott was a kind, friendly soul, but for me the sole attraction at her house was a rough little Irish terrier, called Paddy.

I simply adored Paddy, and the greatest treat would be to take him down to the beach with us. Holding on to his lead, I would pretend he was my very own. Paddy's favourite place in his house was at the top of the stairs, where he could lie and watch the life of the street through the fanlight over the front door. Whenever we were not out I would join him there and happily loving him, my cheek resting on his rough little head, and my arm round his neck. Dear little Paddy! He never complained or tried to escape me, but put up good naturedly with me. Leaving Paddy behind was always the worst part of the holiday, there were long fond farewells.

"You ought to take him home with you!" Mrs Scott would tease me, and I would gaze beseechingly at Mama.

"Can we?" Mama would shake her head.

"No, this is his home, and besides, think how he would miss the beach."

19. PETS IN PERIL

As a child, I was totally and utterly dog mad. I would ask for a dog for birthdays, Christmas and any other opportunity; a near fanatical cat and dog lover even now. I shudder at the way dogs and cats came and went during our childhood. Mama and Papa were both fond of animals and were kind to them, but neither had that special dedication that everyone must have before they even think of taking a pet into their home.

When we first settled in Louis Street, Papa brought home a terrier pup called Boy. Sadly, when only a year old he contracted distemper and died. I remember very little about Boy, but I have two memories that remain with me.

One day I found him sitting on the kitchen table, eating a huge piece of meat, I ran to find someone grown up.

"Boy's got something," I told Mama. She didn't take much notice, but later on, when the Sunday joint was missing, she remembered my words, and by then it was too late to scold a replete Boy, or to recover the meat!

My second memory is of the day he died. He was lying quite still in his little basket bed. Mama told me he was dead, but I didn't really understand death. What I noticed was that his snowy white fur was stained bright red.

"He's bleeding!" I said, shocked.

"No, he's not," said Mama, "he wet his blanket and the colour has come off on his fur."

After that we didn't see Boy any more, and in the garden was a little mound of earth that Mama told us was Boy's grave. She said Papa had buried him there. He had also nailed two pieces of wood together in the shape of a cross to mark the spot. I wondered why. It was my first encounter with death and it didn't even sadden me. I was only four years old, after all.

Poor little Boy! Those were the days before vaccinations and antibiotics, a dog had little chance of recovery, once the dreaded distemper attacked him. Nowadays, our dogs are vaccinated against every possible known disease, and distemper does not hold the terrors that it used to.

After Boy, Papa went to the Dog's Home for a replacement. He came back with a fully grown brown and white terrier called Rover. He said he reminded him of Hexe. Rover was a handsome dog, but also too good a house dog. He bit the postman, attacked the milkman and chased all and sundry off the premises. I remember him being tied to a tree, and then Papa took him back to the Dog's Home and exchanged him for a gentler dog. Poor Rover, even now I shudder to think of his fate. Fresh from the awful confines of the Dog's Home, he must have been bewildered and frightened, all he needed was a lot of loving, a little discipline, patience, and a feeling of security.

He never had a chance to make good.

Brown-and-white Rover was replaced by black-and-white Rover. A portly, comfortable terrier, who loved everyone. He encouraged me shamelessly to feed him between meals. I used to fill my hands with dog biscuits illicitly taken from the pantry and we would run and hide in a corner of the garden where he would gorge himself, and I would watch with delight as he polished off a pile of biscuits in two or three mouthfuls.

Black-and-white Rover took a great fancy to the maid we had at the time, no doubt, she too, slipped him the odd tit-bit now and again. He used to follow her home on her day off, and finally Mama let her keep Rover for good. He really did love her more than anyone else.

After that, there were no more dogs until my ninth birthday, by which time we were living in Sunny Bank. On that day, I discovered a dog's lead among my birthday presents. The same day we went to collect my longed-for dog. This was a fawn and white terrier called Oscar, he was just twelve weeks old. My joy however was short-lived.

Oscar was not completely house trained, and left many a puddle on the floor. Once I screamed at the maid for cruelly rubbing his soft little nose into such a puddle.

"It's the only way he'll ever learn to be clean," she told me ruthlessly. As a result, poor little Oscar would be shut out of the house and left in the garden for long periods of time – a cruel and totally useless exercise. He would spend most of the time yapping at the back door, pleading to be let in again.

Next door at number 12, the elderly neighbour, Mr Smith, was laid up with a broken leg, and his sister asked Mama to keep the dog quiet, as it disturbed her brother.

"How can I keep a young dog quiet?" Mama said to the maid. The answer in my opinion now, was easy. Let the little dog in when he'd done his duty in the garden. It didn't seem to occur to anyone that once again a little patience and understanding was needed. So Oscar went back to his former owner, who luckily, so we heard later, found a good home for him. The old man next door had broken more than his leg that winter, he also broke a little girl's heart.

I asked Mama, "Why can't he sleep in one of the front bedrooms?" Why indeed!

Several years later, when I was already at High School, one of the teachers there had found a stray dog. She appealed to the girls in morning assembly for someone to give it a home. I hopefully passed the request on to Mama, and to my utter amazement, she said yes, we could have the dog. This time it was a young liver and white bitch, we called her Judy. Her stay with us was short and sweet. As I was taking her for a walk one day, she pulled the lead out of my hand, and chased after a man on a bicycle. The man got off his bike, and a joyful reunion took place. She was his little dog! So happily for Judy, whose name was really Peggy, but sadly for us, she returned to her original owner.

After that, there were no more dogs until after the war, when I was grown-up and firmly took matters into my own hands. Since which time there have always been much loved and cared for dogs at 10 Sunny Bank.

Cats, before the war, fared little better with us. Dolly, the maid, once brought us a tiny black kitten. The poor wee thing suffered unbelievable cruelty, I am ashamed to record, by my own hand. My only defence is that I was only about five years old at the time, and didn't realise what I was doing. I would wrap it in blankets and force it into my doll's pram and push it around.

Another time, I remember, I tied a string round its neck to walk it up and down the garden like a dog. The poor thing was almost choking its last gasp, when luckily Dolly came to its rescue. She scolded me for being so cruel. Thankfully for the little cat, Dolly took it back to her own home, where no doubt it led a happy, tranquil life away from my thoughtless, unintentionally cruel ministrations.

The next kitten, a tabby and white, arrived on Anita's sixth birthday, complete with red ribbon round its neck. He was a present from Mrs Wagner, the pork butcher's wife, and was delivered by the errand boy. This kitten lasted a little longer, but developed a habit of stealing. Stealing food is natural to dogs and cats if humans are thoughtless enough to leave it lying about. So, in spite of our protests, Pussy was given to Fred. He lived with Fred a considerable time, until one day Fred informed us that he had found Pussy dead in his basket. He had been poisoned, so Fred said, and gave us a horrible imitation of how he had found poor Puss, rolling up his eyes and dropping open his mouth. We were shattered, and for a long time I blamed Mama for giving him to Fred, and Fred for not looking after him properly The real culprit, of course, was the vile person who had put down the poison in the first place, whether for rats, mice or cats is immaterial.

Our next feline pet was a pretty half-grown tabby, that followed Anita and me home one day. Without a thought of taking her back to where we'd found her or trying to trace her owner, we smuggled her into the playroom and sneaked up some milk for her. She settled down happily in a doll's cot, and we went to bed, hugging our lovely secret to ourselves. During the night, her plaintive mewing must have woken the maid, who investigated, for the next morning, rushing up to the playroom, we found no cat! On going downstairs, however, we found our purring little friend enjoying breakfast in the kitchen, delightedly watched by Mama and the maid! She was allowed to stay and proved to be a loveable and entertaining pet. Allowed to stay, that is, until just before the birth of our baby sister, when Mama, fearful of the possibility of a cat lying on the baby's face and smothering it, gave her to our local grocer.

Fortunately, she settled down happily, and we would often see her sunning herself in the shop entrance, even years later, after the war. At first she would always recognise us, rubbing her head against our legs and purring loudly. Later on she would only blink her eyes at us sleepily, and ignore our overtures of friendship.

The only other pets we had as children were a budgerigar and a mouse. The mouse was a birthday present for me from a friend. From November to the following July it lived in a large box in the morning room cupboard. Every night it would come out to be played with, while Pussy was banished to the dining room. It was incredibly tame and an enchanting little creature. From that time on I have admired mice, with their shell-like ears, their tiny fragile pink hands and feet, their soft velvety coats. Vulnerable, exquisite creatures trying to live out their tiny, short lives in peace, yet hounded and persecuted on all sides by the human race, tracked down with poison, cruel traps and such like.

With a cat and a mouse living together in the same house, the inevitable was bound to happen, sooner or later. One summer morning loud shrieks from the maid made us rush downstairs. The cat had caught the mouse, in spite of all our elaborate precautions. We chased Puss into the garden, but it was too late, my dainty, delicate little pet was already dead.

The budgerigar was a Christmas present – we called her Jolly, and spent much time trying to make her talk. She too became quite tame, and would come out of her cage and fly about the room. By then there was no cat to threaten her.

When the summer came we would take her cage into the garden, where she loved to call out to the wild birds. Then one day, when Anita was carrying the cage, the bottom slid out. Jolly was out in a flash and away up in the trees to join her wild feathered friends. We never saw her again, but hopefully left her cage outside for many a day, leaving the door invitingly open and the dishes full of her favourite seeds.

A few months later a school friend, whose house was not far from ours, told me that one day in the summer, her grandfather, who lived with them, had seen a budgie sitting in an open window. He had quickly fetched an old cage and the little budgie had immediately flown in, and they had kept it. It was a green and yellow bird, she told me. It sounded just like Jolly, and though the description fitted millions of other budgies too, I like to think it was.

20. OUT OF BOUNDS

The first winter in Sunny Bank passed and spring came, with all its attendant delights and surprises. In the back garden we saw, for the first time, the beauty of the trees planted there. First the apple trees, with their profusion of pale pink blossom, followed closely in their flowering by the blooms of the Lilac, Laburnum and Red May. In the shrubbery, the Snowball, Syringa, Mock Grange and Red Currants created colour and unforgettable scents, while the flower beds produced Daffodils and Jonquils, and the lawn sprouted Snowdrops and Crocuses. As the days grew warmer we spent a lot of time playing in the garden.

One sunny day I was playing with my dolls on the front porch step, when a voice called out, "Hello." I looked up, and pressed to the iron bars of the gate was a bright, rosy-cheeked face, with laughing blue eyes – the whole topped by a mop of corn coloured hair. It belonged to a small girl, about my age. "Hello," I replied shyly, wondering who this bold little stranger was. The little girl opened the gate and walked up the path. "I'm Betty," she announced, "what's your name? Can you come out to play?" "Rosemarie, I'll go and ask." I answered both her questions, and ran indoors. Mama came out to vet my new intended playmate. "Where do you live?" she asked Betty. "At number forty," replied Betty. "Where do you want to play?" asked Mama.

"Out there on the pavement," said Betty.

We had not played outside the garden before. I looked at Mama. "All right," she said, "but don't go too far away."

Permission granted, Betty and I left the garden, and went off to play in the street. Betty turned out to be the ideal companion, the exact opposite of shy little me, bold, cheeky and full of fun.

She had a fund of wonderful games at her fingertips – Hopscotch, Block, Eggie, French cricket, witches and many more. There was never a dull moment in her company. Apart from becoming Betty's friend and devoted slave, I also envied her enormously. Everything she had seemed to be better than anything I had. Her summer dresses were prettier than mine, her hair was wavy, her downstairs toilet was inside the house, and boasted a carpet! Once I helped her set her tea table and coveted her pretty china plates, all differently patterned with flowers, and some even with crinoline ladies. I longed to eat my tea off a crinoline lady instead of our plain wooden boards!

Betty had a swing in her garden, and a rabbit – she also got pocket money. I was in a constant state of envy. Betty too kept reminding me of my shortcomings, which didn't help much. Betty's mother was a widow and besides Betty there were two older brothers and a sister. No wonder that little Betty was spoiled and indulged.

Then, one day, Papa was in the front garden, cutting the privet hedge, and Betty and I were helping him. Papa was behaving impeccably, not talking German, not saying words like 'Donnerwetter', and not even calling me by my silly nick-name of 'Fette', which dated back to baby days, when Eberhard couldn't get his tongue round the word 'Schwesterchen' and called me Fette instead. Much to my disapproval, this silly name, with its suggestion that I was a fatty, still kept cropping up.

I was relaxed and happy, helping to fill a sack of hedge clippings, which Papa then carried through the house to the back. Betty stood silently for once, watching his retreating back, her eyes were wistful.

"I wish I still had a father," she said.

I felt a great feeling of pity for Betty, and a great glow of delight for myself. Yes, I had a Papa, funny and German though he might be, and poor Betty had only her mother.

Betty, not given to sad reflection for long, was already running across the road to the great iron gates of Hymers College and its grounds.

"Come on," she shouted, "let's go in Hymers!"

I followed her obediently as always, but I never forgot her sad little remark, even though I still envied all her other advantages. The sprawling grounds of Hymers College cover about thirty-two acres and runs the full length of Sunny Bank, the other sides being bordered by the Scarborough, and former Hornsea and Withernsea railway lines. Originally these grounds were known as the Botanical Gardens. Older people remembered skating on the frozen lakes during the cold winters, with chestnut sellers and their small, glowing stoves adding their warmth and colour on the banks.

By the time we lived there, the school had been built some years before, and the only reminder was the small local railway station still called Botanic Gardens. Apparently, at some time, the road of Sunny Bank was widened, and instead of taking the land from the grounds, it was taken from the plots of land destined for building. The result of this was that all houses in Sunny Bank and Spring Bank West had the right to go into the grounds after the school was built. Many households renounced their right, in exchange for a small sum of money, but some retained their right. The first time I set foot in Hymers was a very sedate 'best clothes' occasion.

One Sunday morning in spring, Mama, accompanied by the three of us, armed with her camera, knocked on the door of the pretty little lodge that nestled behind the great iron gates. The lodge keeper appeared in shirt sleeves and braces. "Could we please walk round and take some photographs?" asked Mama. "Do you have the right?" asked the porter.

"I believe so," said Mama, who wasn't sure at all, but remembered that Mrs De Jong had said something about the grounds. "All right," said the man, and hurried back to his fireside, it being a chilly day. We walked sedately down the path, through the woods and back again past the playing fields. Three photographs were taken. We look too good to be true. In one picture I proudly hold up my new book, a free gift from Gibbs toothpaste. I was wearing my black velour hat and best coat trimmed with beaver fur, Eberhard his new tweed coat and matching cap, and Anita her new outfit, a pretty blue coat trimmed with white fur and woolly cap, sent from Germany, where copies of the photos were destined to go. We were seven, six and three years old. After that first visit there were no more walks there with Mama. She preferred the parks, Pearson Park and West Park. There was more to do and see, she thought.

So it wasn't until Betty took me in, about a year later, that I went into Hymers again.

"I've got the right to go in," Betty informed me, "you haven't, but if you come in with me you'll be all right."

I didn't query her statement; everything Betty said was true, it wasn't for me to question her. We ran past the little lodge.

"There's a new porter living there now," said Betty, "he's nice. The old one has gone. We used to call him Gaffer, he always chased us."

Confidently she led the way into the woods, and into a new world for me. A world of trees soaring to the skies, trees that could be climbed, that shed leaves, conkers and blossoms according to the seasons. A world of shrubs and bushes, that made wonderful dens where we could play houses, or sit and just dream, as birds all around rustled, sang, twittered and built their nests.

Elderberry bushes that carried masses of heady scented saucers of miniature, creamy blossoms later on were heavy with juicy berries. The meadows with their long grass and myriads of wildflowers of every type and colour. Betty knew all their names, and avidly I learned them too. The starry Celandines, first out in spring, to be picked in shiny yellow bunches. The buttercups that when held under ones chin revealed that one liked butter if they made a golden glow on one's skin, the daisies for daisy chains, the dandelions for

Betty's rabbit, the blue meadow cranesbills, the Ladies Smocks, delicately pink, which only grew in the grass opposite the lodge. There were Lady's Fingers and silverweed round the running track, pink campions edging the wood, and Jack-go-to-bed-at-noon, which I never managed to see open. Further afield were the bluebells and yellow irises by the lake. The playing fields were enclosed by these areas of woods and rough, uncut grass.

There were boundary posts which showed how far we were allowed to go – a certain number of yards from the fence bordering Sunny Bank. Betty pointed them out to me.

"You're not allowed past these," she pointed out, "and the woods over there at the other side are out of bounds, we're not allowed there either."

I gazed at the forbidden woods beyond the playing fields.

"I've been there," boasted Betty, "our Mick once took me there. It's real creepy."

We were content to play in our allotted part of the grounds. We made up our own names, the 'first' wood was nearest home, the 'second' wood was the best place to be, the bushes were thicker and denser and we had wonderful dens there. Then came the 'meadow' and beyond that the third wood. The forbidden woods we called 'Averil's' wood.

Averil was the youngest daughter of the Deputy Headmaster, who lived in a great, rambling house, behind the school. She was a friend of ours and we sometimes played in her house, which fascinated me. There were so many rooms, it was wonderful to play there. Averil was not allowed to play in the grounds, as not too far from her house was the lake, and it was considered unsafe to play on its banks unsupervised.

We had plenty of scope for our play and imagination in our own woods, and we were largely uninterrupted.

One thing marred our bliss and added a small element of danger to our excursions. This was when gardeners or groundsmen appeared on the horizon; they would chase us if they saw us, said Betty. Surprisingly enough, to me now, they did! We rarely saw them, but if we did Betty would shout "Cave." Her brother Mick, she told me, said it meant "Danger," and we would dive for cover or a handy hole in the fence, to the safety of Sunny Bank. Betty delighted in shouting "Cave," even though many times it was a false alarm.

"I thought you said you were allowed in," I whispered once as we hid in an elderberry bush, "why do we have to hide?"

"Course I'm allowed," said Betty airily, "but you aren't, are you? You don't want to be caught, do you?"

Anything that is forbidden to children immediately becomes more desirable. One day we were lying on our backs in the grass, watching white clouds floating lazily across a Summer blue sky, when Betty suddenly said, "Let's go in Averil's wood!"

Shocked, I sat up. "We're not allowed to, we can't!" I protested.

"Who says so?" said Betty, her mind made up, "as long as no one sees us."

Betty's boldness infected me. We jumped up with one accord and headed for the forbidden territory. It meant going as far as the railway line and then sneaking past the squash courts. Then we were at the start of the path that led through the tangled growth, all the way to the lake. There was barely a way there, a tiny track twisted and turned through tall hogweed, far taller than us, with their thick stems and huge umbrella heads of flowers.

"Those plants are poisonous," Betty informed me inaccurately, but with relish. "If the juice gets on you, you'll die!"

I was nearly dead with fright already, and this remark didn't help!

"Shouldn't we go back?" I suggested, timidly, but Betty was already forging ahead and I had to follow quickly before she disappeared completely.

This was the first time I had been in Averil's wood, and it certainly was not the last. We were to go in over and over again, but every time we went in I would get the same feeling. The tight constriction in my throat that was part fear and part excitement, the leaden feeling in my stomach that was all apprehension, and the delicious weak-kneed relief when we finally returned to our own dear familiar woods!

On this first occasion I followed closely on Betty's heels, through what seemed a veritable jungle. One part was like a small green tunnel and we had to bend double to avoid the twigs and leaves that slapped our faces. The tunnel safely negotiated, Betty suddenly hissed "Cave," and flung herself down into a patch of tall cow parsley! My legs collapsed under me in sheer terror as I fell almost on top of her.

"Cave," in the middle of the unknown territory of Averil's wood was all the more terrifying, as we were too far from our usual haunts and definitely out of bounds. After a while, Betty raised her head.

"It's all right," she said, "nobody's there."

I peeped through the foliage and saw before us a small shed. It was where the groundsmen kept their tools, and used it generally as a base, its double doors stood open, but there was no sign of anyone inside the gloomy interior.

"Come on," whispered Betty, "don't stand up until we get past."

We crawled on all fours until the hut was out of sight and we were back in the woods once more. A few more steps, and ahead of us lay the lake. It seemed enormous with deep muddy depths. Two small islands were situated in it, one quite close to the shore. Someone had made a rough bridge to it with a fallen tree trunk and a few branches.

"Come on," urged Betty, "let's go across."

She put a foot on the shaky structure, which rolled alarmingly. I didn't usually defy Betty, but this time I stood my ground.

"No," I said, "I'm not going on that, it isn't safe!"

Betty taunted me, but she too probably realised the makeshift bridge was unreliable, and after a while came and joined me on firm ground. She took a stick and poked around in the water.

"I bet there are tadpoles in there, next time I'll bring a jam jar," she said.

I didn't want a next time. I'd had enough adventures for one day.

"We'd better go back now," I said, dreading the return walk, and wishing we were safely back on familiar ground.

We turned back, crawled past the hut and the jungle undergrowth, and finally landed, thankfully for me, in our own woods.

As Anita grew older, she began to accompany us in Hymers, and soon there was no need for me to wait for Betty to come out to play. In the summer months, Anita and I would spend most evenings and weekends in the grounds.

Next to home, Hymers was the most important place in our lives. School was way down the bottom of the list of our priorities. School got in the way of our private lives. School was only tolerated because some of the lessons, like art, were quite nice, and some of the teachers were 'all right'.

But homework was the very worst thing about school, especially when I reached the High School stage in my education – there were two subjects set every night, and three at weekends. Little wonder I did the minimal acceptable amount so that I could live my own life as much as possible. Friday and Saturday nights were heaven! No homework was ever touched, unless it was Art, which wasn't work. By Sunday, the shadow of homework waiting to be completed would begin to loom, but it was always put off until after tea, when there was no more escape. For years, Sunday afternoons carried this feeling of doom and gloom as the weekend reached its inevitable close, and one had to unwillingly immerse oneself in one's horrible school books. I always was, and still am, anti-homework. I think the few precious hours a child has to itself and to be with its family should not be used up by school work. The school day is quite long enough. Poor Eberhard, who was so much more conscientious than I ever was, would sit at his little bureau in his room, studiously working every evening and nearly all the weekend.

He was with the family less and less, and missed the family games of Ludo, Snap, Pegotty and Dominoes that we played with Mama and Papa. It just didn't seem fair that he missed all that fun. True, he was always top or nearly top of his class, but in my opinion, his liberty was too high a price to pay for that honour. I, with my place near the bottom of my High School class, was a much happier and more carefree child.

So, Anita and I grew up like country children in our beloved Hymers. There were dogs to be taken out too. Betty and I would take out a beautiful Red Setter called Derry. He was a little too bouncy for his mistress. Her name was Mrs Weldon, but we disrespectfully referred to her as 'Weldy' among ourselves. When we returned Derry after his walk, Weldy would always reward us with a delicious liquorice roll.

One day she was busy baking and told us to go into her pantry and help ourselves to a sweet each from the tin. Betty grabbed a handful of sweets and pushed them deeply into her blazer pocket, and I, with only a small twinge of conscience, followed her example! Weldy must have noticed the depleted supply in her tin later, for she never let us help ourselves again!

After a time, Derry became too boisterous for Weldy, and went to a new home in the country. Weldy acquired instead, a small black Cocker Spaniel. We were not allowed to take 'Doody' out on our own, but we often accompanied Weldy and her new puppy on their walks in Hymers. There, Weldy would sit under a row of poplars, on a fallen log, while we played with Doody. To this day, we still call the row of poplars Weldy's trees.

Another dog friend was Dicky, the Springer Spaniel from the lodge and Punch, a Scottie, who lived at the sweet shop. Our reward for taking Punch out was always a bag of chocolate covered dates. They always tasted soapy, and were probably old stock, but we didn't mind that! Our neighbourhood dogs often joined us at our play in the woods, they came in all shapes and sizes, but our favourite was little black and tan Toby, who lived a few houses up from Betty.

Now, over half a century later, I no longer rely on other peoples' dogs to keep me company, I take my own into Hymers – but how different it all is! For they have 'tidied up' Hymers. The trees, much older and taller now, still soar to the sky, but many have been needlessly felled, the undergrowth and the elderberry bushes have been rooted out, most of the rarer wild flowers have gone, perished forever after the gardeners lavish use of weedkillers. Celandines, happily, still flourish in the first and second wood, but the blue periwinkles no longer peep primly from behind their dark, glossy leaves in the third wood. Daisies still stud the grass, with their inexpressible white faces, but buttercups are few and far between, and the delicately pink Ladies Smocks have completely disappeared from the grass opposite the lodge.

As for Averil's wood, the whole area has been opened out and landscaped. There are banks of snowdrops, crocuses and daffodils which delight the eye, as they flower at the appropriate times, but the bluebells no longer fill the air with their heady scent, in the late spring. Half the lake has been filled in, and only one island remains.

Averil's huge house has been demolished, and a Junior School built in its place. The dreaded gardeners' hut disappeared long ago and the white bluebells that grew beside it, and that only Betty dared to pick, have gone too. The giant hogweeds no longer rear their great umbrellas above our heads, they too have succumbed to a killer more deadly than they ever were.

Sometimes on Sunday's we walk the dogs as far as Averil's wood, and I admire the colourful banks of flowers, and as always I delight in all the beauty the changing seasons bring, but long ago I gave up trying to recapture the magic and mystery that was 'Averil's Wood'.

21. TUSKY'S – V – CURTSYING

When I was eight years old, Miss Sawden retired, and the little school closed forever at the end of the Summer term. The parents had all been informed well in advance, and now Mama was faced with the problem of finding a new school for me.

There was no doubt in my mind which school it was to be.

"Please, can I go to Betty's school?" I begged.

Mama however, had other ideas.

"I thought of the French convent in the park," she said, "then at least you would learn proper French."

I had heard other things about the French convent – my little Jewish friend, Irene, was going there, and she had been to see it with her mother.

"It's all nuns," she reported, "and they have a lesson called Manners, and when the Mother Superior comes in, you have to get out of your desks and curtsey!"

I told Mama what Irene had told me, hoping it would put her off, but Mama was highly impressed.

"It sounds very suitable, and if Irene is going there you'll already have a friend."

"But I'll have Betty at Froebel House, and anyway, Jean is going too, and it's much nearer than the convent," I pleaded.

Either I convinced Mama with my reasoning, or she decided for herself. At any rate, to my delight, Froebel House was to be my next school. In those days, it was simply called "Tusky's," by its pupils, and to this day, it's still going strong over half a century later. The little school in the Avenues is still Tusky's to me!

The school was owned and run by two sisters, the Misses Musgrave, and Tusky was our disrespectful name for the elder. The younger we addressed as Miss Winifred, and behind her back we called her 'Winnie'. I met Tusky for the first time when Mama took me for an interview. The school in Marlborough Avenue, occupied two large double fronted houses. One house was wholly given over to school use, the other was partly a residence and partly a school.

We were ushered into a private sitting room on the ground floor. Details like fees and school uniforms were discussed, and my latest reports were perused. While this was going on I surreptitiously studied Tusky. She appeared to me to be quite terrifying, and I began to wonder if it was such a good idea to come here after all. Maybe the French convent for all its nuns and curtsying would have been better!

Tusky had very dark hair, which was pulled back from a centre parting, arranged over her ears and severely gathered in a large loose bun at the back. Like a pair of heavy curtains joined in the middle and held at the sides with loops. To this day we call curtains arranged in this fashion, Tuskys. Tusky wore glasses, behind which her dark eyes, shiny like pebbles, stared out unblinkingly. Her complexion was sallow, her expression forbidding. Her discipline, as I found out later, was absolute and unquestioned.

The interview over, Mama and I were out in the Avenue again.

"There," said Mama, "that's that. She seems a nice sensible woman. Now we'll see about your uniform."

This was the best part, I thought. At Miss Sawden's we hadn't worn uniform. The uniform consisted of dark green, box-pleated serge tunics, square-necked, long-sleeved, white cotton blouses and dark green V-necked jumpers with white borders. Black velour hats with green hatbands, bearing the motto, 'Esse quam Vedere' were worn in winter. In the summer there were cotton tunics in a lighter shade of green, blazers with the letters F.H.S. in white, entwined on the breast pockets, and Panama hats.

An excited Betty called for me the first day of the autumn term. She looked critically at me, self consciously kitted out in my new uniform.

"Oo, 'eck!" she said, "what a sight. Come on!"

Thoroughly deflated and with some trepidation, I meekly joined her, but I was thankful for her bossy little presence. We entered the school. The floors were all practical brown lino, the doors and woodwork painted brown. A brown staircase curved elegantly upwards.

"Wipe your feet!" ordered Betty, and I obediently followed her example on the large doormat.

Betty led the way into a room behind the staircase. It was full of pegs and pigeon holes. We removed our hats and coats and changed our shoes and then, surrounded by lots of other little girls in green and white, we mounted the staircase. Over the stairwell, on a brown wooden plaque and in gold lettering, hung the school motto – 'Esse quam Vedere'.

"Do you know what that means?" asked Betty. I shook my head, "To be, rather than to seem," Betty enlightened me proudly, but I was none the wiser. Betty led the way into a large room to the right of the top of the stairs.

"You're in Miss Winifred's, with me," she said, and led me to the teacher sitting at the high, old fashioned desk.

Miss Winifred was a much less frightening personage than her sister. She wore glasses, but her hair was cut short, and Marcel waved. Betty had already informed me that Tusky was awful, but that Winnie was all right.

The classroom was really two rooms knocked into one, and both halves contained rows of polished double desks. We were a small class and only filled the desks in one half of the room. Luckily, I was allowed to share Betty's desk. The other side of the room was used only for exams when we sat further apart, or for the odd sinner who had to be isolated. Jean, my friend from Sawdie's, had been brought by her mother and was already established in another desk. She smiled at me across the aisle.

So started my schooling at Tusky's. It was really quite different from Miss Sawdens. Tusky had worked out a most elaborate and comprehensive number scheme for use right through the school. It says a lot for Miss Sawden, that Jean and I were way ahead of anyone else in numbers in Miss Winifred's class. I am no mathematical genius, and Maths was my worst subject at High School later, but the basic rules had been extremely well taught.

I had no difficulty following any of the other subjects either, but when it came to the Art lesson, I was totally useless. Used only to copying pictures at Miss Sawden's, I had no opportunity to develop any imagination. In the first lesson we were told to draw a picture of the caravan in *The Wind in the Willows*, which they had been reading the term before. Too shy to tell the teacher, Miss Bettison, that I didn't know the story, I copied Betty's rather dreadful drawing. Betty was no artist, and it was not until a long time later that I discovered that I had quite a talent for drawing; in fact it became my favourite and best subject.

There were two other classrooms upstairs besides ours. Tusky's class was housed in the adjoining room and came through a door into Miss Winifred's. Miss Barnfather's 'Upper Transition' was across the landing from us. Downstairs was the Kindergarten and Miss Bettison's class, 'Lower Transition'.

Every morning, and at the end of the school day, the three top classes would assemble in Miss Barnfather's room. Miss Barnfather, who was our needlework teacher, would sit at the piano, while Miss Winifred, with her back to one of the great marble surrounded fireplaces, supervised one half of the room, and Tusky, leaning on the fire guard of the other fireplace presided over the rest of us.

We had green hymn books, stamped on the cover with the school motto, Tusky read the prayers, always the same ones. Her eagle eye ran over us nonstop and her chilling voice would call one to order for the slightest fidget, the dropped hymn book, the open eyes during prayers.

The large garden behind the school had been paved over, and this was where we had our morning break. There was no afternoon playtime. It was a new experience for me to go out and play in the middle of lessons. On cold days there was always an organised game of 'chain tag', which kept us all running, and we would return to the classroom out of breath and with glowing cheeks. Further exercise was provided in the afternoons when we had gym or country dancing. This took place in the large Kindergarten room downstairs. The little ones only had morning school. On the wall were some ribstalls, but apart from these our gym lesson consisted of the usual arm and leg exercises, running on the spot and so on. These lessons were taken by a kind old soul, Mrs Garret. She always wore a navy tunic and cream silk shirt blouse. Secretly, I thought she was far too old to dress like a schoolgirl, but in reality she probably wasn't all that old! She tried in vain to teach me the Polka. I had little sense of rhythm, and she would steer me round repeating, "One, two, three, hop. One, two, three, hop!" I would become more and more embarrassed, and made more and more mistakes until she gave up. I always remember her hands, they were very soft and dry, and she smelled of baby powder.

Music lessons were taken in Tusky and Winnie's parlour. We would sit on the carpet round the piano and sing to Miss Winifred's playing. I enjoyed these lessons, as they were not a bit like school. It was more like home, with the pictures, ornaments, cushions and lace curtains. I would gaze curiously at all the little family treasures, and perhaps realised that Tusky and Winnie were quite normal people after all.

In the summer term there was one very special day a week. This was called 'field' day. Instead of afternoon school we went to a playing field on the outskirts, where we played rounders and other games. We had to take the tram to the terminus, and always we sat on the top deck, and at the end of the trip helped the conductor to move the back of the seats over, ready for the return journey.

Once a year we had a sports afternoon in the same field, an event at which I did not shine, winning not a single point for my house – the Yellows. Luckily, there were plenty of other children winning points for the coveted cup, which would then be decorated with the appropriate colour ribbons for a whole year.

Another annual summer event was the 'outing'. We had to bring a packed lunch and we all piled into a hired coach and set off for Hornsea, where we played games on the beach, paddled and came home tired and sunburnt, singing Polly Wolly Doodle, and similar songs, led by remarkably jolly teachers.

Christmas at Tusky's was celebrated by the top classes by the singing of carols; there was no truck with paper decorations, seasonal pictures or Christmas trees. Downstairs, the little ones in the Kindergarten and Lower Transition classes, learnt their lessons in rooms hung with paper chains that they had made themselves. The Kindergarten even had a Christmas tree. We used to peep enviously into these fairy grottoes on our way to bleaker classrooms upstairs.

There was one treat for us all however, and that was the annual Christmas party, generously given by Tusky and Winnie. It was held after school hours, and the mere fact of going back to school in the dark and wearing party dresses was enough to make it a special occasion. In the gaily decorated Kindergarten room, we played fiercely organised party games. Tusky, Winnie and the other teachers almost let their hair down, but we children were all on our very best behaviour. Sandwiches, jelly, cakes and lemonade followed the games, and then parents would call to collect their somewhat subdued offspring!

On the last day of term it was tradition to sing the hymn Lord Dismiss Us With Thy Blessing, and I used to think the line 'All who here shall meet no more' unbearably sad. The big girls who stood on the back row usually had a few leavers among their ranks every end of term. In those days the official school leaving age was fourteen, a very young and tender age to be finishing one's education. Girls who didn't pass for the High School stayed on at Tusky's and invariably left at fourteen.

One end of term Betty nudged me during the singing of the final hymn.

"Look," she whispered, "Elsie's crying!" and to my horror, I saw one of the goddesses in the top class with tears trickling unashamedly down her face.

"How awful!" I thought, "how awful to leave! I wonder if I'll cry when it's my turn?"

When I was nearly ten, I moved up into Tusky's class. Both sides of the room were occupied – the young ones at the garden end, and the older ones at the other side. All of us in our part of the room, were to take the entrance exam to Newland High School. Tusky coped remarkably well with the considerable age range in her class, but she was an excellent teacher, and never ever in my whole school life was I as well taught as I was at Tusky's.

One summer Saturday, our entire class went up to Newland High School, to take our exam. We sat in the dining hall along with other little girls in various coloured uniforms. We tackled the easy papers. Children from the Council school took the scholarship exam, but in those days there were still fee paying places for the children from private schools.

We had just started when there was a commotion at the door. A girl had arrived late, and her father was explaining to the teacher in charge. The little girl was placed at a table by the window near me. She looked at me and grinned, and I recognised her. It was Irene, who had gone to the nuns, and learnt manners and curtsying.

Between papers we had a short break in the playground. The final paper completed, we were free to go. On the bus going home we chattered about our chances of passing, and of the papers we had just done.

"Easy, wasn't it," said Betty confidently, and we all agreed with her. It had been easy. Too easy. Maybe they were short of funds, and needed the fee paying pupils for an extra boost! But at only two guineas a term, I doubt it. Although it was practically a foregone conclusion that we would all pass the exam, nevertheless we were pleasantly surprised when we did!

We all arrived at school, chattering excitedly about the letters our parents had received, informing them that their daughters had passed the entrance exam for Newland High School. Enclosed with this piece of news were details of school uniform, school rules, and a list of text books to be bought. Betty had brought her copy of the school rules. We all shouted with laughter over the one that forbade the wearing of corsets at school! The rules had obviously been laid down in the last century, and never been updated. Tusky, for once, looked at us benignly, and told us that she was very pleased with us. Praise indeed!

All too soon, the last day of term was upon us, and we were singing the lines 'All who here shall meet no more'. This time it applied to me and my young classmates. Studiously avoiding looking at Betty, whose put on lugubrious expression would have sent me off giggling hysterically, I tried to feel sad and regretful on this, my very last day ever at Tusky's. I tried hard, but failed completely for I was bubbling with excitement inside. Not because next term I would be starting at Newland, nor because my pristine new uniform was already hanging in the wardrobe at home, nor even the thought of the pile of new books, neatly covered with brown paper by Papa. No, my excitement did not concern any of these. My thoughts were already on the holidays ahead.

At home, Papa had already brought the great cabin trunk down from the box room, and Mama was busy packing. Just a few more days and we would be in Hannover again, with Oma and Tante Mane, and of course, our beloved Steinman twins.

22. TANTE ANNA

Rudolf and Wilhelm, the Steinman twins, were not related to us; they lived opposite Oma in the Simrockstrasse and were our very special friends. Handsome boys, with blonde curly hair and blue eyes, they were a few years older than Eberhard and were really his playmates. Anita and I adored them, and when the boys went out to play we always tagged along behind them. They would call on us as soon as we settled in at Oma's, politely shaking hands all round, with a little bow and clicking heels that impressed us enormously.

Then we would go out and play with them, either in the street or further afield to the Stephansplatz, where there was a sandpit and children's play area. Whatever games we played, they always included all of us, treating Anita and me as equals to them, and not condescendingly as most boys of their age would have done. Small wonder then that we worshipped them! Anita and I had our own plans for the future, I would marry Rudi when we were all grown up and Anita would have Willi.

Needless to say, the boys knew nothing of this cosy domestic arrangement in store for them. It came to naught anyway, as both boys lost their lives in the war that was so soon to tear Europe apart. They belonged to a generation where so many did not live to become middle-aged or old. Forever, I shall remember them, full of life, blue eyes shining in their young fresh faces, the sunlight glinting on their blonde hair, as we played the happy carefree games of childhood together.

In Hannover and its neighbourhood, Mama had a host of relations, uncles, aunts and cousins in various degrees of cousinship. Though depleted by the 1914-1918 war, there were a fair amount to be visited, or who called to see us on our annual visits to the city. Most of them left very little impression on me, they were all much of a muchness. They called us "Kleine Engländer," commented on how much we had grown and asked us if we could still speak German or had we forgotten it by now. We would answer "Ja" and "Nein," which presumably satisfied their queries and we were allowed to continue with our play. One of Mama's cousins, however, stood out above the rest. This was cousin Aenne, who was straightforward and jolly and treated us children as equals. She had been on a visit to America on the S.S. Bremen, which in my opinion made her unique. She worked at the Post Office in Lauenstein, and we would take the local train and visit her. Then we would go on lovely long country walks with her, and the woods and meadows around would ring with her happy boisterous laugh.

Then there was Tante Anna, who, next to Oma and Tante Mane was the most important relation on Mama's side. As the second eldest daughter in the Daues clan, Tante Anna still was the undisputed, if self-appointed, head of the family. The other sisters and their families more or less resentfully danced to her tune.

Anna's word, at least when she was present, was the law. As soon as we settled at Oma's, Oma would announce "Tante Anna is coming tomorrow." Mama, who lived too far away to be greatly influenced by Tante Anna's whims and moods could take Anna's visits in her stride. She could cope with her for a few weeks and then happily return to England and freedom.

Mane, on the other hand, as strong willed as Anna herself, had many clashes of temperament with the good lady. To get her own back, she would egg us on as soon as the impending visit drew near.

"Go and look out of the corner window," she would urge us, "then as soon as you see her turn the corner, shout and wave, and run down to meet her and hug her."

Once, she even produced a small tin trumpet for Eberhard to blow as soon as the tall, stately figure, dressed from head to toe in black, turned the corner into the Simrockstrasse. We would shout "Hurra, sie kommt!" and wave frantically, and Anna, pleased at the reception, would wave her stick from afar. I used to feel slightly guilty at this overdone welcome, as we next rushed down the stairs and into the street to embrace her. We would be enfolded to her black, voluminously clad bosom, that always smelled of moth balls, and all of us together holding on to her arms and hands would climb the stairs back to Oma's apartment, Tante Anna asking questions, and we politely answering them. After all, Anita was her godchild, there were always silver cake forks every birthday, to prove it.

Papa would be greeted and then we would all sit down to repast. Anna loved food, especially cakes, and Mama had a fund of little stories of Anna and her cakes. Once, when asked to help herself to a cake, the delicious Mohrenkopf she coveted was on the side of the plate furthest away from her. Not to be put off by this, Tante Anna turned the cake platter until the desired Mohrenkopf was opposite her.

"I'll just take the nearest one," she said modestly, helping herself to the coveted pastry! We used to scream with laughter over that one, and it was one of our ritual family jokes, turning the plate to get the biggest piece and quoting Tante Anna. Another little oft repeated anecdote, concerned a coffee and cake session Oma and Tante Anna had at the Stadthalle Cafe. They regularly visited this cafe, and took it in turns to pay the bill. Once, when it was Oma's turn to pay, she was a pfennig short, and borrowed one from Tante Anna. It was a negligible amount even in those days, but the next time they were out together, Tante Anna reminded Oma.

"See, you still owe me that pfennig – why don't you give me it now, then I don't need to think about it anymore!"

Oma paid up, but it rankled somewhat, as Tante Anna always had the most luscious cakes, whereas Oma's tastes were more frugal!

Many times Tante Anna would accompany us to the zoo or Tiergarten. On these occasions she would dive into the large black cloth reticule she always carried and produce a paper bag of assorted biscuits. She would regale us with these. They always tasted of soap, but we were well brought up and polished off every crumb. On her bag were her embroidered initials A. S.

"Do you know what A. S. stands for?" whispered Eberhard once, as we sat in the grass behind the grown-ups seat in the Tiergarten, munching the soapy biscuits. "Anna Schmidt," I said.

"No," said Eberhard, "it stands for Alles Seife." (All Soap).

We tittered and giggled over that, thinking it was a rare piece of wit, and couldn't wait to pass it on to Mane.

Once, in every holiday, there was the ceremonial visit to Tante Anna's apartment. Dressed in our best, we would board the tram to the other side of Hannover, where she lived. Her apartment was in an old house. The rooms were enormous, filled with dark, heavy furniture, with dark red drapes and thick white lace curtains at the tall windows.

While the grown-ups talked in the salon, we children were sent to play in the study. Tante Anna would produce some old fashioned books and card games and we were left to amuse ourselves until summoned for coffee.

On the enormous desk, that had belonged to her ill-fated school master son, Wilhelm, there stood an enchanting ornament. It was a heavy metal ash tray on which was fixed the model of a horse – Mama said it was Nil. It was complete with saddle and bridle and about six inches high. There wasn't much I could do with it, but I loved it dearly, stroking its hard little head and wishing it were mine.

Joining the grown-ups in the dining room for afternoon coffee, we children would sit at a small table by ourselves. For us there was no coffee. We drank cocoa out of the thick blue and white kitchen cups, and cake was passed to us from the top table. We did not dare take the choicest pieces of cake as we were encouraged to at Oma's, and no matter how hard we tried not to spill our cocoa, or perhaps because we tried too hard, we always managed to get stains on the crisp white embroidered cloth that covered our little table.

An intriguing aspect of Tante Anna's place was her toilet. For some reason or another, probably because the property was of an older type, its toilet was not actually in the apartment itself, it was, as she called it, 'half stairs'. This meant one had to go out of her front door and down a short flight of steps to reach it. For this reason it was always kept locked. The key hung on a hook by the front door and if one needed to visit the lavatory it was always a great performance of unlocking doors and locking them up again.

On one such occasion, having been ushered in and out by Tante Anna, who always checked up to make sure the door was properly locked, instead of going straight back into the salon I peeped through an open door which led off the hall. It was a bedroom, with two great beds covered with enormous white feather beds. On a washstand stood two large jug and ewer sets. Tante Anna came up behind me and rested her old gnarled hand on my shoulder.

"See," she said, "I have so much room, you could all come and stay with me sometime."

I was only a little girl, with my head full of selfish thoughts, but strangely, at that moment the hand on my shoulder and the wistful voice communicated to me the loneliness of Tante Anna, who lived all alone, who had lost a husband and two sons. My soft little heart ached for her and the great empty beds, where nobody slept anymore.

"Ask your Mama," said Tante Anna, "if you can stay with me sometime."

"Yes, Tante Anna, I will." I reassured her.

On the tram going back to the Simrockstrasse, I broached the subject with Mama.

"Why don't we ever stay with Tante Anna?" I asked her, "she says she has lots of room."

"You wouldn't like it," said Mama, "she wouldn't spoil you like Oma does. She's very strict."

"Couldn't we just once?" I pleaded.

"What about Oma?" said Mama, "she'd be very sad if we didn't stay with her."

"Maybe just one night, then," I persisted, "nobody ever sleeps in her beds now."

"Don't worry about Tante Anna," said Mama, "everybody who visits Hannover stays with her, they daren't stay anywhere else!"

Of course, as I found out much later, this was quite true, cousins, nephews, nieces, any relative, no matter how remote, stayed with Tante Anna on their visits to the city.

But the great white beds, that nobody wanted, haunted my childhood, and I vowed to myself that when I was grown up I would go and stay with Tante Anna, all by myself.

It was never to be; Tante Anna, in her eighties, died one month before the war broke out, when I was still a long way from being grown up. Mane told us later that after Tante Anna's death all the relatives descended like vultures, and shared her things between them. She, Mane, only got a set of teaspoons and a table cloth or two, which were later lost in an air raid. Years later, cousin Aenne gave us a small tray cloth that Tante Anna had embroidered as a child. I treasure this small heirloom, but even now I wonder what happened to the one thing I would have really loved – the little metal horse.

23. LITTLE BERLINER!

Papa's two sisters; Agnes and Hanny, lived in Berlin, and visiting them was always part of our summer holiday. Tante Agnes and her husband, Onkel Karl, had no children, and with them lived an old uncle, known as 'Der alte Onkel Karl'. He was a brother of Papa's father, a dear old fellow, but we children had little to do with him. Tante Hanny was married to a Police Inspector, Onkel Willi, and they had one child, Konrad, our cousin. Konrad, Mama used to say, was a proper little, 'Berliner'.

He was two years my junior in age, but in all other matters he was light years ahead of us. He was a handsome, charming, forward child, who oozed self-confidence, said outrageous things in public, interrupted grown ups, and joined in their conversation. He mimicked our funny way of talking German, yet we adored him, and were his devoted slaves from the moment we arrived. He was possessive with his toys, only allowing us to have his oldest cast-offs to play with, and taking away any that Tante Hanny had given us, just as soon as her back was turned.

Tante Agnes had the larger apartment, and we mostly all stayed with her. Once, however, I stayed alone with Tante Hanny, Onkel Willi and Konrad. As far as I was concerned, it was not a success. Konrad had a fine rocking horse, covered with real fur, and more than anything in the world, I longed to ride it. So when it was suggested that I might like to stay with Tante Hanny, I agreed, thinking of the noble horse, and how I would be able to ride it all day long. Once the rest of the family had gone off to Tante Agnes, and I was on my own, doubt crept in!

For a start, Konrad wouldn't let me ride his horse, nor could I mount it myself. I couldn't boldly fling one leg over the saddle the way bragging little Konrad did, so I had to content myself with stroking it. Once, when I dragged a footstool up, and was trying unsuccessfully to mount again, Konrad pulled me off. He then managed to pick up the heavy horse, and began belabouring me with it, while I cowed on the floor, screaming for Tante Hanny.

At night, I slept on a little sofa at the foot of Tante Hanny and Onkel Willi's beds. I was frightened of Onkel Willi; he was strict and brusque, but luckily he wasn't home much, and I avoided him whenever I could. One night I woke up, knowing I was going to be sick. I was! All over the bedclothes! Tante Hanny was up in a minute, fussing about, changing my nightie, washing my hands and face. Then while she changed my bedding, she popped me into her own bed. All this time Onkel Willi lay in his bed, totally unsympathetic, muttering and mumbling and being cross with me for being sick. It was not a kind way to treat a frightened and embarrassed little girl, I was thankful to get back to my little sofa.

Happily, Tante Hanny and family moved to another apartment in the same house as Tante Agnes, in the suburb of Wilmersdorf. It made visiting much easier, for we three children would share the big bedroom at Hanny's with Konrad, all four of us sleeping in the two great beds. Mama and Papa would stay with Tante Agnes.

We four would have an uproarious time, laughing and giggling till late, when Onkel Willi would bang on the door and threaten us with dire punishment if we didn't go to sleep at once. Even the ebullient Konrad would then subside under the covers, muttering defiantly about 'der Olle' as he disrespectfully referred to his father, while we stifled our hysterical laughter under the pillows.

Konrad's family, like many others in large German cities, rented a garden. This was a few minutes' walk away, a place of tranquillity and cool shade, so welcome in the hot Berlin summers. It was a sizeable plot, surrounded by others, and bounded on the perimeter by the usual large apartment blocks of the city. The garden sported fruit trees, vegetable and flower beds, ornamental shrubs, a small patch of grass and a delightful little summer house-cum-shed. There were cane chairs and an old table covered with oil cloth, for picnics and al fresco meals.

We would spend hours in that garden making up strange games with Konrad, while the grown-ups sat at the table, in the shade, drinking beer. The evenings were always warm, so there was no rush to get back to the stuffy apartments.

When the warm scented dusk fell, Tante Hanny would light candles and place them into delicately coloured, fragile paper shades. These she would hang romantically in the trees and about the summer house. It used to amaze me that the candles in the dainty shades did not set the whole frail lamps alight. As the light faded completely the glowing lanterns seemed to float in the air above us. It was a time filled with the wonder and enchantment of a magical land. The adults could only be located by the hum of their voices and the glowing tips of the cigars that Papa and the uncles smoked.

It has been said that before the second world war, Berlin was the most corrupt capital in Europe – if not the world. It may have been for some, but we rarely left the pleasant suburb of Wilmersdorf. Mama and the aunts would go on shopping trips to the city without us. Only once do I remember going on a bus to the city centre. We went down the famous Unter den Linden, and under the great Brandenburger Tor.

"This is the most famous street in Germany," Mama told us, "Now you can say you've been down it too." So it made an impression on me, and I remember it.

But for the most part, our little world in Berlin consisted of the homes of aunts and uncles, the pretty garden, and in the centre – the bright little sun we all revolved around – cousin Konrad – our very own little "Berliner!"

24. KAPUTT HITLER!

After Hitler's rise to power, in 1933, life in Germany began subtly to change. Even we children could not fail to notice this. For a start, the streets of Berlin and Hannover seemed to be permanently festooned with flags. Not the traditional black, white and red horizontally striped German flags, but blood red, with a white central circular patch containing a strange black device.

"That's called a "Hakenkreuz," explained Mama, "horrible, aren't they? What was wrong with our nice old flags?"

Actually, I thought the new flags were quite pretty and certainly unusual.

While we stayed in Berlin, Papa, Mama and the aunts and uncles, tactfully, never discussed politics. Onkel Willi, as a Police Inspector, sported an armband with the Swastika over his uniform. Konrad belonged to some sort of pre Hitler youth movement, which was called the 'Kukenschaar', and as for Hanny, she seemed to be quite an admirer of Hitler!

Once, she and Mama went to a concert and the Führer himself put in an appearance, walking up the centre aisle with his bodyguard once the audience had settled in its seats. Mama was staggered at the reception the audience gave him. They rose from their seats in one accord and cheered, clapped and shouted "Heil." Mama thought Hitler looked very ordinary, but as for Tante Hanny, Mama was really quite embarrassed for her! She shouted and clapped with the rest and kept on repeating over and over again, "Oh, isn't he blond, isn't he blond!"

Finally she subsided ecstatically in her seat and sighed romantically, "Oh, I wish I could be his bedside rug!"

It was such a funny thing to want to be, that when Mama told us later we thought it was hilarious, but the fact that

Hanny should be so besotted was also, for Papa and Mama, slightly disturbing. Still, it was quite an achievement for Mama to have seen Hitler, and when we got back to Hull, I casually informed Betty that Mama had actually seen Hitler.

"Who?" asked Betty, with crushing disinterest, "is that?"

I did not bother to enlighten her.

In Hannover, however, Oma and Mane were definitely anti-Hitler, but their views were only aired in low voices and behind closed doors.

As soon as we arrived at Oma's apartment now, and the hugging and kissing was over, Mama and Papa would lower their voices and ask, how things were, and a sotto voce discussion of the political situation would begin. We children were not particularly interested in the whys and wherefores of the Nazi party, but some of the more obvious features fascinated us. Instead of the usual greetings of "Guten Morgen," "Guten Tag," or "Auf Wiedersehen," the National greeting was now "Heil Hitler." Oma, Mama and Tante Mane would pointedly use the old forms of greetings, ignoring the shopkeeper's Heil Hitler. But Anita and I, if sent on an errand would boldly shout "Heil Hitler!" when entering or leaving a shop. It made us feel important and up to date.

Then also, Mane told us that there was a Nazi living in the house, whose duty it was to keep an eye on the other tenants. To us, it sounded sinister and rather frightening, and we used to tiptoe silently past his apartment door on our way up and down the stairs.

The Steinman twins too had changed, they were growing up, and belonged to the Hitler Youth. They looked very smart and handsome in their uniform. As usual, Rudi came to visit. He walked into Oma's living room where we were all assembled and said, "Heil Hitler!" For a moment there was a stunned silence, the greeting was totally out of place in Oma's gentle, old fashioned room. Then Anita piped up cheekily, "Kaputt Hitler!" And everybody laughed in a slightly embarrassed way. Even Rudi could not help smiling, but then his face became serious.

"Don't ever," he said solemnly, "say that outside in the street, or you'll be in big trouble."

"Why?" asked the incorrigible Anita.

"Because you mustn't," said Rudi firmly, "this is Germany, not England."

So we didn't say, "Kaputt Hitler," outside, but that night in bed, Anita put her head under the bedclothes and whispered the forbidden phrase, I joined in, and we got louder and louder and sillier and sillier, until Mama came in.

"For heaven's sake, be quiet and go to sleep. What's so funny anyway?" she said.

We didn't tell her, it suddenly seemed very childish.

One warm afternoon, while the grown-ups were resting, Anita and I went out to play. For us, the elegant, suburban streets of Hannover Sudstadt with their tall, imposing houses, were as familiar as our own so different surroundings in Hull. We wandered off to the Stefansplatz to gaze into the toy shop window at a doll we coveted, then on to the sandpit, which was another favourite haunt. Finally, we went back to the Simrockstrasse and sat on the step outside Oma's house. We chatted and giggled together and maybe because it was such a warm still afternoon, our voices carried on the quiet air. Suddenly a voice from an open window above us shouted down a torrent of German, would we be still, and kindly consider people who were trying to rest etc. etc. We were obedient children, and subsided immediately.

Then Anita whispered, "Do you think that was the Nazi? I bet it was. Anyway, we'll pretend we can't understand his silly old German." Then she put her mouth close to my ear and hissed daringly, "Kaputt Hitler." It tickled my ear, and her bravado amused me. I hissed back at her, and we got the giggles, getting louder and louder, until the irate voice boomed out again.

We waited to hear no more; and ran to the street corner. We heard martial music playing and saw a strange procession approaching. A small military band, clad in brown with the familiar Swastika armbands, was being followed, Pied Piper fashion, by dozens of children of all ages, all waving small paper Swastika flags. As we stared, a tall girl, dressed in the uniform of the 'Bund Deutscher Mädel' , came up to us. She carried a bunch of flags, and handing us two apiece, told us to join in the marching. Eagerly we followed the others, waving our little flags with gusto. We traversed a large part of the Sudstadt, and finally were deposited back at the Simrockstrasse. An anxious Mama was pacing the pavement, looking for us. She did not look overly pleased. We left the procession and joined her. The B. D. M. girl explained that we hadn't been far, just a little march. Mama glanced at her, but didn't reply. Instead, she spoke to us rather loudly in English.

"We've been looking all over for you," she said, "we've been really worried."

The B.D.M. girl said disparagingly, "Ach, Engländer," and rejoined her column.

"Why did you speak English?" we asked Mama.

"I couldn't have been cross in German," said Mama, "I might have got into trouble."

We were intrigued, it didn't make sense to us that grown-ups could get into trouble, but we kept our little Swastika flags, and later that year, they decorated our sand castles by the Baltic Sea.

Mama and Papa now increasingly spoke in English when we were in the street, on the tram or in the shops, especially after one small, ugly incident that happened to Papa and Eberhard once when they were out for a walk. They both came back to Oma's one day, and Papa looked visibly shaken. Mama immediately wanted to know what was wrong. Papa hedged a little, it wasn't important, he said, best forgotten. He and Eberhard had simply been walking along, and Eberhard commented on the large number of flags that adorned the balconies, and hung from the buildings.

"He only asked me why there were so many flags," said Papa, "and all I said was I didn't know."

Knowing Papa, I should think he would have said rather more than that. He probably was quite insulting and derogatory about the ridiculous amount of flags hung about the place. He didn't realise that this was the new Germany, and not England, where free speech was taken for granted. He would also have spoken quite loudly for the benefit of passers-by to show that here was a man not taken in by Nazi propaganda, a man who was still free to think as he wished. He was in for a shock! One of the men going past, immediately turned on him, and began to berate him loudly.

"A good German," he thundered, "knows exactly what day it is, and why the flags are out!"

Papa explained he had just come from England, hoping this would appease the irate stranger, but the belligerent fellow assumed a threatening attitude, and suddenly a hostile crowd had collected round them. Papa's bravado evaporated, he clutched Eberhard's arm, and made quickly for the nearest house entrance. Luckily, it was open. They hurried up the stairs, and were thankful that no one followed them. After a decent interval had elapsed, they emerged cautiously, and hurried back to Oma's.

Papa tried to make light of the whole incident, and even laughed a little at the way they had fled into just any house.

"Good job the door was open," he said, "heaven knows what would have happened if it had been locked."

"Well," said Mama, "you were lucky, in future, it is better to always speak English when we are out."

So they did, and contrary as children are, we didn't like it. At home in England we disapproved of their, speaking German in public, and here, in Germany, the position was reversed! Even though we children only conversed between ourselves in English, we liked Mama and Papa to speak German while we were in Germany!

Apart from Oma's whisperings about the Nazi party's attitude to Jews, there were also for us, small outward signs.

There were some shops that displayed a sinister notice 'Juden nicht erwünscht'.

"Why don't they want Jews?" I asked Mama. "What's wrong with them?"

My friend, Irene, was Jewish, and I liked her very much. She was such fun to be with, and her birthday parties were always a great treat. Her father owned a car and sometimes on rainy days he would collect Irene, and I always got a lift as far as the railway crossing. So what was wrong with Jews?

"Well," said Mama, "I don't really know. I suppose they always have lots of money and Hitler wants it."

That figured, Irene's father had a car – that, in my opinion, was being rich! "But how can they tell if people are Jews or not?" asked Anita, "do they ask them first."

"You can usually see," said Mama vaguely, "they have different features, you know, bigger noses, dark eyes, things like that."

"But Irene hasn't got a big nose," I said, "she looks just like me, except her hair is naturally wavy," I added enviously.

Then once, somewhere in a park, there was an empty bench, painted bright yellow. We went to sit on it. Then Mama saw the writing on the back, "Nur für Juden' it stated simply.

"We can't sit here," said Mama, "it's for Jews only."

We were hot and tired, "Why not?" we said defiantly, "we can pretend we're English and don't understand their daft German." "No," said Mama, firmly, "I wouldn't risk it. Come on, we'll find another seat." "But what would happen if we sat on it?" Anita wanted to know. "I daren't think," said Mama, "Germany just isn't Germany any more, with these horrible goings on."

"I'm so glad we live in England," said Papa, "at least all this Nazi business can't reach us there!"

But there he was wrong, for it could, and did, reach us, even in Hull!

25. THE PARTY

As the Nazi party gained its hold in Germany, so its tentacles began to creep further afield to seek out Germans who had, so to speak, escaped the net by living in other countries. Good party men, in the guise of business men, were sent abroad to form small groups of supporters in various cities in England.

One such man appeared in Hull, and contacted the handful of German businessmen who lived and worked there. He approached Papa one fine day, and suggested that as a good patriotic German he should join the party. Papa flatly refused. For a start, he had no interest in politics, and secondly, he had no sympathy with the party, in spite of its glowing propaganda.

These views were not allowed, and a little pressure was applied. It would be much better for his business, it was suggested. Was there even a hint of a threat? Papa talked it over with Mama. His family and his business were important to him; he could join, and pretend to support it, he could always leave if things got too involved. So, Papa reasoned, and discussed it with another German, who was also being unwillingly pressured. This one too, suggested they join, just to keep the peace.

So it was arranged, and the Nazi infiltrator had his little group of four or five reluctant candidates. While all this was going on, the Nazi had been a regular visitor to our house. We children knew nothing of what was being planned, but from the day I first set eyes on him I hated that man with such a fierce burning hatred that I had never felt for anyone before. The reason had nothing whatever to do with politics, nor had he ever harmed me in any way. On the contrary, I doubt if he was even the slightest bit interested in my existence.

He was a large, fat man, whose neck bulged over the collar of the leather coat he wore. It was the coat that started it all. The first time I saw him was when I happened to be in the dining room doing a jig-saw, when he called. Papa was out, and Mama made polite conversation. The fire was burning brightly, and the room was warm. The sweat began to trickle down his brow, and he mopped it. Mama could see she was not going to get rid of him easily.

"Why don't you take your coat off, and have a glass of wine?" she asked with reluctant hospitality.

"Thank you," he said, and removed his heavy coat, it was fully lined with patches of variously coloured fur. He hung it on the back of a chair, and went on talking.

"It's a very warm coat," he said, "I suffer with rheumatism, so it's lined with cat's fur."

A shock, like an electric one, passed through me. Cat's fur! Had I heard right? I looked at the coat, and saw clearly for the first time, the terrible lining. The tabbies, the bright gingers, the soft greys, and sooty black. I saw the silky whites, the tortoiseshells and the little patchy ones. I felt sick to my very soul. My vivid imagination sprang into action. I could picture the podgy hands ruthlessly killing and then tearing off the little coats of the poor darling cats. I couldn't be in the same room as him and his coat, I had to get away. I left my jig-saw and hurried out. I stood outside the door, raging at the monster, the cat killer, who sat under our roof, in our chair, beside our fireside, about to drink our wine.

I gave vent to my feelings, behind the safety of the heavy door. I stuck out my tongue and pulled horrible faces at the ogre within. Mama, opening the door at that moment, and seeing my contorted face, let out a muffled exclamation. Hastily, she shut the door behind her. "Whatever are you doing?" she hissed. "He's horrible, I hate him!" I hissed back.

"I can't stand him either," whispered Mama, "I'll get some wine, and then we'll get rid of him."

I thought Mama disliked him for the same reason I did. I followed her into the pantry, still obsessed with the coat.

"Did he kill all those cats?" I asked, still whispering, although we were out of earshot. Mama had other things on her mind. She was looking at two started bottles of wine which stood on the stone pantry floor. She was muttering to herself.

"This wine will do for him, no need to give him the best."

"Give him poison," I whispered.

Mama opened the biscuit tin and took out a few very plain biscuits which she arranged on an ordinary plate, not the usual silver reserved for honoured guests. She set the frugal offering on a small tray and returned to the dining room with me following close behind.

"If he didn't kill the cats, ask him who did," I persisted.

We had reached the dining room door. Mama's eyes focused on me in surprise.

"What on earth are you talking about? What cats? Open the door for me please."

She arranged her face into a bright, false smile as she went into the room, as I held the door open.

"Here we are!" she cried gaily, "In vino veritas!"

I closed the door angrily. "Really," I thought, "Grown-ups! How can they be so good at pretending?" I would have thrown the whole lot in his face!

The coat, lined with cat fur, was to grace our hall stand on many a future occasion, and it had a fearful fascination for me. Whenever I saw it hanging there, it drew me with an irresistible force. I would sit on the floor beside it, surreptitiously stroking the fur of the dear departed little cats. I mourned them and pitied their cruel fate. They had so needlessly given all of their nine lives to keep a fat man warm. I grieved for them all; the tabbies, the bright gingers, the soft greys, and sooty blacks, the silky whites, the tortoiseshell and the little patchy ones.

Once the Hull branch of the party was formed, meetings were held in strict rotation at the various members' houses.

The first time it was at our house, we became aware of a tense atmosphere as soon as teatime was over. Mama had arranged for the maid to have the evening off, she didn't want any outsiders around.

The dining room was tidied, and we children were told that we would spend the evening with Mama in the morning room. Mama laid a dark blue, plush cloth on the dining table, and in the centre Papa placed a most enchanting little bauble. It was a small brass flagpole, holding a tiny silken Swastika flag, complete with miniature golden ropes and tassels. Anita and I gazed at it in delight, it was the dearest little banner we have ever seen. "Why have you put it on the table?" asked Anita, "can we play with it?" "You can touch it if you like, but don't break it," said Papa, distractedly. He was walking about the room like a cat on hot bricks, wearing what we called in later years, his glassy look. His face had a kind of sickly expression, and his eyes behind his glasses were vague and unfocussed. "What's this meeting all about?" Eberhard asked, "what do you talk about?" "That's a secret," said Papa, "nobody must ever know!" The doorbell rang.

"Out!" said Mama sharply. She and Eberhard went into the morning room, but Anita and I flew upstairs as Papa went to open the front door. Peeping over the banisters, we watched the men arrive, one by one. Finally all had arrived – the fat man was the last. He was the only one who said "Heil Hitler!" as he went into the room. The dining room door was firmly closed, and a faint murmur of voices came from within. Anita and I looked at one another, remembering the words Papa had spoken. "Nobody must ever know!"

We'd see about that! We tiptoed down the stairs and pressed our ears close to the panels of the dining room door. I caught Anita's eye close to mine, and we both got the giggles. Clapping our hands to our mouths, we strained our ears to catch the mumbled words spoken in the room. The door of the morning room opened suddenly, and Mama came out, she flapped her hands at us, and silently shooed us away. We rushed upstairs, our giggles exploding as we ran into our bedroom, which was over the dining room. We crept across the room and folded back the bedside rug. Then we lay on the floor, and, pressing our ears to the cold lino, continued our eavesdropping.

It was impossible to distinguish even one word from the rumble of voices below, and finally we rose from our uncomfortable positions and joined Mama and Eberhard in the morning room.

At future meetings we occasionally eavesdropped, more out of bravado than curiosity, but we always played with the little flag before the men assembled. "When you've finished with it, can we have it for our dolls?" asked Anita. "When I've finished with it, it's going straight on the fire!" said Papa, with unusual vehemence.

As time went on, Papa realised his mistake in joining the party and made tentative attempts to leave it. All his efforts were met with open threats from the fat leader. He told Papa that his business would be ruined if he gave up his membership. This shocked Papa into action, and he took an unexpected trip to his firm of suppliers in Elmshora. It was run by two brothers, whose political views were moderate. Nothing, they assured Papa would wreck their business relationship. Reassured, Papa returned to the bosom of his family, and he brought back, among other presents, two very strange objects. He took them out of his pocket, and placed them on the table. Our delighted eyes beheld with joy, two tiny soldiers of Hitler's army, one in black, S.S. Papa told us, and one in brown, S. A. – what the initials stood for we didn't know.

On their left arms they wore minute Swastika armbands, and their right arms were raised in permanent Nazi salute. Anita grabbed the black one, "He's mine," she announced, "I'll call him Hans." I took the brown one, "And this is Heinz," I said.

We played with the little soldiers for hours on end, they marched about, they had adventures, they talked German in funny gruff voices. We adored them.

Why Papa ever brought them in the first place, knowing how he felt, is a mystery to me. He had got them as a free gift with something or other, and they had not cost him a penny. He could have dropped them overboard from the ship coming over, but he'd kept them, for a free gift is after all a free gift, whatever shape it takes.

After a while, Hans and Heinz ceased to be a novelty, and they were relegated to the playroom mantelpiece. There they stood for many moons – their tiny arms permanently saluting the two other occupants on their shelf, a soap dog, destined never to touch water, who had a sickly smell and whose feet were beginning to crumble, and a silver paper covered chocolate dog that had stood there so long that its smell rivalled that of the soap dog!

By now, Papa's mind was firmly made up. He was going to leave the party and apply for naturalisation. His latest visit to Germany had convinced him that he could never reconcile himself to that Government. He and Mama decided that England was now their permanent home. There was no point in going back as they had once planned to, when Papa retired. Papa had, up to now, been very sentimental about his German origins. His cradle had stood in Germany, he used to say, why bother to change nationality? Now he saw naturalisation as the only way out.

He officially left the party and sent his application for naturalisation to the Home Office. There were, we heard later, a lot of threats and a great amount of ill feeling, but Papa stood firm. His business did not suffer in the least, and the coat with its controversial lining never hung on our hall stand again. Whether Papa burned the little flag, or handed it in, I don't know. It disappeared, and we never saw it again!

26. "GOOD MORNING PEOPLE!"

Long before I started at Newland High School in September, 1935, I knew that the school boasted a ginger haired games mistress. Miss Ellis never tired of telling us how she had almost been expelled from Newland. During a game of hockey, this particular mistress had gained the ball and was heading for the goal, when Miss Ellis screamed out, "Tackle the ginger bitch!"

She had been overheard, and brought before the headmistress. In the interview that then took place, expulsion was threatened, but in the end, she was let off with a severe reprimand.

In my sweet innocence, I thought it was the word ginger that was objected to! Bitch, to me meant a female dog, a piece of dog lore gleaned from Weldy. As I adored all dogs, male or female, to be referred to as a bitch was therefore an accolade akin to 'angel' or 'princess'. Armed with this interesting, if useless, snippet of information, concerning the games mistress, I set off with Betty for our first day at High School.

Proudly, we wore our new uniforms. Newland had become liberated and cast out the old-fashioned serge box-pleated tunics. Instead, we wore a rather unflattering garment designed for freedom of movement. A sort of V-necked Greek tunic in fine navy woollen material, with an elasticated waist, and slits at the side of the skirt. Under this was worn a white square-necked short-sleeved blouse. Mama had thriftily shortened the sleeves of my Tusky blouses, I hoped Betty wouldn't notice this pauperising.

The jumpers, navy and trimmed with the school colours of orange and yellow, were normal, but perched on our heads was the most hideous form of headgear ever devised for schoolgirls, and yet very popular too with other High Schools in Hull. These were ghastly pork pie hats with the school badge in the centre. New girls wore them plonked straight on their heads in an unbecoming fashion.

As time went by, we learned to tuck in the back of these hats as the older girls did, and also to make sure that not even half an inch of navy blue knicker was revealed by the split skirts. Only discreetly clad brown lisle-stockinged legs were allowed to show!

Tusky's had been large compared to Miss Sawden's little school, but Newland seemed enormous to us small newcomers. A vast neo-classical, creeper covered building with hundreds of windows, and inside, long corridors, endless classrooms, and teeming with swarms of navy and white clad girls. This was the first time for me to be in a 'real' school, and I was suitably awed. As it was we were gently broken in to High School life.

The five of us from Tusky's, together with twenty other new girls, most of them from private schools, were placed in Form 3D. Our form mistress was Miss Davy; she was kind, but firm. She appeared to be permanently smiling even when reprimanding us, for she had very prominent teeth. She told us that as a small girl, she had fallen and caught her teeth on the window ledge, and they had been like that ever since.

A wise woman, for instead of laughing behind her back at her strange expression, we sympathised with her in her misfortune, and accepted her as she was.

When I came home that day, I told Mama all about Miss Davy and her teeth.

Mama smiled reminiscently, "When I started school," she said, "My very first teacher had teeth like that, and I told everybody that I liked her because she had such friendly teeth!"

Miss Davy took us for most subjects and we had little to do with the rest of Newland's large staff of mistresses. A plump, motherly body taught us French, another taught singing, a fierce little soul was in charge of our needlework, and yes, the ginger haired mistress took us for gym and games.

We did not take to each other, the 'ginger bitch' and I. She didn't care for me as I was hopeless at gym, hockey and netball and I didn't like her because she didn't like me!

As time went on, and I became more familiar with the other mistresses, I compared notes with Miss Ellis. I found out that, apart from a few younger members of staff, all the others had been there in Miss Ellis' schooldays.

"Gosh," I said, "they must be ancient."

"Oh, yes," grinned Miss Ellis, "as old as the hills, the lot of 'em."

Without exception, in those days, all the mistresses at Newland were single women, and they ran the school with dedication and efficiency. There was only one man in this wholly female academy, and that was the master who taught Maths to the senior girls. He was a benevolent looking, white haired gentleman, who invariably sang the part of Good King Wenceslas at the Christmas Carol concert. His looks belied him, for we heard that he had a short temper and was inclined to throw chalk at girls who answered his rapped out questions stupidly.

All the mistresses had their little quirks and idiosyncrasies, but the most outstanding eccentric of them all was dear old "Tinny," the senior History teacher.

From the moment she strode into the classroom calling out, "Good morning, people!" we would sit spellbound throughout the duration of the lesson. Not so much because of the historical information she imparted, but because of her strange antics while doing this! She would ramble round the room, hands clasped behind her back, regaling us with tales of wars and Kings and Queens in her inimitable and picturesque fashion. She would suddenly stop and gaze into space, peer out of the window, or rummage in the waste paper basket. She would pick up objects lying on our desks and scrutinise them intently, or sort through the books and papers in her small attaché case. All the time her discourse never ceased.

"And the flame of freedom spread through Europe," she would intone, as she rearranged the vases on the windowsill. Sometimes, she would open the classroom door, step out into the corridor, peer up and down without a single pause in her speech. Occasionally, she would come to, with a start, and stare at us all, as though surprised to see a class of girls before her. Then she would come out with gems like,

"Are you people normal this morning?"

She always wore severely tailored suits. She had three in all, one brown, one navy blue and one clerical grey, and with these she wore shirts and ties. In the summer, on warm days, she would blossom out in striped Macclesfield silk shirt dresses, which hung strangely on her angular frame. She then wore flat leather sandals, like an overgrown child. Her outdoor wear was a belted raincoat and a flat felt hat.

For all her eccentricities, she was a strict disciplinarian, and we had a healthy respect for her as well as a great affection. Dear Tinny! They don't make them like that anymore.

The excellent teaching and disciplines of learning I had received at Sawden's and Tusky's stood me in good stead that first year at Newland. I worked diligently and conscientiously, and at the end of that year was awarded the form prize. This was to be my only burst of glory at High School.

I was promoted to the A class the following term, and immediately sank to my rightful place at the bottom of the class. For here I had met the real brains, the crème de la crème. These were mostly brilliant, ambitious girls, who absorbed knowledge like sponges. Thankfully, I gave up the struggle and became my true lazy, dreamy self, getting by with the minimum of work and effort.

I was not even there to hear my name read out at assembly on the last day of term, so missed my small moment of triumph. I had left school a few days earlier, as we had to catch the ship to Hamburg for our annual holiday in Germany. However, the following Speech Day I climbed on to the platform to collect my prize, a book. We could wear long-sleeved, collared blouses and ties for special occasions like Speech Days, and as a reward Mama had bought me a navy, orange and yellow striped tie, which I wore with one of Eberhard's white shirts.

27. SORROW AND JOY

That summer visit of 1936 was to be our last to Germany for many a long year, but we did not realise it at the time. The Swastika flags festooning the streets of Hannover and Berlin were now joined by other, and to my eyes, more beautiful flags. A white one adorned with brightly coloured circles, the flag of the Olympic Games, for this year was the year the Olympics were held in Berlin.

At Oma's too, things had changed; her little canary, Charlie, had died, and no longer did his sweet trilling little song so enchantingly delight us. Oma herself was not the same bubbling little person she usually was. Her heart was bad, we were told, and she had to go to Bad Nenndorf for the 'cure'.

We saw little of her that holiday, she did not join us when we went to the Baltic Sea for two weeks, but Mama spent time with her at Nenndorf before we all went on to Berlin.

Berlin was in the grip of Olympic fever, with flags and souvenirs abounding. We each acquired a silk handkerchief on which all the flags of the competing Nations were printed, and a brooch of the Olympic rings. We treasured these small mementoes. We stayed longer in Berlin than we usually did, for the cure had done little for Oma, and she was not well enough to have us romping about her apartment. We only had a couple of days in Hannover before leaving again for Bremen and Hull. We went to say goodbye to Oma. She sat white and still in her chair, a camel blanket over her knees. I kissed her soft, wrinkled cheek.

"Auf Wiedersehen, Oma," I said, but this was not my laughing, happy little Oma anymore. This was a very old lady, almost a stranger to me, and suddenly I felt shy and tongue tied.

There was to be no Wiedersehen for us and Oma. She died the following November 11th. I came home that day at lunch-time, and saw the telegram on the morning room table. It's message was simple – Oma had died in her sleep. I could hear Mama and Papa talking in the kitchen, but I didn't want to speak to anybody just then. I rushed upstairs to my bedroom, and stared out of the window unseeingly.

I couldn't cope with death. I took refuge in my childish make believe, "It's not true," I told myself, "they've made a mistake, she's all right, she's not really dead. She'll wake up soon." But even as I was thinking this I knew that all the imagining away in the world could not change the awful fact that my Oma was dead.

Mama came into the room, her voice was full of tears as she said, "We've just heard, Oma died last night."

I didn't even turn round, I only said, "Oh," and went on staring at nothing out of the window.

If Mama was surprised at my reception of her sad news, she did not comment on it. She left me alone with my grief and disbelief. Later on, Anita and I went into town with Mama to choose material for Mama's mourning dress.

"Not all black," said Mama, "I want something with a white pattern."

Together we chose a silky crepe material. It was black, patterned with tiny white windmills, trees, cows and little people in Dutch costume. It reminded me of Oma's pinnies.

Life for us continued at a leisurely pace. There was no such thing as television to rush us into a precocious maturity, we were so incredibly innocent. The thirties were pleasant years to grow up in for a middle class child.

If there was no television, there was the radio, but this was only switched on for music, the news, and Children's Hour, where Aunt Muriel and Aunt Doris wandered happily through the countryside accompanied by Romany and Raq, his dog. Nevertheless, we had already lived through a King's death, an abdication, and a coronation, all of which we followed avidly, step by step on our radio.

"The King's life is drawing peacefully to its close," and we went to bed silently and thoughtfully. We had once seen George V and Queen Mary on one of their rare visits to Hull. We had worn red, white, and blue crocheted berets, and waved little Union Jack's as they passed. When the news of Edward and Mrs Simpson broke, we sang cheeky ditties about the pair, at the tops of our voices. We discussed the situation with girls and teachers at school, using long words like 'morganatic' which we didn't really understand. We heard the abdication speech, and felt sorry for the ex King; he sounded so sad and lonely.

Then came the coronation. Mama made us coronation dresses. They were white with a pattern of tiny red and blue flowers. We wore them proudly all summer. We saw the coronation on newsreels at the cinema. The two little princesses were about our age, and we watched them enviously as they paraded in their miniature robes.

As the summer holidays of 1937 approached, Mama told us that we wouldn't be going to Germany that year.

"Not even to Berlin?" we asked, disappointedly.

"No," said Mama firmly, "not while Hitler is still around, we're better off in England."

"But where will we go?" we cried, "where else is there to go?"

"We're going to stay on a farm at Littlebeck, on the Yorkshire Moors," said Mama, "I've already booked it."

The holiday was a huge success. The farmhouse was old, there was no electricity and we went to bed by candlelight. There were cats, chickens, calves, and a lovely, affectionate sheepdog, called Gyp. She was always tied up in the stable, and I used to sit with her in the sweet smelling straw, loving her and talking to her. In the evenings the farmer's son would release her, and together they would bring home the cows at milking time. If I was around I was allowed to go too. I watched fascinated as Gyp obeyed strange commands like 'cush' and 'gerraway bye' as she cleverly rounded up her gentle, cud chewing herd.

Desmond, the boy, let me shout the commands at times, but Gyp ignored my feeble attempts and had ears and eyes only for her young master. When our holiday was over, I gave Gyp one last cuddle.

"Can we come back again, soon?" we begged.

"Perhaps," said Mama, "we'll see."

But we didn't, and years later, driving in the area, we saw the signpost 'Littlebeck', and drove down the steep lane to the farm. How changed it was! Landscaped gardens sloped down to the little stream, where once only wild flowers had mingled with the long grass that fringed the water's edge. The stables where Gyp, the cats, and chickens had all cosily lived together with the calves and the cows had been turned into garages. The farmhouse was modernised almost beyond recognition, and even the old derelict mill behind the farm had been done up, and appeared to be inhabited. One shouldn't really go back, I suppose.

Another year passed. My reports from High School were littered with 'could do better' and 'has made no effort this term'. Strangely, neither Mama or Papa were upset at these shocking remarks! Papa merely said indulgently that girls didn't need to be clever, as long as they could cook and sew, while Mama only said she didn't understand the English school system at all. It was no good compared with German education! So I cashed in on their attitudes, and happily muddled my way through school, always at the bottom of the A class. Why I wasn't demoted is still a mystery to me.

1938 brought the 'crisis' and everyone began talking about war. We did not take it seriously, after all, Neville Chamberlain would sort it all out. We went to collect gas masks, which we treated as a huge joke. That summer we returned to the Yorkshire Moors again. This time we stayed in a camping coach, an old railway coach, cleverly adapted to live in, with bedrooms, sitting room and kitchen. We loved it.

On September 30th, 1938, Neville Chamberlain signed his historical agreement with Adolf Hitler. There was to be 'Peace in our time', but our family had another celebration that day. I was in the playroom when Anita came racing up the stairs. "Rosie! Rosie!" she shouted, "we've got a sister!"

Babies were not discussed in our family, the stork brought them, and that, very firmly, was that. When I did hear the true facts of life from a school friend, who told me on the bus coming home from school, I didn't believe her. I thought she was making it up. I much preferred the cosy myth about the stork, it was much easier and far less performance! When Anita shouted her news, I immediately pictured a fully grown child, walking and talking just like us.

We all went to visit Mama and the new baby at the maternity home. The baby was tiny and very sweet. On her wrist she wore a tape which read "Baby Dalheim." "What shall we call her then?" asked Mama. Anita and I answered together, "Margot," we chorused. We had once had a German sea captain's daughter stay with us, to improve her English. She was a lovely, funny, outgoing girl and we all worshipped her. Anita and I planned that to keep her in the family, Eberhard would marry her when we were all grown up. Her name was Margot. Mama, however, had other ideas about names.

She said, "We need a name that's right for England and Germany. Margot isn't really English. I thought of Barbara or Erika."

So we chose Erika, because Mama said it meant heather, and we all loved the moors and the tiny purple flowers that covered them. However, Anita and I saved our money and bought Erika her first doll, which we called Margot!

When Erika Agnes Elisabeth was to be christened, there was no need to take her all the way to Germany, as we had done with Anita. She was to be christened in Hull, for by now, we had our own German Church.

153

28. THE CHURCH AND PASTORS

There had been a German Lutheran Church in Hull since 1848. In those far off days, there was a considerable number of Germans living in the area, merchants, importers, pork butchers, bakers and such like. They must have been prosperous, for they bought St. Luke's Church in Nile Street, in the old part of the city. They refurbished it, put in beautiful stained glass windows depicting biblical scenes and a large portrait of Martin Luther. The house adjoining had accommodation for the caretakers on the ground and second floors, and the whole of the first floor was turned into a large schoolroom. Here, the German children attended classes run by the pastor, who ensured that their mother tongue would not be forgotten.

After the 1914-1918 war, the little church had been closed indefinitely, but with the dawn of the thirties, the remnants of the old congregation decided to reopen it. It was not an easy task; Papa and his friends wrote letters, attended meetings, visited Germans residing in the area, and removed one official obstacle after another.

Now that German ships in ever increasing numbers were regularly visiting the port of Hull, the church was to be a seamen's church and mission. It would be a centre to cater for, presumably needy sailors. There would be socials, outings and practical or spiritual help as required. The idea caught on with the German Government, or whoever was in charge of these things. They agreed to give financial support and send a seaman's pastor as soon as a suitable applicant had been appointed. The church buildings were put into the capable hands of local builders and decorators, and gradually were restored to their former glory.

The new pastor arrived before the restoration was complete, and anxious to start his pastoral duties immediately. The church elders found a small house that was already being used as a Christian mission meeting house, and rented it for the time being. A few services were held there, but it proved inadequate and instead the Danish Church in Osborne Street became the temporary venue for the German Sunday services.

The only memory I have of those services is the beautiful model of a schooner which hung above us in the nave. I didn't understand the service or attempt to follow the hymns, my eyes roved round the church, and always came back to that perfect little ship hanging aloft. At last, our own church was ready, and there was to be a grand re-opening on July 21st, 1935. It was a very special day, Anita and I wore our best summer dresses with matching knickers. On our heads we wore our school Panama's with the green bands removed. We carried small leather clutch bags which contained our pennies for the collection. We felt grown up and virtuous, but the service was long, and we began to fidget; we also lost our dignity and got the giggles!

The reopened church flourished, the congregation was small, but enthusiastic. Services were held every Sunday morning at 11am. Our family always sat in the same pew, and gradually we children got used to the order of service, singing the responses with the adults. We would importantly find the hymns in our special small hymn books, and follow the words in their strange Gothic print. The hymns were not like the jolly, tuneful ones we sang at school. These were typical slow, Lutheran dirges. I would read the words to myself and on reaching the last verse would be surprised to hear the rest of the congregation still droning away at the first or second verse!

The sermons were always way above our heads. This was the time when Anita and I would begin to fidget and play about, and invariably start to giggle. I would feel Anita's shoulders starting to shake, and move away, only to have her slide closer. Finally, Mama had had enough, and we had to sit on either side of her. In winter when the church was cold, we would cuddle up to her fur coat.

The only time we really took an interest in the proceedings was Harvest Festival, when the church was a riot of colour, with fruit, flowers and vegetables; and at Christmas.

At Christmas, there would be a real tree in front of the altar, with lighted candles. We would then sit waiting for the candles to ignite the tree. This invariably happened.

A candle that had been thoughtlessly placed too near a twig, would suddenly catch the needles, and a small, spluttering fire would start.

We would nudge Papa, and he would leave his seat, even in the middle of the sermon, and pat and blow until the little conflagration was extinguished. It enlivened the proceedings, but Christmas was always specially nice at church. The Christmas hymns were more tuneful than the normal ones, and we could join in with gusto, for we knew them off by heart.

Once, a pastor decided to stage a Nativity play. Eberhard was chosen to be a shepherd, and wore his striped bath robe, and a towel on his head.

"Looks as though he's just had a bath, and washed his hair!" tittered Anita.

Another time, dressed in our best, we girls had to sing, 'Ihr Kinderlein kommet', beside a tableau of Mary, Joseph and the crib. It was a terrible performance, our reedy voices were barely audible and in the background, Mama and Lucy, the pork butcher's daughter, sang lustily to reinforce our efforts.

Another year Anita, a girl called Annie and I had to stand up in front of the altar and recite the Christmas verses from the bible. We practised for weeks, and became word perfect, my bit beginning 'And there were shepherds'. When the time came to repeat the lesson before the congregation Anita and I stood shivering in the cold church in our pale blue, crêpe de Chine party dresses, our coats and cardigans left in the pew.

Annie said her part perfectly first, she enjoyed the limelight. Anita repeated the last bit clearly in her treble voice, but I, sandwiched in between them, made a total hash of my shepherds. It was quite awful. I forgot bits, my voice stuck in my throat, and I wanted to giggle. The pastor prompted me at every single turn.

"Never again," I muttered to Mama, in the safety of our pew, "Never, ever again!"

"You weren't too bad, really," whispered Mama, as the congregation thankfully sang, 'O, Du Fröhliche', "you were only a little bit nervous, I used to hate saying things in public too."

Apart from the Sunday services there was also a flourishing social side to the church activities. The women formed a 'Frauenkreis' which met weekly to knit comforts for the sailors. In those days, sailors still needed comforts. The ladies clicking needles produced an endless supply of scarves, caps, socks and gloves. The afternoon meetings were held upstairs in the old schoolroom, but every now and again, the ladies took it in turns at having the meetings in their homes. Then it was more of a social occasion with coffee and home baked cakes, clacking tongues replaced the clicking needles.

At Christmas the woollen garments would be parcelled in fancy paper, each with a toilet article, a bottle of brilliantine, a shaving stick, a bar of soap and so on. These were then distributed amongst the seamen who visited the mission in the festive season.

Every week, there was a social evening for sailors in port, consisting of dancing and simple refreshments. Miss Ellis, lured by the prospect of shoals of young, unattached men in need of feminine company, was a regular visitor, as were several friends of hers. To our delight, she met a young officer called Sigmund. He was blonde and blue eyed and very handsome. Anita and I approved even more after we had met him.

The romance blossomed, and Miss Ellis was invited to spend her summer holiday with Sigmund and his sister, Elfriede, in Flensburg, near the Danish border. She set off starry-eyed, expecting to get engaged.

Eagerly, we awaited her return. She sent Mama and Papa a postcard from Flensburg. She was having a wonderful holiday, she wrote, Elfriede was so kind, and they got on like a house on fire, but as for Sigmund, well, "The dream is over!"

We couldn't wait for her to return and explain herself. She came back suntanned and sparkling. Not a bit like someone whose heart had been broken. Anita and I questioned her closely. "What happened?" we wailed. How could she let a lovely man like Sigmund go? Miss Ellis was philosophical.

"I always had my doubts," she said "and when I saw him in his own surroundings, I knew we were too different. Anyway, I had the most wonderful holiday, Elfriede and I thoroughly enjoyed ourselves!"

"But what about Sigmund?" we cried, "what did he say when you said goodbye to him?"

Miss Ellis' eyes grew misty.

"I didn't say goodbye," she said, "I had to leave early in the morning, and I went into his bedroom, but he was still asleep. So I kissed his cheek, and tiptoed out."

We sighed with her, at least it had ended romantically, no harsh words or vulgar quarrel, and I pictured her going off into the sunset to the accompaniment of soft music, the way it happened in films, regardless of the fact that it was already morning.

Miss Ellis and Elfriede kept up a spasmodic correspondence, which still continued after the war, when a sad Elfriede informed Miss Ellis that Sigmund had joined the German Navy at the outbreak of the war, and had tragically gone down with his ship.

We children only attended the social evenings at Christmas time. We would sit, squashed into a corner, watching the festivities through a haze of cigarette smoke.

The old schoolroom, which was not very large, would be crowded. There were candles on the tables and a Christmas tree ablaze with lights on the platform. There was music and laughter – Papa always played the piano and led the singing of German Christmas Carols. Then cakes and coffee would be brought up from the kitchen, and this was the cue for Papa to unobtrusively remove himself from the room.

He would return several minutes later, wearing Mama's red dressing gown and a rather battered Father Christmas mask, specially bought for these occasions. Previously, he would have counted the sailors present, and filled a sack with the appropriate number of gifts. These he would hand out to the somewhat bemused seamen with much ceremony and flourish, while we sat in our corner, feeling faintly embarrassed.

In the summertime, outings to local beauty spots were arranged for the congregation and any seamen who happened to be in port. Our family never missed a single one; we would all pile into the hired double-decker bus, with us three children always managing to sit on the front seats upstairs. There would invariably be a sailor who brought his harmonica or accordion, and we would travel merrily along the country lanes to the accompaniment of singing and music. Arriving at the appointed place, the picnics would be unpacked and there would be dancing, games and football for the more energetic, until it was time to return to the bus and home.

We had a succession of pastors. The first one stayed for nearly three years. He was very popular with the grown-ups, but we children didn't care for him overly much. He was pompous, and had no way with children. The second pastor only stayed for a year – he was tall and thin, and wore round, owl-like glasses. He understood children, coming from, I believe, a large family himself. We adored him, he always had time for us, and we were sorry when he went back to Germany.

His successor was a very large, plump young man. He stayed at our house until he found suitable accommodation. His bedroom had a peculiar smell; our current maid said it was "sweaty feet, you know!" A phrase gleefully repeated by us many times.

We couldn't stand him, and avoided being in the same room with him on our own. To our great relief, he finally found 'digs', and moved away, but not very far. He would still come in through our back way and help himself to a deckchair from our summer house. Then he would sit in the garden, sunning himself, while everybody else was busy. Mama, irritated by his presence, and fearing for the groaning chairs, locked the summer house, and hid the key.

The next sunny day, the pastor flounced into the kitchen.

"Where on earth," he called out peevishly, "is the key to the summer house?"

"It's lost," said Mama mendaciously, and to relieve her conscience for lying to a man of the cloth, she proceeded to try very hard to forget where she had put it. Whether she succeeded or not, I don't know, but the summer house remained locked for a week or two, and even we had to forego our own deck chairs!

Then we went on holiday. On our return, the key miraculously turned up, but by then the plump pastor had either got the message, or the weather was too inclement to be sitting outside.

Later his mother, a lady as large as her son, joined him in England, and they settled in the small rooms in the mission house, originally intended for the caretaker. There they lived happily, she cooking enormous meals in the small, cramped kitchen. The floorboards and the small twisty stairs must have creaked alarmingly under their combined weight!

Having settled her son into his new quarters, the lady returned to her native land, reluctantly leaving him to fend for himself. Her plump offspring was not without charm, and after his mother had left him, he put on his helpless little boy act. It worked, the kindly women of the congregation rallied round, and invited him to share their lunches or teas, so he happily munched his way through the plentiful and nourishing meals they provided.

He always had lunch or tea at our house, when he came to give Eberhard and me our confirmation lessons. These lessons were, as far as I was concerned, a complete farce and utter waste of time. For a start, they were on Saturday afternoons, that precious time that should have been all our own. To give up even one hour was to me the worst thing possible, so my mood was already peevish and resentful. Then, they were held in our little office, which, rarely used by Papa, was our own cosy little den. There was a book case full of my favourite books, an old piano for our practising, and a maple wood rocking chair, which was my special reading place.

Usually, when the pastor arrived for our lesson, Anita and I would be already in the room, hammering out a made up duet on the piano – we called it our rhapsody. The pastor would stand in the doorway, while we calmly ignored him, and carried on. The din must have been terrible. He would shout above it.

"Time for ze lesson."

"We haven't finished yet," we'd reply cheekily, and carry on playing. Finally, after many resounding final chords, Anita would leave, Eberhard would come in, and we'd settle ourselves round the small table. We each had an exercise book in which we wrote down various parts of the Catechism. Important parts were underlined in red ink.

Eberhard's book was neat and perfect, an example to all, but mine was an absolute mess; I wouldn't have got away with work like that at school. The pages were smudged, the red lines a disgrace, but I knew the pastor could do nothing about it. I pretended I couldn't understand his German, so he had to explain in English, which was even worse. For me, there was no feeling of reverence or religion about the whole thing.

"Come in and interrupt us," I'd egg Anita on, and she, the lucky free one, would pertly open the door, grin and say, "Sorry, I've left something," and rummage noisily about, and set me off giggling, until the pastor sent her packing. She would run up and down the corridor outside, singing silly songs, which made me titter loudly. Finally, the pastor would fling open the door with a cry of, "Enough of zis!" and Anita would skip off to the comparative safety of the garden, or the playroom upstairs.

At last, however, much to everyone's relief, we were through the set lessons of the confirmation class. The actual confirmation now loomed horribly. There should have been an oral examination before the congregation, in which we had to prove that we had fully taken in and understood the Catechism. The pastor, for obvious reasons, waived this formality.

"I know they know it all," he informed Mama and Papa.

Thankful that this ordeal, at least, had been spared us, we only had the confirmation itself to worry about. After the next church service, the pastor had a little rehearsal for the two of us, showing us where we would stand, and the cushions to kneel on. I muttered things like 'daft' and 'rubbish' under my breath and showed a distinct lack of interest. In that frame of mind I should never have been accepted into the church, little heathen and rebel that I was!

The seventh of May, 1939, the dreaded day arrived. Eberhard wore a brand new navy blue suit for the occasion. In Germany, in those days, girls wore black for their confirmation. Mama, realising that I would never wear that colour, so it would be a complete waste of money to buy me the correct garment, decided that my summer Sunday dress would do. This was a flowered silk, in brilliant colours. In honour of the occasion, I also wore light coloured lisle stockings. More in keeping, said Mama, than white ankle socks.

"Don't you dare make me laugh when I'm out there in front," I threatened Anita, "I'll murder you if you do!"

162

Lucky Anita! She'd be sitting safely in the pew, while I stood before the altar, looking and feeling silly.

In this highly irreverent frame of mind, I entered the church with my family. It wasn't nearly such an ordeal as I'd imagined. The actual confirmation took up only a few minutes of the service. Eberhard and I had to go up to the front and answer "Ja" to a couple of questions and then kneel to accept our first communion, and receive the pastor's hand on our heads in a formal blessing.

"What if I choke over the wine?" I thought in panic, "how awful to be choking and spluttering in front of everybody!"

But everything passed off smoothly, and I didn't even get the urge to giggle. Nevertheless, I had no sense of the solemnity of the occasion, I just felt all kinds of a fool, and was glad when we could return to our pew.

After the service, Eberhard and I stood next to the pastor in the church porch, and shook hands with everyone as they left, a grinning Anita joining in the queue.

In the afternoon there was a tea party for us with some of Mama and Papa's friends. The pastor came too, and a couple of photographs were taken to mark another milestone in our lives. Surprisingly, we even received gifts, my favourite one being a comb, brush and mirror set in a pretty shade of blue. From Germany some relations sent a parcel and eagerly we opened it.

For Eberhard, a lovely volume of photographs of the German countryside. For me, a very strange present to give a fourteen year old on her confirmation. It was a large book called "Der Führer unter den Kindern," or something like that. It was crammed with pictures of Hitler – Hitler patting children on the head, Hitler receiving bouquets of flowers from flaxen haired little girls, Hitler surrounded by laughing, waving children.

Mama and Papa didn't really like it lying around. This was the early summer of 1939 and the personage of Herr Hitler was hardly popular in England. The book was finally hidden in the bookcase, out of sight. After the war, I burnt it.

Silly really, I should have kept it, it would be quite a collector's item by now.

In my diary, that 7th May, 1939, I recorded laconically. "Got confirmed in morning. Had a do in afternoon. Took some crude pictures."

29. URSULA'S HAT

Anita and I had been keeping diaries since January 1939. Anita started Newland High in 1938, and every year it was possible to buy a schoolgirl's diary, which bore the Newland crest and motto.

I was already the proud possessor of one of these much coveted journals. Mine I had acquired in 1937, and in it I had made but two entries, and not used it since. When Anita bought her diary for 1939, we decided to write in them every night without fail; I could use up my old one, all I had to do was alter the names of the weekdays.

We were very determined to keep up our new resolution, so every night, after putting in our curlers, we recorded the most important of the day's events. Putting in curlers had been part of our bedtime routine for a while now. Instead of straight hair held in place by a hair slide or ribbon, most girls at school now made some attempt to have curly hair, inspired as we were by the pretty child star, Shirley Temple, and our own little Princesses. Mama had read somewhere that the younger one's curls had to be 'helped', as only the elder princess had natural waves. What was good enough for a princess, was good enough for us! We persuaded Mama to buy us curlers.

They were sharp metal, and most uncomfortable for us to sleep in. Never did a saying apply to us more aptly than. "II faut souffrir pour être belle!" We certainly suffered, but whether the results were beautiful is a moot point. The curlers had a habit of dropping out during the night, and the result was usually an untidy sort of page boy bob. Nevertheless, we felt we were doing our bit to make the world a more aesthetic place!

In 1939, Anita's godmother, Tante Gertrud, sent her a special calendar from Germany. It consisted of pretty postcards to be coloured in and sent to one's friends for birthdays and other festive occasions. For the month of April there was a sketch of Hitler's hideaway in the Bavarian Alps.

"Colour this carefully," stated the caption underneath, "and send it to the Führer for his birthday on the 20th."

Anita duly painted it with great care.

"Shall I send it to him?" she asked me.

"I don't know," I answered, "would you dare?"

The previous month it had been Neville Chamberlain's birthday, Anita and I had sent him a card. It was a type very popular in those days, a glossy sepia photo of a country scene, surrounded by roses, in a lurid pink. To our surprise and delight, we had received in return, a printed card thanking us for our good wishes. On the back of the envelope was printed '10 Downing Street, London Wl.' This prized possession now reposed in a sideboard drawer, to be taken out and gloated over occasionally.

Anita broached the subject of Hitler's birthday again at teatime.

"If I send Hitler a birthday card, maybe I'll get a reply from him too," she said hopefully.

"I still haven't heard if my application for naturalisation had been granted, so the last thing I want in this house, is a letter from Adolf Hitler!" said Papa firmly.

So the pretty card remained unsent, instead Anita pinned it to the playroom wall.

Hitler was fast becoming a most unpopular person in England, and one now heard daily reports of Jewish and political refugees seeking asylum in Great Britain and America. I too, had my own personal experience of this.

Irene's mother rang Mama one morning. She sounded desperate. "Please, Mrs Dalheim," she begged, "would you send Rosemarie round. We need her as an interpreter. We've taken in a little Jewish girl from Berlin. She's supposed to understand English, but she won't even speak to us."

Full of self importance, I hurried off to Irene's house. Her mother, looking distraught, met me at the door.

"She's upstairs with Irene," she told me, "we've treated her like our own daughter, we've given her everything. I just don't know what to do with her."

She broke off as we entered Irene's bedroom. It was a pretty room, with twin beds covered with green silk bedspreads, I noted approvingly. Then I saw the child in question. She was a girl of about 12 years old, wearing a shabby tight coat, and a most unbecoming sort of a beret pulled down on her head. Irene, next to her, in her smart outdoor clothes, made the child look even dowdier.

"This is Ursula. We want to take her to town to buy a new hat," said Irene, "but she won't come."

"Did you ever see such a terrible cap!" said her mother, "I mean I can't possibly take her anywhere looking like that!"

I agreed silently. Irene's mother was what I called 'posh' and Irene herself was always exquisitely dressed. Once she had been to an elegant wedding in London, and I had listened raptly as she described the hotel where they stayed, the beautiful dress she had worn, the lace edged petticoat, the shoes and the gloves. But what had impressed me more than all these outward trappings was the fact that she even had new knickers to wear underneath it all! New knickers! That had seemed to me the height of reckless and unnecessary extravagance.

Irene's mother went on. "Tell her she must do as she is told."

I looked again at the child. She stood before us without appearing to notice what was going on round about her. In dumb misery, she stared at nothing in particular, isolated in her own lonely little world of grief and bewilderment. What could the three of us, complacent in our comfortable, unthreatened existence, know of what could be going through her young mind. Separated from all she had known and loved, parents, family, home, school, familiar surroundings, and suddenly abandoned in a foreign country with total strangers, no matter how kindly intentioned. In all probability she would have been learning English at school, but at her age it would have still been at the simple stage of, 'Where is the cup?' 'The cup is on the saucer', or other equally inane sentences that school books deem it necessary for us to master.

The fact that up to now Ursula had completely ignored me, added to my own discomfort. I had expected a child that would immediately start talking German, which I would fluently and cleverly translate to an admiring audience. Faced with this total wall of silence, I became tongue-tied and shy. Irene and her mother were looking at me expectantly. I cleared my throat to gain time. My mind seemed to have gone a blank, for the life of me I couldn't think of the right German words.

"Go on," encouraged Irene.

I translated literally, "Du musst wie Du gesagt bist."

I knew as soon as I said it that it was completely wrong, and felt silly. The child's gaze for the first time, focused on me, with a look of faint contempt.

"Tell her we're going to town, then," said Irene, "to get her a new hat."

I told Ursula, hoping it would cheer her up, after all, one didn't get a new hat every day. For the first time Ursula spoke.

"I don't need a new hat," she said sullenly, in German.

"What does she say?" asked the others.

"She doesn't want one," said I.

"Nonsense," said Irene's mother, "off you go, here's your bus fare. Go to Thornton Varleys and charge it to my account. "

Ursula, probably realising she was outnumbered, moved to the door with Irene and me on either side, like small gaolers.

We took the bus to town, we went to Thornton Varley's and Irene and I had a lovely time trying on hats in the children's department, while Ursula stood silently by, with studied disinterest.

Finally, a helpful assistant chose a hat for us. It had a turned up brim, and was in rather a hideous shade of tan. The assistant assured us that it would 'go' with Ursula's coat.

"Does the little girl want to wear it now?" she asked kindly, "I'll put her old one in the bag."

But Ursula refused to be parted from her cap, so Irene had the new one wrapped instead. The serious part of our errand completed, Irene and I set off to enjoy ourselves, going round the store, just looking at things. Ursula tagged along.

Kind little Irene kept saying, "Look, Ursula, isn't this pretty?" or "do you like that?" But everything we pointed out or showed her, received the same response.

"We have all this in Berlin, but it's much better there!"

Irene and I weren't in the same form at school, and some time later I met her in the school lane. She told me that Ursula had gone to live with another family in another city.

"What about that hat?" I asked, "did she ever wear it?"

"No," said Irene, "she wouldn't, so Mummy took it back and changed it for a different one for me."

Poor little Ursula, I hope she found some measure of happiness, somewhere, somehow, in her shattered young life.

As the Summer of 1939 progressed, the political situation worsened. For the moment, it did not concern me, I had problems nearer home to worry about. At school, the teachers were beginning to talk about NEXT YEAR and the SCHOOL CERTIFICATE and MATRICULATION exams that loomed. We were even given letters by our form mistress, Miss Ward, to take home. They invited our parents to a meeting at school with the staff.

"Before your parents come," said Miss Ward, "perhaps you could discuss with them what you want to do when you leave school, and what subjects you will take in your exams, and which you will drop."

There was no problem about choosing a future career, as Anita and I since being very small girls, had played schools with our dolls. When we grew up, we always said that we would have a little school, like Tusky's, but instead of having real desks we would have Mickey Mouse desks.

This ambition had been reinforced for me by a small occurrence at school. One day, one of the older girls was visiting her friends in our form. She was leaving school at the end of the summer term, she told us excitedly. She had already got a job in an office. She told us how much she would be earning, which sounded to be a very generous wage.

"When do you start?" I asked, "after the summer holiday?"

"Oh, no," said the girl, "the Monday after we break up. When I've been there a year, I get a whole week's holiday with pay."

She went on telling the other girls about her new duties. I sat in stunned silence. For the first time in my life it dawned on me that when one left school, the lovely long and frequent holidays would cease. Then I cheered up, for the thought struck me that the teachers had the same holidays as their pupils. That settled it, my mind was made up. Sooner than forego the holidays, I would definitely be a teacher.

Now safely retired from the teaching profession, I can state with perfect honesty, that it was not idealism or dedication, or a great desire to set young children on to the path of learning that kept me going as a teacher. It was purely and simply the holidays! Twelve glorious weeks a year. Indeed, if it wasn't for the holidays, I doubt if many teachers would stay the course!

Family discussions usually took place at teatime. I handed over our form mistress's note reluctantly, I didn't believe in parents and school getting together.

"There's no need for you to go," I told Mama and Papa. "They just want to know which subjects we're going to drop,

170

and what we're going to do when we leave school, things like that. I think I'll drop Physics, Biology, Latin, History, Geography," I reeled off a list of practically every lesson I didn't exactly shine in.

"Drop subjects?" said Mama, "I never heard of such a thing – I just don't understand this school system. When I was at school we took exams in every subject. If it wasn't for Hitler I'd send you to Germany for a year, to get a decent education."

Thank goodness for Hitler, I thought. He had his uses. The mere thought of being in a class of German girls, beavering away at every subject under the sun, gave me the cold shudders. I was perfectly happy in my little rut in Lower 5A at Newland.

"Anyway," said Mama, "what do you want to do when you leave school?"

"She doesn't need a job," said Papa, indulgently, "she can help in my office."

"I'm going to be a teacher," I announced.

Mama was pleased and surprised, as she mentally reviewed my meagre scholastic achievements.

"But what will you teach?" she asked.

"I don't know," I replied, for I hadn't planned any further than the Mickey Mouse desks and the holidays.

"German," suggested Papa.

"Wish we'd learn German at school," I said, and off I went into one of my favourite daydreams. In my dreams, we had German lessons at school, and for once, I would be the shining light, the brilliant star pupil of the class. The teacher would hardly dare open her mouth without first consulting me on vocabulary, pronunciation and so on. She would anxiously turn to me for confirmation and approval in everything she said. I had just reached the most satisfactory part in my dreams, where the teacher was beginning to grovel, though why she should grovel, I don't know, I just liked the thought of it, when Mama, who had been giving my future a little more positive thought said, "I know! Domestic Science!"

"Domestic Science!" I echoed.

"Yes, cooking and sewing and things like that," said Mama.

Our domestic science lessons and needlework lessons were extremely thin on the ground at Newland. We had made some shapeless garments over the years, and baked the usual rock cakes and sausage rolls.

I gave the matter some thought. My greedy mind focused on jam tarts, chocolate buns, home-made sweets and biscuits. If one taught baking, then, who ate the demonstration models, so to speak? It must be the teacher, of course. I saw a rosy future ahead, where I happily munched my way through my lessons.

"All right," I said, "I'll be a domestic science teacher. No need for you to go to the meeting, I'll tell Miss Ward myself."

In spite of all my discouraging remarks, Mama and Papa went to the parents' meeting after all.

I was still awake and worrying when they came home. Who knew what those teachers had been saying about me? "What happened," I shouted when I heard Mama and Papa coming upstairs. Mama came into my bedroom.

"There was such a crowd there," she said, "we didn't really speak to anybody, we had a cup of tea and left early." Thankfully, I sank back onto my pillow. "Told you it was a waste of time," I said.

"Well we did have a word with one teacher," was Mama's parting shot, as she left the room, "she said you didn't make the most of your abilities, and if you want to do well in your exam next year, you'll have to work a lot harder!"

I consoled myself with the thought that next year was still an awfully long way away. A lot could happen before the dreaded exams. There might even be a war…

Eberhard, Mama and Rosie on the moor

Mama, Eberhard and Rosie, Kaltenweide

Rosie, Papa, Eberhard and Hexe the dog, Kaltenweide

Anita's christening

*Rosie with Boy the dog,
Louis St*

*In the garden with
Oma and Tante
Mane, Louis St*

First day at school

*With Dolly in
Louis St*

Oma and Tante Anna

Boating in Bridlington

On Oma's balcony

Crossing to Germany

Rosie, Eberhard and Anita on the donkeys, Hornsea

Summer 1936 on the Boltic

Berlin Zoo, 1936

With family in Berlin

Hymers Grounds, 1931

With Miss Ellis in the garden, Sunny Bank

Summer 1938 on holiday in Lealholm

On the beach with swastika flags, Baltic Sea

Summer 1939 on holiday in Sigglesthorne

Last photo before the camera was confiscated, August 1939

The family on the Isle of Man, autumn 1942

Isle of Man, spring 1943, Rosie, Eberhard and Anita

30. LAST DAYS OF PEACE

Every day now, it became increasingly clear to us all that in spite of Neville Chamberlain's peace efforts, we were on a very slippery slope rushing inevitably into war. Unless, of course, a miracle occurred.

Already, there were too many sinister signs that could not be ignored any longer. Apart from the gas masks lurking in our wardrobes, we had numerous A.R.P. leaflets around the house. These gave frightening advice and details about how to cope in an air raid. There were hints on first aid, the use of stirrup pumps, emergency rations to keep in ones shelter, if one had one. For the less prudent folk, who had still not dug themselves one in the garden, there were instructions on how to turn a room or cellar into a temporary place of safety.

From our classroom window we could see one of the new barrage balloons. These were springing up all over the place; we were told they would intercept enemy aircraft, which would crash into them and become entangled in their steel ropes. There was great excitement at school when one afternoon a girl shrieked, "the barrage balloon!" and we all looked out in time to see the whole thing burst into flames, and disintegrate. Not much protection there, after all.

At school, a new word was being bandied about – evacuation. We had taken letters and forms to be filled in, to our parents, in case they wanted us to be evacuated to a safe place, should war break out. There was even a list of essential clothing and other things the evacuee should have ready, when the call came. Mama and Papa studied our letters.

"There isn't going to be a war," said Mama, "surely everybody has too much sense to start one. In any case, we're not signing anything, wait and see what happens first."

"What about holidays?" we asked, "where are we going this summer?"

"Papa and I have decided that come what may, we're going to have two holidays this year."

"Two!" we cried, delightedly, "where are we going?"

"You remember Jessie, where we used to stay in Hornsea?" asked Mama, "well, she's married a farmer and lives in Siggles home now. We're going to stay with her first."

"And the second holiday?" asked Anita.

"I've written to Mrs Wise in Bridlington to see if we can rent her house again. We'll be going there for the last week in August, and the first week in September."

School broke up, and the longed for holidays began. We had a lovely time at Jessie's farm. It was Baby's first holiday, and she wore a little muslin sun bonnet. Outwardly, everything was peaceful, and we were not going to let the political situation spoil these idyllic days.

We returned home for a few weeks before our Bridlington holiday. Life went on as usual, we played in the garden, took Baby to the park and ate ice-cream. These events were duly recorded in my diary. Mama bought us new bathing costumes for our seaside holiday.

Our complacency was rudely shattered on the 24th August, two days before we were due to leave for Bridlington. The German consul rang Papa.

"There's a ship leaving for Germany tomorrow," he said "if you want to get yourself and your family out of England, it's your last chance. I'd advise you to take it, don't forget, you're still not naturalised. When war breaks out, things could be very unpleasant for you in England."

Papa noticed he said "when" and not "if". He told Mama what the consul had said.

"There is no question of us leaving our home," he said, "things in Germany will be worse for us than here."

Mama quite agreed with him.

"It would be ridiculous for us to stand there with four children. Where would we stay? What would we live on?"

We children, listening to them, now saw for the first time, the gravity of the situation. The thought of leaving home, and all that was dear and familiar filled me with horror. Germany was nice, yes, it was a lovely place, but Hull was home and always had been. Besides we were supposed to be going to Bridlington in two days' time.

"What about Bridlington?" we asked, "can we still go?"

"I really don't know," said Mama, "we'll have to think about it."

That night we went to bed gloomily.

"Hope we go to Brid.," I wrote in my diary.

The next morning, Mama came into our bedroom, bright and early. She was smiling.

"We've decided to go to Bridlington, after all," she told us. "Why should we let all this silly talk of war spoil things for us. As for the ship, it can go to Germany without us."

Jubilantly, we jumped out of bed, to get our own bits and pieces ready to pack.

We arrived at Bridlington on Saturday, 26th August. Gleefully, I wrote in my diary that we would miss the evacuation practice at school the following Monday. Who wanted to go to school in holiday time anyway, war or no war!

The last five days of August were warm and sunny. We wore our new bathing costumes, we paddled in the sea, we rode the gentle beach ponies, at sixpence a time.

"We're having a lovely time," I recorded in my diary, and so we were, as was everybody on those sunlit beaches. But not for much longer, for on the other side of the North Sea, in which we were splashing with such abandon, Hitler was marshalling his troops. They were ready to invade the luckless Poland, and on the 1st September they would march across the border.

World War Two was about to begin.

31. "IT'S ONE OF OURS"

The first of September started off with our usual first of the month ritual. Anita shouted "White rabbits, white rabbits, white rabbits!" as she jumped out of bed. I followed suit. We had our breakfast, and raced down the beach. Mama, Papa and Eberhard followed with Baby and the deck chairs. Papa bought a newspaper. The news was bad. "It looks as if war is inevitable, after all," he said.

We went back to the house for lunch. Mama and Papa discussed the situation throughout the meal. We listened in silence.

"If only there was a radio in the house," said Papa, "at least we'd know what was going on."

In the afternoon Anita and I went back to the beach, armed with our sixpence and sugar lumps, to ride the ponies. After our ride we hung about petting and stroking them, feeding them the sugar lumps. The beach was crowded, and looked, so normal and colourful. There isn't going to be a war, I thought – nobody's bothered. There couldn't be. What was war like, anyway? The A.R.P. leaflets were terrifying. There would be bombs and gas, and dead and hurt people. Not here, not in Hull, not in Sunny Bank. I just couldn't imagine it. The soft little pony nose that I had been stroking, nudged me. "You've had all my sugar lumps," I said, and looked around for Anita. She too had used up her supply of sugar. We decided it must be nearly time for tea, and walked slowly back. We were halfway through our meal when the doorbell rang. "I'll go," said Papa.

We could hear him talking in the small entrance hall, then he came back into the room, closely followed by two men. We stared at the strangers, then Papa spoke, his voice sounded odd and choked.

"These gentlemen," he informed us, "are from the police. They have come to intern me."

After a stunned silence, Mama found her voice.

"Why?" she said, "there isn't even a war on!"

The men were non-committal, "No, there isn't yet, but there's going to be one."

"But we're on holiday," said Mama, as though that made any difference.

"It may be only for a few days," said Papa. He was, after all, the expert on internment. "It must all be a mistake, as I have applied for naturalisation. They won't keep me long."

We were not a family that indulged in scenes and hysterics, besides, Papa had always warned us that this might happen.

"Finish your tea," Mama told us, "I'll go and pack a few things for Papa."

She, Papa and the two plain clothes men left the room.

Too shocked to do much else, we hastily finished our tea, and rushed upstairs to see what was going on. Mama and Papa were alone, packing.

"Have the men gone?" asked Anita, "where are they?"

Papa pulled a wry face, "They're searching the house," he said, "what they're looking for I can't imagine. "

"They're upstairs in your bedroom," said Mama.

Anita and I shared the big attic, and intrigued that anybody could be searching for anything there, we raced up the stairs. In the doorway, we stopped and stared. The two C.I.D. men were looking through the chest of drawers. One of them had Anita's diary in his hand, it was open and he was reading it. The sight of somebody reading her very own private little diary, aroused Anita to fury.

"Put that down!" she cried, shrilly, "that's my diary, you can't read that!"

Her protest was ignored. With a smile the man turned over a page and went on reading. Goaded by his attitude, I said boldly.

"Fancy a grown man reading a little girl's diary. What d'you think you'll find in there?"

Anita grew even bolder.

"Ha, ha, you must be daft," she mocked, "it's only about school, and silly things like that!"

The men had had enough of our cheek. They took a step towards us, and we flew downstairs, I could feel my legs trembling. The men didn't bother to follow us, and after a time, all came downstairs. The police waited in the hall while Papa came into the dining room, and kissed us all goodbye.

"Cheer up," he said, "it won't be for long, look after your Mama, won't you?"

When Papa and escorts had gone, the house suddenly felt empty.

"What are we going to do now?" we asked Mama.

"Nothing," said Mama, "we'll just have to wait and see. If there isn't a war, then Papa will be back in a day or two; we've still booked another week in this house, let's enjoy the rest of our holiday."

The next day, Anita and I went for a walk on our own. The town seemed to be milling with children of all ages – evacuation had begun. To our immense surprise, we met a crocodile of Newland girls, accompanied by teachers. One teacher spoke to us.

"What are you doing here?" she asked.

"We're on holiday," we replied sheepishly, feeling guilty that we should really be among the column of girls, being marshalled to their billets. We rushed back and told Mama, who looked serious.

"That means there probably will be a war," she said, "otherwise why go to all this bother of getting children out of Hull?"

That afternoon another incident occurred. Anita and I were playing ball on the promenade when a strange man retrieved our ball, and proceeded to ask us all manner of questions. Where had we come from? Where were we staying? How long were we staying? When were we going back? Having been warned never to speak to strangers, we only answered briefly, and ran back to tell Mama.

"He could have been from the secret police," she said intriguingly," trying to find out if you knew anything."

"Anything about what?" I asked, fascinated by the thought of being caught up in political intrigue and espionage.

"Well, I don't really know," said Mama, vaguely.

In my diary that night I wrote, "Man spoke to us – mystery."

Sunday the 3rd of September was a typical late summer day. After breakfast, we went for a walk down to the sea front. The sun shone out of a cloudless sky, the air was warm, and the sea a soft, shimmering blue.

Mama bought a newspaper, avidly we read it. There was going to be a war! England had declared war on Germany! This was it – it had happened. The placards outside all the newsagents bore just one terrible word WAR.

Mama went into a call box and rang Miss Ellis for advice. Miss Ellis told Mama that she'd heard from Papa. He was in Hull Prison, and could be visited. He had given her instructions about his business. She suggested we had better all come home. She would come to Bridlington by the afternoon train, and help Mama with the packing, and the journey home. Mama came out of the telephone box and told us – selfishly we were cross at having our holiday shortened in this manner.

When Miss Ellis arrived we all had tea, then she and Mama saw to the packing, and informed Mrs Wise of our departure. While this was going on, we had a quick walk round our favourite haunts. Everywhere we went we bumped into girls or teachers we knew.

"Thank goodness!" I thought, "we'll be getting away from that lot!" To meet teachers on holiday was definitely something to be avoided. At last we were ready to go, and Mrs Wise was there to collect the key, and take over her own home again. She wished us well. "Perhaps it will all blow over," she said reassuringly.

Soon we were on the train going home. It was evening, and a brilliant sunset lit the sky. I looked out at the peaceful countryside, with the backcloth of flaming sky.

"War," I thought dramatically, "this is what it will be like. Flames shooting into the sky as bombs fall and buildings burn."

My thoughts roamed sensationally on, fed by the A.R.P. leaflets that depicted gory scenes and situations.

"People will be lying in ruins, screaming in agony. There will be black, choking smoke and gas everywhere." So I went on, revelling in my gloomy imaginings.

I didn't know then, that, though for many, many people the war would be just that, and far, far worse. I and my family would be among the lucky ones, barely touched by the tragedies of war. For me, the only fires would be the golden gorse, blazing against a blue sea, the only cries would be the plaintive ones of seagulls. The smoke would be the soft white mists rolling in from the sea. I didn't know then, that for me, the memory of war in later years would be of great happiness and laughter and funny little anecdotes. For me, memory, like the sundial, would mark naught but sunny hours.

Daylight was fading as we reached Hull. Home was blissfully normal, with the late summer flowers colouring the front garden. Inside the house smelled sweetly of apples, the way it always did after our summer holidays. For while we were away, Miss Ellis and Fred would diligently pick up the early windfalls and store them on trays about the house. As soon as we and our luggage were inside the house, Miss Ellis took charge.

"Before we do anything else," she said briskly, "we must see to your blackout."

"Blackout!" cried Mama, "Oh, my goodness, I'd forgotten all about that!"

She and Miss Ellis toured the house. The bedrooms and most of the downstairs rooms were well curtained, and passed the test. Mama liked dark, heavy curtains, and though I longed for dainty chintz in my bedroom, the kind we usually had in holiday houses, our bedroom was curtained in dark green material. Kitchen, bathroom and scullery were devoid of over curtains.

"You'll have to go straight out tomorrow, and buy blackout material," said Miss Ellis, "in the meantime, just have candles in the kitchen, and leave the landing light on upstairs, that should be all right for tonight."

It was really quite exciting, like preparing for a siege! Eberhard, conscientiously, collected all the items listed in the A.R.P. booklet. We did not have an air raid shelter, in fact most people didn't. Just a few prudent householders had provided themselves with some sort of dugout shelter in their garden.

"The safest place," Eberhard read, "if you haven't a shelter, is to sit by an inside wall. That will be the dining room."

He arranged torches, bicycle lamp, first aid kit and so on, on the dining room table. "Have a blanket ready soaking in the bath, to hang over the door in case of a gas attack."

Anita, wanting to help, rushed up to the attic, switching on lights, regardless of the fact that the window was uncurtained, and dragged an old blanket off the spare bed. She filled the bath with water, and immersed the blanket in it.

Miss Ellis went home to collect her night necessities, she would stay the night with us, for at the time we had no live-in maid, only a daily help.

At last we went to bed, gas masks beside us, ready for the worst. Anita slept with Mama and Baby, Miss Ellis shared my room. I was asleep before Miss Ellis came upstairs, worn out by the excitement and activity of the day. It must have been about 4 o'clock in the morning, when I was awakened by Miss Ellis, saying loudly.

"Air raid warning! Oh my God, they're coming already."

She switched on the bedside lamp, as Mama came agitatedly into the room.

"Can you hear it?" she said. Then I could hear it too, the awful wail of the siren, that up to now had only been heard at practices in broad daylight. In the middle of the night, at the unearthly hour of 4 am, it sounded eerie and spine-chilling.

I sat up in bed, rigid with fear, we were all frightened, even Miss Ellis, who was a veteran of Zeppelin raids in the First World War. She had often told us how they used to sit in the fields outside Hull, and watch the bombs dropping.

Fear is catching, and we stood on the landing huddled together, wondering what to do.

"Get your dressing gowns and gas masks," said Miss Ellis, recovering her wits, "and go into the dining room, quick!"

The urgency in her voice scattered us, and we collected the necessary items.

"Baby hasn't got a gas mask yet!" wailed Mama.

Anita had read the A.R.P. leaflets thoroughly, "you have to hold a wet towel over her face, then," she said, running into the bathroom and plunging a towel into the bath. Squeezing it out, she pushed it at Mama, who was passing, carrying Baby. Not daring to put on the downstairs light because the front door was not blacked out, we went down by the light of the upstairs landing. Nobody was aware of the fact that the skylight had been overlooked, and, totally uncovered, was blazing away a message to Hitler, or any other German who happened to be flying over!

Down the stairs we trailed, Anita last, dragging the heavy, soaking wet blanket behind her. We arranged the dining chairs along the inside wall, and waited, for what, we didn't know.

Baby, who had awakened briefly, slept soundly again, cuddled safely in Mama's arms.

Then we heard it! The dreaded sound of a plane passing overhead.

"Here they come!" whispered Miss Ellis, in sepulchral tones, and reached for her gas mask. She put it on – in the light of the bicycle lamp on the table, she looked weird and horrible. We hastily followed her example, my fingers were stiff with fear as I pulled the rubber strap over my head. Mama put her mask on with one hand, and it hung lopsidedly. Then she took the wet towel and held it over Baby's nose and mouth. Baby woke up, and the sight of the strange apparition bending over her face, set her off screaming with terror and anger. She pushed at the unwanted cloth, and tried to pull it off. Through her gas mask, Mama tried to soothe her. The strange distorted voice only made matters worse! Mama wrenched the mask off her face and took the towel off Baby's. She concentrated on calming her little daughter. From behind our grotesque disguises our voices screamed at her to put her mask on, and cover Baby's face again.

On the lino, between the door and the sideboard, the blanket lay gently oozing water, already the corner of the carpet was darkly wet. Nobody noticed or cared, if there really had been a gas attack it would have been impossible to fix the blanket over the door, there was nothing to secure it with. What good would it have done? That door led into the hall, gas would have come merrily seeping in through the great draughty French windows that led straight into the garden!

Baby quietened at last and fell asleep again. Silence reigned, and we realised that no bombs were dropping, indeed all was quiet outside, not even a plane droning overhead. Yet, with the exception of Mama, we still sat masked and huddled against the wall. After a while, Miss Ellis too, removed her mask.

"That's better," she said.

After an interval, we three followed suit.

"What do you think is happening?" whispered Mama.

Miss Ellis was not very reassuring.

"That was probably the reconnaissance plane," she said.

"What's that?" I asked fearfully.

"That's the one that comes first and has a look, then it tells the others where to drop their bombs. Just you wait and see, they'll be back."

We waited, nothing happened. Later Miss Ellis said, "I'm going to look out at the front."

Cowards that we were, we let her go alone! Miss Ellis walked boldly out of the front door and down the garden path. She peered into the gloom, that already seemed less dark. A shape in a tin hat went by. It was a neighbour we children referred to as 'young Prudie', who was an air raid warden.

"What's happening?" Miss Ellis hissed at her.

Young Prudie stopped, surprised "Why nothing," she said, "the all clear went ages ago, didn't you hear it?" "We only heard the plane," said Miss Ellis, "did it drop any bombs?" "Of course not," said young Prudie, heading for home and bed, "it was one of ours!" Miss Ellis came back with her information.

"We've been sitting here like idiots all the time," she giggled, "I'll bet it was just a practice!"

Thankfully, we all went back to bed, leaving gas masks, wet blanket and all the rest of the paraphernalia in the dining room, to be cleared up the next day.

We laughed at ourselves the next morning, and never forgot the first night of the war. Other people had equally funny experiences, and now one screams with laughter when they are recounted, but at the time it wasn't really funny, and I had my first taste of real fear.

Despite the nightmarish events of the preceding night, breakfast the following morning was quite a hilarious affair. Partly due, no doubt, to the almost hysterical relief we all felt, and partly to Miss Ellis' bubbly personality. She and Mama were downstairs before us, and had cleared away all traces of the dramatic siege of the previous night. All that remained to remind us of it was the wet corner of the carpet. We woke to the delicious aroma of coffee, and went down to the dining room to find the others already round the table, with Baby banging her plate and spoon on the tray of the high chair. She was none the worse for her interrupted sleep. It was all so reassuringly normal and safe.

Mama and Miss Ellis were making plans for the day. That afternoon they were going to visit Papa in Hull Prison. Mama said that she didn't dare go on her own, so Miss Ellis volunteered to accompany her. Dear Morgel Ellis! What a staunch friend and ally she was to Mama in those bewildering early days of the war.

Within the grim confines of the prison, they found a surprisingly cheerful and optimistic Papa. He told them not to worry, he had seen his solicitor, who by now would have written to the Home Office pleading his case. Soon he would be released. In the meantime, he was all right, the food wasn't bad – no herrings with maggots, at least! If he had plenty of cigars he would survive. Luckily, Mama, ever thoughtful, had brought with her a large box of Papa's favourite brand, as well as several changes of clothing.

Mama and Miss Ellis came home and told us all about it. We were quite surprised to hear that Papa was allowed to wear normal clothes, not the arrow-patterned overalls depicted in cartoons and comics!

"Of course he doesn't wear things like that," said Mama, laughing at the very idea, "he's not a criminal, he's just a German!"

The outbreak of war had actually very little effect on our everyday life. Apart from Papa not being there – it was only as if he were away on a business trip, and Miss Ellis staying the nights with us – everything was as usual

Outside, everyone went about their normal lives with only small indications that there was a war on. Most people carried gas masks slung over their shoulders. Air raid posts, heavily sand-bagged, sprang up here and there, and many houses and shops now sported a criss-cross pattern of gummed paper strips on their windows. We went with Mama to a local school to collect a gas mask for Baby. It was a hideous contraption. The entire top half of the baby was encased in a rubber bag, which tied around the waist. A large window in the rubber enabled one to see the child's face, and at the side was a large hand pump. This had to be pumped continually to keep the air inside fresh. Luckily, all this was demonstrated on a doll, otherwise, no doubt, the hall would have been filled with hysterically screaming babies and their mothers!

Fortunately, there was no need to try it on Baby, for after that first air raid warning there were no more alarms, and no more disturbed nights for the time being. There was also no more school. With all the mistresses and many of the pupils evacuated to Bridlington, Newland High School remained closed.

On the day we should have donned our uniforms and returned to our desks and studies, Anita and I gleefully ran off to play in Hymers instead. But our glee was to be short-lived.

32. EVACUEES

On the 13th of September, Mama had a phone call from Miss Dawkins, Anita's form mistress. She said it was a pity we were missing out on our schooling by staying in Hull, and would Mama consider sending us to Bridlington as evacuees. Mama promised to think about it and told us about her telephone conversation. Our reaction was decidedly cool. Leave home? Leave Mama and the others to go to school?

What was wrong with staying at home we argued, there was no air raids, and we didn't want to stay in a hotel sharing bedrooms with other girls, and least of all did we want to go to school! We were enjoying our extended holiday, why spoil everything? Mama was not overly impressed with our arguments. She didn't really want us to leave home, but as a former school teacher education ranked high on her list of priorities. She came up with a compromise.

"I'll write to Mrs Wise," she said, "and ask her if she will take you as private evacuees. Then you won't have to share a room in a boarding house, and things like that. You can come home for weekends now and again, and maybe I can get over to visit you occasionally."

Put that way, it didn't sound quite so bad, in fact the phrase 'private evacuees' sounded rather exclusive!

Mama wrote to Mrs Wise and within a day or two the reply came. Mrs Wise would be delighted to have us. A billeting officer had already been to her house to ask about accommodation for evacuees, and she would rather have a family she knew than complete strangers. She could claim eight shillings and sixpence a week for each of us and if Mama paid an extra ten shillings a week she would see to it that we received extra food and comforts. Mama decided to take up her offer and made definite arrangements for our departure.

Half wanting to go and half not, we made the most of our last days of freedom. The weather was still warm and pleasant and we spent much of our time playing in Hymers with Betty, who had no intention of ever being evacuated, and said she pitied us. Hymers was not the same anymore for a huge barrage balloon was now moored on the running track and there was lots of intriguing activity involving soldiers in camouflage battle dress. We would go and watch them but were constantly told to go away, which, needless to say, we didn't!

One evening, Miss Ellis said she would take us for a walk in the blackout. It was an eerie experience. Used as we were to street lighting, the total blackness that enveloped us once we left the house was, at first, quite alarming. We clung to Miss Ellis as we tottered along beside her. Gradually, our eyes became accustomed to the dark, and we could make out far more landmarks than we could at first. After that first outing our attitude to the blackout became as nonchalant as that of Miss Ellis! In fact, a few days later, Betty and I went for a walk by ourselves.

At last all the arrangements with Mrs Wise were completed. We were to travel alone on the train to Bridlington and Mrs Wise would meet us at the station. Mama promised to visit us when we were settled and see how things were for herself, but she knew we couldn't be in better hands.

Our few possessions were soon packed. Mama had received an official list of what an evacuee should be equipped with, but she had ignored it. It was too impersonal for her, so she packed what she thought would be best, and we put in our beloved paint boxes and books. We decided that Peggy and David had better stay at home, and for the first time, travelled without our beloved dolls.

Mama took us to the station and settled us into an empty compartment. She gave us last minute instructions and advice, a purse with spending money, our tickets, and two comics. She kissed us goodbye, slammed the door shut, the whistle blew, the train gave a jerk, and we were off!

We waved to Mama until she was out of sight then flung ourselves back in our seats and gave ourselves up to the sheer excitement of travelling alone for the first time in our lives.

We felt tremendously grown up and independent. "Hymers," shrieked Anita suddenly and rushed to the windows, for the train was passing Hymers' grounds and the bottom end of Sunny Bank. We hung precariously out of the window screaming "Goodbye, Hymers," and "Goodbye Sunny Bank!" until the train left them behind. It was only twenty-five days since we had last been on a train returning from Bridlington and now we were going back once more.

The train sped over the by now familiar route, passing the little villages and farmsteads, all of which now lay basking in the warm autumn sunshine, so incredibly peaceful. Yet we were being evacuated, presumably to get away from air raids. It seemed ridiculous, looking at the placid countryside, to even think of war, but it was because of war that we were returning to Bridlington. We hung out of the small carriage window practically all the way, waving to all and sundry as we passed.

All too soon the journey was over and we steamed into Bridlington station. Our little independent interlude was over. With a sigh, I lifted our suitcase from the rack, Anita opened the door, and we jumped out, wondering what to do next. We followed the crowd through the ticket barrier and looked about us for Mrs Wise. I didn't really know what she looked like, I had a vague picture of her in my mind, plump and wearing glasses. However, I needn't have worried, for it was Mrs Wise who spotted us first, and came hurrying over.

"Hello," said the kind Yorkshire voice behind us.

We turned round and there was Mrs Wise. She was really just as I'd remembered her, a comfortable Yorkshire woman, her hair scraped back into a rather untidy knot, and glasses perched on the end of her nose. Thankfully, we let her take charge.

"Is your case very heavy?" she asked, "if it isn't, we can walk."

I assured her it was not at all heavy, and we set off for 26 Richmond Street. It was a longer walk than I remembered and the case felt heavier and heavier, but between us we managed it, and as last we were there. Mrs Wise unlocked and we entered her house once more.

It was strange to be back at Mrs Wise's. We looked round and nothing had really changed, apart from the fact that there was more clutter, like cushions, ornaments and so on, about the place. In the living room a fire crackled cosily in the grate and the table was set for lunch.

Lunch was an excellent, if rather silent meal. Mrs Wise did her best to put us at our ease, but it must have been an uphill struggle. This was the first of the many delicious meals we were to have there, for Mrs Wise was a fantastic cook. We were good eaters and she used to say that it was a pleasure to cook for us. Lunch over, Mrs Wise took us to our bedroom, which overlooked the garden.

"When you're unpacked," she said, "why don't you go down to the sea? It's a lovely day and you can stay out till tea-time, about 5 o'clock."

We didn't need telling twice. It did not take us long to stow away our few bits and pieces. Then we hurried downstairs, collected our coats from the hallstand and sedately walked out of the front door. Then our reserve dropped from us like a cloak, and giggling and chattering we skipped down the well known way to the beach.

The promenade at that time of day was deserted and we had the beach to ourselves.

The season was over, and Bridlington had a completely different aspect. Feeling very grown up we wandered round the town and shops and finally went back to Mrs Wise and tea. Tea was another silent meal, then, with the tea things cleared away, we sat primly by the fire, wondering what to do next.

Mrs Wise bustled about in her kitchen and called out, "Do you know how to play Rummy?"

"No," we chorused.

"Never mind," she said, "I'll teach you."

She set out a card table by the fireside, produced several well thumbed packs of cards and proceeded to instruct us in the intricacies of the game. It certainly broke the ice, we laughed at the mistakes we made, and by the end of the evening had mastered the really quite simple rules. Time passed quickly and pleasantly, and at 9 o'clock Mrs Wise packed up the cards, made cocoa, and sent us up to bed.

"Tomorrow morning," she said, "you can have your breakfast in bed, then when you're dressed you can wait by the gate until some of your girls go by. They'll show you where your school is."

Bright and early the next morning, we were woken by a knock on the bedroom door.

"Breakfast out here!" called Mrs Wise, and Anita, who slept on that side of the bed, climbed out, and brought back a charmingly set breakfast tray. We arranged our pillows comfortably and thoroughly enjoyed our meal.

This was indeed a rare treat, for at home breakfast in bed was provided only in times of illness. As it turned out we were to have breakfast in bed every Saturday and Sunday as long as we stayed with Mrs Wise. How kind she was, and how she spoilt us. It amazes me now, that all the time we were there, we were never expected to help with the washing-up. It was the least we could have done – but she never asked us and we never offered to.

But we had not been evacuated simply to lead a life of slothful ease, or even to escape the, for the moment, non-existent, air raids. The prime reason for our being in Bridlington was to continue our education. We therefore, reluctantly, prised ourselves out of our cosy nest, put on school uniform, and ran downstairs.

Mrs Wise was already at her garden gate, flagging down a couple of Newland girls. One of them turned out to be a classmate of mine and we fell upon each other with shrieks of delight. School, I decided, wouldn't be so bad after all.

Newland had its wartime premises at Bridlington High School, and on arriving there, Anita and I duly presented ourselves to 'Daisy' Pearson, the mistress in charge of the evacuees. She took us to our respective classrooms. These were spread about the school in various huts, annexes and a large building at the back of the playing fields known as the 'White House'. In peacetime this had been the adult education centre. Anita was based in the White House, while I was with the Upper Fifth in a large hut overlooking the playing fields. Assembly every morning was in a small chapel, just outside the school. The only part of the main school building we were allowed to use was the library. Off this was a small special room called the 'Bickersteth library'. The imposing white panelled school hall we used only once while I was there, and that was for the Christmas carol service.

All the Upper Fifth girls had been amalgamated into one form, and there were about thirty of us. Most of the girls I already knew, so I settled in quite happily. My desk was by the window next to a great iron radiator and there I spent a very warm and cosy winter term, gazing over the fields, sleepy with the warmth beside me, and not really taking any notice at all of the teachers striving to educate me.

As most of the girls were billeted in the larger hotels, with little possibility of peace and quiet, there was no homework. All this suited me down to the ground, and then I discovered the libraries. This was my total undoing! I soon found out, especially after many of the staff and girls had returned to Hull leaving only the more elderly mistresses in charge, that there was very little supervision.

In the Upper Fifth we attended only the lessons we were to take for the matriculation exam so that for many lessons only half the girls were present. This was the perfect excuse. I appeared only for the subjects I liked, such as English and French, the rest I skipped shamelessly. I spent hour after hour in the small Bickersteth library which sported a roaring coal fire at either end, and there, like the bookworm I was, worked my way through the books. Only the sixth Form of the High School used this room and usually it was totally deserted. The small navy blue clad figure permanently curled up by the fire with a book became part of the furnishings!

The weeks passed in a pleasant, carefree manner, school and evenings of rummy on weekdays, walks to the sea and shops with the other girls at weekends. Mama visited us once to see the set-up for herself and we had a heavenly afternoon off school. Papa, she told us, had left Hull Prison and was now in a camp in Seaton, Devon.

"Lucky Papa," I said, "Devon is where people go for holidays, isn't it?"

"Yes," said Mama, "but he won't be able to go on the beach like you do here. Being interned isn't like being evacuated."

"No, I suppose it isn't," I agreed, "being evacuated is rather fun," and indeed it was. It was a pleasant interlude in our lives.

One day a school friend introduced us to a new entertainment, the troop concerts in the Spa Theatre. These, she told us, were free, and anyone could go. We asked Mrs Wise if we could accompany our friend, and on receiving her permission we attended a concert. We thoroughly enjoyed it and never missed a single one after that if we could help it. Entertainment was for, and by, the troops, with assistance from the local talent. There were comedians, singing and tap dancing. We lustily joined in the choruses of 'Run, rabbit', 'The Siegfried Line' and all the old favourites. It amazes me now how all that winter we came and went to those concerts in the blackout without anybody giving a thought as to whether it was safe or not, for apart from evacuees, Bridlington was swarming with troops.

We had our own front door key in case Mrs Wise was out and enjoyed a real measure of independence. Sometimes Mrs Wise would be out for tea, and she would leave ours on the table, covered with a snowy white cloth. We would feel very grown up as we brewed our own tea. We also got to know Mrs Wise's friends and her two sisters. Sometimes she would take us visiting with her to their homes. There we would play the inevitable rummy or whist – a newly acquired skill – which was always followed by a generous tasty supper.

As the winter approached, Mrs Wise's house became chillier and chillier, in spite of the blazing fire. Mrs Wise would drape a large tartan stole round our shoulders. It was in the Cameron tartan and she was entitled to wear it, she told us proudly. Not to be outdone, Anita and I also solemnly placed our own tartan scarves upon our shoulders. The label pronounced them to be 'Ancient Drummond', and we were definitely not entitled to wear them! An odd trio we must have made, crouched over the little card table by the fire, draped in tartan, like Scottish chieftains!

Mrs Wise also knitted sea boot stockings for the Merchant Navy. She had two huge balls of 'ab' wool rotating in her lap, as her needles clicked busily above a stocking, huge, and long enough for a giant. Following her example, we bought wool and knitting needles, not to knit patriotically for the troops, but to knit ourselves some mittens. Our knitting, we said, was not good enough to knit balaclava helmets and scarves, as a lot of our school friends did. Indeed, it took us long enough to knit our mittens, their shape would have made an expert knitter's hair stand on end, but when they were finished they fitted quite well with a bit of pulling here and there. They also kept our hands beautifully warm.

There had been a couple of air raid warnings in Bridlington, but both had been in broad daylight. There had been no panicky rush to the shelters by the inhabitants of the town. Instead, they had come nonchalantly out of their houses and stood about in little groups, peering at the sky, calling out remarks like, "it's only a practice" and "they wouldn't come this time of day, we'd spot 'em and soon shoot 'em down." The all clear following a few minutes later, proved them right, and dispelled any fear one might have had, but one dour passer-by said grimly, "when they come, it'll be dark, just mark my words, then we'll really know about it."

His gloomy prediction left a small icy chill round my heart, and I remembered his words the first time the warning sounded after dark. We were engrossed in our evening session of rummy, when the banshee wail of the siren penetrated our minds. We put our cards down on the table and gasped fearfully, "Air raid warning!" waiting for Mrs Wise's reaction. She was totally unconcerned, and calmly rearranging her hand of cards. She looked at us over her glasses.

"No it isn't," she reassured us, "it's the seven o'clock train."

She triumphantly placed some cards on the table. "Two fivers!" she said firmly.

We were too frightened to be impressed by this display of good luck.

"It isn't," we insisted, "it's the air raid warning!"'

Mrs Wise calmly discarded the card and surreptitiously peeped at the top card on the pick-up pile. We were too agitated to comment on this flagrant breach of the rules.

"No," she said again, "it's the seven o'clock train."

We were saved any further agony by a violent knocking on the back door. It was the neighbour.

"Air raid!" she shouted dramatically.

Mrs Wise moved at last. She went to the door and opened it, and light streamed out into the garden.

"Put that light out, and come into our shelter," called the neighbour, already hurrying off.

"If I'm going to go, I'll go on my own property," said Mrs Wise, defiantly.

"Well just bring the girls then, and hurry!" insisted the neighbour, pausing at her garden gate.

"All right," said Mrs Wise, "I'll just get my handbag and lock up, do you girls want anything?"

All we wanted to do was go with the neighbour, and quickly, but Mrs Wise went back into her house for what seemed ages, but at last she came out and we were led to the neighbour's 'shelter'. This turned out to be, as far as I could see, simply a small wooden shed at the back of the garden. Squashed among the gardening implements and other junk were a few old chairs and stools. A sack hung over the doorway. Useless in a gas attack, I thought," it was dry instead of wet. A solitary candle spluttered in a jam jar perched on a pile of boxes. The neighbour's husband and daughter were already seated, and after a bit of shuffling around we were all settled.

"It's cold," stated Mrs Wise, "shall we get our coats?"

"No, no!" I gibbered with chattering teeth, "I've got my scarf, I'm not a bit cold, are you Anita?"

"Of course not," said Anita, shivering and shaking beside me.

For a while we sat in silence, then the husband became restless. "Shall I have a look out and see what's going on?"

"Don't you move," said his wife, "listen!"

You could have heard a pin drop in the little shed. A faint droning noise sounded overhead. "One of ours," said the husband.

"How do you know?" asked the daughter, who was sitting on a stool with her back to the curtained doorway. "German planes sound different," explained her father, "sort of brr-brr-brr."

"If there are any German planes up there," I prayed silently, "tell them we're down here, Germans like they are."

There was a sudden wild shriek, and the daughter literally disappeared from sight. She had forgotten that there was only a curtain behind her, and had leant back. In the noise and confusion that followed the candle went out and we were rooted to our seats in sheer terror. However, in no time at all, the daughter was reinstated on her stool, and the candle relit.

"Oo!" gasped her mother, clutching her bosom, "I thought they'd got her!" The sheer improbability of such a ridiculous statement was a blessed relief. We screamed with hysterical laughter until the tears ran down our cheeks.

"Oh, my goodness!" said the neighbour, wiping her eyes, "I'll go and make a cup of tea."

She and her daughter, with a reckless disregard for their safety, went out into the night. They returned with hot cups of tea for all. We gratefully drank the scalding liquid, which was well sugared to counteract the shock we had all sustained, and the atmosphere became light-hearted and party-like. The husband regaled us with funny tales of the last war, and told outrageous jokes. The walls of the flimsy little shed echoed with our mirth. The all clear sounded, and reluctantly the little party broke up.

Back in Mrs Wise's cosy room the card table was as we had left it, the two five's flaunting themselves indisputably at Mrs Wise's place. She poked up the fire, picked up her remaining cards and said, "Your turn to pick up, Rosemarie. Can I buy?"

Caught unawares, I nodded, and she picked up the card she had peeped at previously. It was a two – a highly desirable 'wild' card.

That was the only time we ever used the next door shelter. In future, when the warnings went, we stayed where we were, warm and cosy by the fire, with the light out.

"If Hitler's going to get us," Mrs Wise would say "we might as well be comfortable while we're waiting," and we wholeheartedly agreed with her. Not that we had much choice in the matter.

Anyway they had said, "It would all be over by Christmas." Hadn't they?

33. "INTERN THE LOT"

As Christmas drew nearer however, it became quite obvious that the war would by no means be over in time for the festive days. There were still a few optimists, who now stated, "It will be over and done with by Easter," but they said it with less conviction.

For our family, at least part of the war would be over, for Mama had heard from Papa that he would definitely be home for Christmas. Sure enough on the 9th December at 10pm, a jubilant Papa returned safely to Sunny Bank.

A few days later we received a letter from Mama telling us the good news. She also wrote that we could come home for the Christmas holidays, and enclosed ten shillings for our bus fare, the change from which we could spend on presents.

There had, of course, been no air raids whatsoever in Hull, in fact when the sirens went at night nobody even bothered to get out of bed anymore, and by day people went about their usual business, warning or no warning.

The last few weeks of the school term flew by, most of the girls were going home for the holidays and many were not coming back to Bridlington. They had heard that Newland would be reopening next term. Excitedly, we packed a few essentials, and counted the hours to going home.

Mrs Wise escorted us to the bus, wished us Happy Christmas, and waved us off. There were other children on the bus also returning home, and their shrill chatter entertained us all the way. Especially one little girl who kept shouting, "Oo, me Ma's pot's broke!" a remark which triggered off shrieks of mirth from her companions. Presumably her gift for her Mother had come to grief when she inadvertently sat on it!

Papa met us at the bus station in Hull, and there was a joyful reunion. It was lovely to be home again. Baby had changed beyond all recognition and was walking and starting to talk.

There was a festive air about our first family meal together after nearly four months apart. The dining table was set with our second best china, and Mama had baked our favourite 'marble' cake. Papa regaled us with tales of his recent internment. He told us how, on the journey down to Devon on the train, the Germans had been manacled together in twos, each couple in the charge of an escort. Papa's partner had been an elderly gentleman who unfortunately suffered from a weak bladder. This necessitated frequent trips to the train toilet, and Papa's description of the three of them easing themselves in and out of this tiny room at regular intervals had us nearly falling off our chairs with mirth.

"Why on earth didn't the escort wait outside?" we cried.

"He had his orders not to let us out of his sight," said Papa, "and he took his duties very seriously!"

Another time, at the camp in Devon, a soldier had brought in an elderly German. He had brought him through the barrier, and then, his duty done, abandoned him. In the blackout and in unfamiliar surroundings the old man had panicked. The other men locked in their huts had heard him calling out.

"Don't leave me, soldier! Don't leave me!" as he blundered about in the dark.

Finally, someone in authority had taken pity on him, and removed him to a place of safety.

Papa had a way of lapsing into the Berlin dialect, which made these little tales sound funnier than they really were. We did not spare a thought for the pathetic old man. We were safe in our comfortable safe surroundings. On the mantelpiece, flanked by colourful Christmas cards stood our three little wooden Advent figures, and from the front room emanated the fragrant scent of pine, assuring us that the tree was already there. Christmas Eve was only four days away.

We were happy, we were together again, and we were going to have a lovely, lovely Christmas.

Christmas Eve was as exciting and special as ever, but there was one aspect markedly different about it. Instead of the candlelit tree standing in the bay-window, it now stood in an alcove by the fireplace and the heavy tapestry curtains were drawn across the window to comply with the blackout regulations. Still, it was Christmas, and the family were together, and that was all that mattered.

We could not have guessed then, that six years would pass before we had another Christmas all together in Sunny Bank. All too soon, the holidays were over, and we were back in Bridlington with Mrs Wise. For the moment, Mama thought it was better. If Newland was reopened, as was rumoured, we could come home then, she promised us.

Life in Bridlington resumed as before, with school, and evenings of rummy or whist. Mrs Wise dutifully wore the shiny 'art silk' tea apron we had presented her with at Christmas. Her work-roughened hands made crackling sounds as she smoothed the pinny over her ample bosom. We were delighted that Mama had chosen such a pretty and useful gift for her.

The weather became colder and colder, and to our delight there was lots of snow. The number of girls still evacuated had dwindled to a mere handful, and back in Hull, Newland had reopened. True to her promise, Mama decided that Anita and I would return home for good at half term, in February. Glad to be going home, but sad to be leaving Mrs Wise, we climbed on to the bus for home with mixed feelings, waving frantically to our kind landlady until the bus turned the corner and we could see her no more. Sometime later I heard from a school friend who had remained behind, that Mrs Wise had a new evacuee, no less than the august personage of Newland's head girl herself. For some reason this irritated me; she was, after all, *our* Mrs Wise, and selfishly I begrudged the poor girl the breakfast in bed and the cosy evenings of cards and cocoa round the fireside.

Back in Hull, life continued very pleasantly. Newland was the same as ever, but we now had pegs at the back of the classrooms, to accommodate our coats and gas masks, ready for any emergency that might arise. Apart from the blackout, the sand-bagged A.R.P. posts, and the numerous uniform-clad young men about, it was hard to believe there really was a war on.

We occasionally had twelve-word messages from Mane, through the Red Cross network. In one, she informed us that she had recently married a Bavarian from Munich. His name was Leo Hofbauer.

The days grew warmer, spring flowers brightened the gardens and public parks, and in April we acquired a new pet. A large black cat had adopted us, and refused to leave. At first, Anita and I surreptitiously fed him milk and scraps, but finally even Mama saved him titbits. As yet he was not allowed into the house, but Anita and I were working on it!

Papa's business, of course, was non-existent, and Miss Ellis had found herself another job, but Papa occupied himself in his office, sorting out this and that. He also spent a lot of time in his new allotment, busy with digging, sowing and planting. We had no money worries, for Papa had enough put by to see us through this crisis. In fact, all in all, we were quite happy and contented with our lot. But it was not to last.

There were people in high places, worrying about the number of German nationals still loose about the British Isles. It was, they declared, not a 'Good Thing!! So one day, someone, somewhere, ordered, "Intern the lot!" and the British police sprang into action.

34. INTERNMENT BEGINS

It was Whit Sunday, the 12th May, 1940, when we awoke to a commotion going on in the house. Voices raised, doors banging, running up and down the stairs.

"What's happening?" I said, sitting up in bed.

These were not the usual Sunday morning sounds. Anita opened sleepy eyes. "What?" she murmured. Mama came into our room.

"The police have come," she said, without preamble, "they've come to intern Papa again, and this time Eberhard is going too!"

"What?" we both shrieked, now fully awake, "why Eberhard? He's still at school, they can't take him!"

"He's over sixteen now," said Mania, "and every man and boy between the ages of sixteen and sixty is being interned today."

"Shall we get up?" asked Anita.

"You might as well," said Mama, "but don't get in anybody's way, we've got a lot of packing to do."

We leapt out of bed, and rushed to Eberhard's room. He was still in his pyjamas, looking bewildered.

"Where are you going? What will they do with you? Will they put you in prison?" we asked.

"I don't know," said Eberhard, "perhaps."

We gazed at him in awe, and for once were speechless.

"Go away," said Eberhard, "I have to get dressed."

We scuttled back to our room, and got dressed ourselves, then we ran downstairs. Although we had been told to keep out of the way we hung about, being more of a hindrance than a help. Papa and Eberhard had a hasty breakfast. Upstairs, two plain clothes policemen were going through Papa's office. In spite of everything Papa was cheerful.

"It's all right," he kept on saying, "I'll be home in a few days, and if I'm not Eberhard will, they wouldn't keep a schoolboy."

"Of course not," said Mama, "the whole idea is quite ridiculous. At least you'll be together – don't let them separate you."

Papa promised he would do what he could. Eberhard remarked that it was quite an interesting experience and he was looking forward to it. We all laughed at that.

"Even prison?" asked the irrepressible Anita.

"Even prison," said Eberhard boldly.

The policemen came into the dining room, breaking up the family party with officialdom and terse voices.

"Ready?" they asked, "It's time we got going."

Goodbyes were said all round; we were getting used to it, we had learned that wartime was a time of partings. Eberhard reached for his black and red quartered Grammar School cap. He put it on his head and followed Papa and the police out to the waiting police car. In his school cap and grey summer flannels he looked young, slight, and very vulnerable.

"How daft!" I thought, as we waved them goodbye, "how could anyone ever think that Eberhard or Papa could be spies!"

There was a mention in the newspaper the following day of the internment of German men. "They included," the report read, "a schoolboy in a Grammar School cap."

We went back into the house with Baby excitedly shouting a new word she had learnt – "Go bye bye, go bye!"

Now that the menfolk had gone, the house seemed strangely empty. While Mama got our belated breakfast ready, I wandered into the garden. The day was already warm and sunny; the apple tree in full bloom had never been more beautiful, a breathtaking canopy of pink and white. Underneath the tree sat the big black cat. I picked him up and buried my face in his soft furry coat.

"Next to Mama," I thought, "I'm the oldest person at home now."

At that moment I grew up a little, not a lot, just a little.

The black cat straggled out of my arms and jumped to the ground. He started playing with the petals that drifted from the tree. I laughed at his antics, and the growing up process temporarily stopped while I played with him, showering him with petals like confetti.

That evening, Mama took stock of the situation.

"Now that we're alone in the house," she said, "we'll all sleep together in the front bedroom, I shall feel safer."

So that night, I slept with Mama in the double bed, Anita had her bed made up on the divan, and Baby's cot was in the corner, as usual. We all went to bed early, and lay awake whispering, so as not to disturb Baby.

"I wonder where Papa and Eberhard are sleeping tonight?" said Anita, "will they be in the prison?"

"I shouldn't think so," said Mama, more to console herself than us, "they surely wouldn't put a mere schoolboy into a prison. At least they're not soldiers being sent to the front, we can be thankful for that!" she added.

As we found out later, Papa and Eberhard were not all that far away. Seven miles precisely, in Beverley Barracks. Later they were to be sent to a camp at Huyton, near Liverpool, and eventually from there to Douglas, on the Isle of Man.

The following day, life once again returned to routine and near normal. Anita and I went to school, and Mama cared for Baby and the house. For two weeks, everything was as usual, apart from the 15th May, when Mama had to go before a tribunal which was to decide her 'fate'. I gleefully had the day off school to look after Baby, Anita mendaciously telling my form mistress that I had a headache. Mama returned home happy with the decision of the tribunal.

"Exempt from internment!" she announced, "but I have to report to the police every week."

"Surely they wouldn't intern women?" I said shocked, "that would be daft."

School by now was really beginning to worry me. The School Certificate and Matriculation exams were looming perilously close, and they were to be taken, war or no war. There was barely a month left to do any revision. My pigeons had finally come home to roost! I was aware of the huge gap in my education.

"I wish something would happen," I thought frantically, nothing awful like the school being bombed, but apart from this I could think of no other solution.

My classmate Jean, and I trailed along our homeward way that Friday, 24th May, gloomily discussing our prospects in the coming exams. We arrived at my bus stop, stood for a minute talking, then Jean walked on. I watched her go, her shapeless school hat crammed down on her head, her bulging satchel swinging from one shoulder.

"Bye" I called out after her, "see you on Monday."

But I was not to see her on Monday; in fact the next time I saw Jean, she would be quite grown up, married and pregnant! For, once again, fate was taking a hand in my life and the dreaded exams were to be postponed for me, and in the nicest possible way. A way I could not even have dreamt of in my wildest imaginings!

35. GOODBYE SUNNY BANK

Sunday, the 26th May was, as I noted in my diary, very hot. We wore summer dresses, and spent most of the day in the garden. The lilac tree was in full bloom, and its sweet scent drifted down. I decided to pick some of the blossoms to take to school the following morning. The blooms were high on the old tree, but with the aid of a broom and a pair of steps we managed to pick a large bunch. We stuffed it into a bucket of water so that it would be ready to take to school. Alas, the blossoms were doomed never to go to school, or anywhere else!

The next day, Monday 27th May, I was roused from my slumbers by Mama's voice. Sleepily, I opened my eyes. Mama was standing by the open window, speaking to someone outside. She had been woken at 7am by the sound of loud knocking on the porch door. On going to the window she saw three people standing on the path, two men and one woman.

"Yes," called Mama, "what do you want?"

One of the men spoke.

"Come downstairs and let us in," he said, "we're from the police, we've come to intern you."

"O Gott!" said Mama loudly.

I sat up in bed. When Mama said "O Gott!" in that tone of voice it really meant something.

Mama turned from the window. By now, Anita too had awoken.

"They've come to intern me," said Mama.

"What?" we cried out, now fully awake, "why? when?"

"I'd better let them in," said Mama, pulling on her dressing gown, "it must be a mistake."

She went downstairs, and soon after we heard voices in the hall. We strained our ears to catch the conversation, but could distinguish nothing. Then footsteps on the stairs, and Mama came slowly back into the bedroom, a distraught expression on her face, close on her heels came a severe, unfriendly looking policewoman, in plain clothes.

"It's no mistake," said Mama, "and we're all going, all four of us!"

From the doorway, the policewoman's voice rang out, peremptorily, "Come along now, get up and get dressed you girls, we haven't got all day!"

The sound of her voice, so hostile, so rude, and so out of place in our home, triggered off feelings of fear, resentment and defiance in us. How dared she speak to us like that! Who did she think she was? We were flabbergasted, unable to cope with this situation.

Anita took the line of least resistance. She flung herself back onto her pillow and began to sob loudly. Within seconds, I had followed her example, and we both lay there weeping copiously. It was so out of character for me especially, that even now I am surprised at myself!

Baby, with the noise and din around her, had woken too, and was standing up in her cot, screaming and rattling the bars. She was totally ignored.

Mama was getting dressed, and saying that only a few days ago she had been pronounced exempt from internment, and what next, interning women and children, and it was worse than Hitler, and so on and so on!

We still lay crying, but I peeped surreptitiously at the policewoman, who stood rather helpless by the door. Then she regained her wits and her authority.

"That's enough, you girls," she ordered, "help your mother, and don't make such a fuss."

We ignored her – Mama was attending to Baby now.

The policewoman, seeing she was getting nowhere, said briskly, "I'll go down and see to breakfast. Will I find everything in the kitchen?"

"No," said Mama, "I'd better see to it myself, I'll be down in a minute."

"I can be putting the kettle on anyway," said the policewoman, and went downstairs.

The minute we were alone, our crying stopped. We jumped out of bed.

"What shall we wear? Where will they take us? What's going to happen?" we cried.

"I don't know any more than you do," said Mama. "It's a lovely sunny day, it's going to be warm. Wear your pleated skirts and short sleeved jumpers. We'll have to pack too, although it may only be for a few days, at least so they say."

We pulled on our navy pleated skirts, and with mine I wore an apple green lacy jumper with puff sleeves and gathered neck, Anita's was the same in lemon.

By now, Mama and Baby were downstairs too. We went into the morning room, where the policewoman had already set the table with a strange array of crockery and food; yesterday's blancmange and cheese and sausage. From the kitchen came the delicious aroma of frying eggs. We never had fried breakfasts and this diversion from the normal, we found intriguing.

Baby was eating rusks and milk, and Mama had made coffee and toast. The policewoman brought in the fried eggs, which Anita and I sat and ate in appreciative silence, but Mama said, "I can't eat this, I'm not hungry."

"I should eat while you can," said the policewoman, not unkindly, "you never know when you'll get your next meal."

The two policemen, one a Sergeant McCloud, and the other, a younger man, were searching Papa's office upstairs. What they were looking for I can't imagine, but they were very busy.

Breakfast over and the table cleared, the policewoman said, "I'll wash up, you go and pack a few things. Girls, go and help your mother."

Obediently, we trailed upstairs and collected our suitcases from the box room. Mama rummaged in drawers and wardrobes, looking for suitable garments. Anita and I went into our own bedroom to fetch our 'essential' curlers, diaries, and sponge bags.

"In a way," I thought grudgingly, "it's quite exciting really, like going on holiday."

I remembered suddenly that it was Monday. "Better than school, anyway"

The policewoman, having tidied up downstairs, was now upstairs, following Mama about, watching her pack. She said a strange thing, which none of us ever forgot.

"Take a little tea apron, you might need one."

"A tea apron?" repeated Mama, "whatever for?" but she packed her silk tea apron, just in case.

Our own bits and pieces collected and stowed away in the cases, I stood and watched Mama packing. The policewoman came up with another piece of advice.

"Take your bathing suits," she suggested, "you may be going to the Isle of Man."

This sounded more promising and positive than anything said before, so I eagerly rushed to the cupboard where our suits were kept, and they too were packed.

"Empty Baby's potty please," said Mama, fastening the, by now, bulging suitcases. I did as I was told, and coming out of the toilet heard Sergeant McCloud calling out to me from the office.

"I say, come here a minute, will you?"

I froze, I couldn't go and confront him clutching the potty, it was too undignified! I pretended I hadn't heard him, and walked away.

"I said, come here!" bellowed the Sergeant at my retreating back, and I hurried back to the bedroom to push the potty under the cot. What he wanted I'll never know, for when I came out of the bedroom there was no sign of the Sergeant or the other man, for they were now rummaging in the 'little office'.

The cases were in the hall, Mama was in the kitchen packing up iron rations for Baby. Rusks, milk in a flask, biscuits and so on. Anita and I went about our pre-holiday routine of saying goodbye to the house. We went up to the playroom to start.

"Goodbye, playroom," said Anita.

"Goodbye," I echoed, looking round our beloved room, at the toys and books.

I was saying goodbye to more than the room at that moment, for I finally, at the age of fifteen, was saying goodbye to my childhood, that had been so happy and secure.

Anita was busy putting all the dolls into their beds. A voice at the door made us jump. It was the Sergeant.

"Hurry up," he said, "we're ready to go."

Anita, lovingly straightened a cot cover. Then she spotted the box of artificial 'dummy' chocolates we had acquired from somewhere. Cheekily she picked them up and offered them to the Sergeant.

"Have a chocolate," she said invitingly.

"No thank you," he said, no doubt smelling a rat.

"Yes, go on," I said daringly, longing to see him take a bite and nearly break his teeth, "we can't take them with us, they'll only go bad!"

"No, really," he said politely, "thank you very much. Why don't you eat them."

"Not at this time of day," said Anita, with a disappointed look, and returned them to the shelf.

The Sergeant, with another "hurry up" went downstairs, and we followed more slowly, looking into every room.

"Goodbye maid's room, goodbye bedroom, goodbye lav, goodbye bathroom."

We finished the routine; the back door was already locked and bolted, but I opened it and went into the garden and down the path. The big black cat was sitting there, sunning himself, probably waiting for the breakfast that was not to come. I picked him up and held his furry, purring body close to my face.

"Goodbye Pussy," I murmured, and suddenly felt very sad. I put him down and he began to wash himself vigorously. Who would look after him now I wondered, we were all he had. Actually, I needn't have worried, for some kind neighbour took him in and gave him a wonderful home. He lived to a very ripe old age, and for many years after the war was over we would see him sitting on the garden wall, the picture of smug contentment.

A shout from the back door brought me back to reality.

"What are you doing out there? Do come along, we're waiting."

The policewoman was becoming impatient.

"Goodbye garden," I said softly, and went back to the house. Under the lilac tree, I stopped short. The bucket that had held the lilac blooms was empty, and the beautiful blossoms had been dumped on the compost heap. "Cheek," I muttered, suspecting the policewoman.

Defiantly, I retrieved the flowers and stuffed them back into their bucket of water. There, they resumed their hopeful waiting.

Back in the house, Sergeant McCloud was ringing for a taxi. It was impossible to accommodate six people, one baby and several suitcases into a police car. Anita and I donned our light blue tweed summer coats, and because they were our best we also put on our Sunday hats. Anita's was a brown velvet Juliet cap, and mine, which had once belonged to Mama, was a brown petersham 'beanie' trimmed with a rather mangy brown feather. We were certainly going out in style!

The taxi arrived and we piled in our bags, baggage and the policewoman, the two men going in the police car. I took a last look at the house – empty, locked up, the wallflowers and tulips bright in the front garden in the hot morning sun. Across the square I could see the 'Prudies' in their porch, peering out. "Nosy things," I thought, and felt a strong urge to poke my tongue out. The taxi moved off, another look at home and we were round the corner, waving cheekily to the Prudies through the back window of the cab. I don't think they noticed, but it was a small last gesture of defiance.

The taxi drove into town and deposited us at the Central Police Station. Luggage and people were extracted and we were led to a waiting room. A policeman stood behind a kind of counter, and glanced at us without curiosity. For a while we waited alone, the minutes on the large wall clock ticked by. Then two young women, who looked like twins, were brought in to join us. They looked bewildered, and one of them was crying. Mama spoke to them soothingly, and gradually they cheered up. Still we waited for something to happen, cups of tea were passed round once and milk for Baby, who was remarkably good.

Then suddenly, all was bustle again – our friend the policewoman and the young detective returned and once more luggage and people were loaded into a taxi, but only our family; the two sisters were left behind. This time the taxi took us to the railway station, the detective and policewoman surprisingly carried our suitcases, Mama had Baby in her arms and Anita and I carried the smaller bags.

"Where are we going now?" asked Mama.

"We're just taking you as far as Bradford," said the detective, and seemed disinclined to discuss the matter further.

We had a compartment to ourselves. Our escorts arranged themselves in opposite corner seats and we settled ourselves about the remaining seats.

A train journey was always exciting – who cared where we were going, anyway!

36. THE LONG JOURNEY

As the train sped on its way, our escorts talked among themselves. They agreed, they said, with the internment of aliens, made no attempt to converse with us, nor did we encourage them. We kept ourselves to ourselves and took it in turns to amuse Baby and hold her on our laps. An eighteen month old child is not the ideal companion for a train journey, but she was surprisingly good. It was not, however, to be a long journey. The train, after an hour and half or so, pulled into a large and bustling station. Our escorts started taking the luggage down from the racks. "Here we are," said one.

"Where?" asked Mama, peering out to see if she could see any sign. "Leeds," they replied shortly, and opened the carriage door. We stepped down, Mama carrying the baby, and the police the luggage. Unencumbered with anything to carry, Anita and I skipped along in front.

"Come back here!" shouted the detective unnecessarily, for there was nowhere for us to run, even if we wanted to escape.

We slowed down, and together our little party descended into the station restaurant. We settled at a small table, and the police woman ordered tea and sandwiches all round. Mama looked askance at the proffered meal. She didn't approve of white bread, and the tea looked strong. She made a little stand. "I don't think I want that," she said.

The policewoman said crisply, "You'd better eat while you can. You don't know when your next meal will be."

Anita and I were already hungrily demolishing the sandwiches set before us, for by now it was well past noon, and breakfast seemed a long time ago. Baby had milk, and bread and butter, which she ate without a murmur, and Mama polished off her own portion too, as hunger won the day!

Lunch partaken, we set off on the next stage of our journey, the train to Bradford. This was only a short trip, and soon we were in a taxi again, bowling through the city streets. Three taxi rides in one day was really an extravagance, I thought, and we weren't even paying.

This time the taxi dropped us at a large building, which on closer inspection proved to be a school. We were led down a long corridor and into a large classroom, where some women, chattering in German, nineteen to the dozen, were already sitting on some of the chairs which were arranged around the four sides.

"This is where we leave you," said our policewoman, and she and the young detective shook hands with Mama, said goodbye to Anita and me, and left. We settled ourselves and our luggage in a corner, and wondered what would happen next.

*

The whole school seemed to have been taken over as a collection point, and we could more or less move about the various classrooms without restriction, as Anita and I discovered when we decided to explore our new surroundings. We found toilets and washbasins, and freshened up. Police guarded the school exits, and all the afternoon more and more women arrived, some with babies even younger than our Baby. There were also several children of varying ages. We four stayed mainly in the corner we had staked out for ourselves, a small family unit, occupied mostly with keeping the youngest member happy and amused. Later on, large plates of stew were handed round – this was tasty and well cooked, as even Mama had grudgingly to admit.

The evening wore on tediously. Our classroom had once obviously been the art room of the school, for as well as the A.R.P. posters and instructions that adorned the walls, there were also some highly coloured pictures and patterns brightening the decor. I had read the posters and instructions over and over again. I knew exactly how to work a stirrup pump, administer first aid, or put out an incendiary bomb. There was nowhere left to go. The other rooms were full by now, we had walked about enough and were bored and tired.

"If only," I thought, "this would have been the library. The books I could have been reading all these hours!"

Then at last, some action! A clattering sound came from the doorway, and some men brought in a stack of green metal stretchers – no doubt part of the A.R.P: equipment. We watched disbelievingly as they began to arrange them in rows, up and down the room.

"Surely we're not supposed to sleep on those!" said Mama.

But we were. Next came pillows and grey army blankets, and everyone in the room claimed a stretcher for herself. Our family acquired four in a row. There was nothing else to do but try to get some sleep. Some of the women began to get undressed with an abandon that shocked Anita and me! Our sense of propriety outraged, we modestly looked away, but kept on casting furtive glances at each other, and the near naked women.

"Aren't they rude!" hissed Anita.

Mama in the meantime, had undressed Baby, and put her in her little night-gown. She laid her on a stretcher with a blanket doubled up underneath for a mattress and another one to cover her. She was almost asleep, probably unaware that she was anywhere but in her cosy little cot at home.

Anita and I whispered to Mama, "Do we have to get undressed?"

"Just take off your skirts and jumpers," she replied "and sleep in your vests and knickers. I shall sleep in my underskirt."

Reluctantly, we removed our outer garments and hung them over a chair, then huddled under the blankets.

"Curlers and diaries," said Anita, and climbed off her stretcher to fetch our sponge bags. Quickly we screwed in our curlers and wrote our diaries.

A voice from the doorway called out "Everyone ready? lights out!" and snapped the switches. A light still glowed in the corridor outside, and shone through the open door. A few women were still holding a whispered conversation. A loud "Sshh" from an irate woman trying to sleep silenced them. The only sound now was the creaking of the stretchers and the deep breathing of those lucky enough to be asleep.

I turned this way and that on my uncomfortable bed and tried to follow their example. The unresisting wire mesh dug into my back through the blanket, the pillow was hard and lumpy, my curlers stuck into my head, and the rough blanket scratched my arms and face. I lay on my back and gave up all attempts at trying to sleep. My thoughts went over the day's events. Who would have thought, last night at this time, that we would be here, in a school in Bradford! What would happen next? Perhaps it wasn't true about the Isle of Man. Perhaps this was internment, a horrible school, and forever sleeping on these awful stretchers!

Next to me, Baby had woken up. She lay with her eyes open and like a little budgerigar, was chattering through her repertoire of words. In the semi-darkness I smiled. How cute she was! Finally, I dropped off, only to be woken minutes later by the most fearsome bloodcurdling shrieks and screams! Footsteps raced down the corridor, lights were switched on, and nearly everyone in the room sat up, demanding to know what was going on. One poor woman was looking upset and shamefaced.

"It's all right," she explained, "I've just had a nightmare!"

Peace restored, sleep had to be wooed again, and at last, I fell asleep.

The rattle of stretchers being removed and stacked, woke me early the next day. I lay still with my eyes closed, wondering what on earth it was. Then memory came flooding back, and reluctantly I opened my eyes.

Most women were already up, their stretchers neatly piled into a corner of the room. Women with towels and sponge bags were coming and going from the wash rooms. I peered at my watch – it was only 5am. Mama, washed and dressed, was attending to Baby. Next to me Anita was still fast asleep.

"How did you sleep?" asked Mama. "I didn't sleep a wink myself."

"I slept a bit," I answered, "but I feel stiff all over."

I dressed and woke Anita. It took her a while to come to, and realise where she was. Together, we went to get washed. The toilets and washrooms were crowded, so we hurried through our ablutions as quickly as we could. A lick and a promise was all we had that morning. We didn't like the smell, and the sight of some women stripped to the waist embarrassed us. It wasn't necessary, we thought. Back in our classroom, the W.V.S. women were dishing out plates of steaming porridge, with milk and sugar. There was the inevitable strong tea and thick slices of bread and butter. But who was complaining, we enjoyed the meal immensely, for porridge was always a treat.

The diversion of breakfast over, we settled down to wait once more, but not for long. We were told to pack our things as we were moving on. Glad to see some action, we fastened up our suitcases, put on our coats, and awaited directions.

This time, we were loaded into buses; settled comfortably in my seat, I slept most of the ensuing journey, tired out after the restless night. When I awoke the bus was travelling through the streets of a large city. "Liverpool," somebody near me was saying. Our bus stopped outside a large building, and once more we collected our baggage and followed the crowd. This time we entered, of all places, a boxing stadium!

Tier upon tier of seats stretched upward into the gloomy heights. Many seats were already filled with women, and the gabbling and chattering was almost deafening. We found four seats together, and settled down to await further events.

217

Then began one of the most boring days of my life, for precisely nothing happened!

Apart from more and more women and children flooding in at regular intervals, there were no diversions. The seat in front of us was occupied by a woman with a baby so tiny, it seemed only hours old. She changed its nappy constantly, and the sight and smell revolted us.

"Why don't you walk about a bit and take Baby with you," suggested Mama after a while.

We looked at the vast stadium around us, the steps, the aisles, the different levels.

"We'll lose you," we said, "we'll never find you again."

"Yes you will," said Mama, "all these blocks and rows are numbered and lettered, remember which are ours, and you can't get lost."

We noted our places and off we went, an endless walk, round the top, up steps, down steps, back to our seats, and round the other way. We took it in turns to walk or sit, like mice in a wheel getting nowhere, but at least it was exercise. The hours dragged on, the seats uncomfortable, as they tipped up easily. The woman in front placed her tiny baby on one and the seat obligingly tipped up, baby and all!

"It's dead!" I thought dramatically, as its mother, with hysterical shrieks retrieved it. But the baby was a survivor, its tiny face grew scarlet as it yelled loud protests from incredibly strong lungs. Thankfully, the mother changed its nappy for the umpteenth time.

Morning turned into afternoon and I suffered strange pains in my stomach. For the first time in my spoilt and well regulated young life, I was experiencing hunger pangs! I was not the only one, for around us people were asking when we were going to get something to eat. It was long past lunchtime and nobody had made any effort to feed us. Baby was the only one who was contentedly munching biscuits.

"I daren't give you any," said Mama, "you'll just have to do without. After all, we did have a big breakfast."

"But it must be nearly tea time," I said, "and we haven't had any dinner yet." Rumours were flying round, we were going to spend the night in the stadium! Oh no! Last night had been bad enough. Surely we didn't have to sit in these awful seats a whole night.

Then, at long last, a welcome sight. Plates of sandwiches were being passed around. It seemed an endless time before any reached us. Hungrily, we bit into them. Fish paste. Someone near us had a cheese sandwich. What luxury! The next plate passed round was fish paste sandwiches again. The crowd grew restless.

Near us, an English woman, married to a German, was shouting "Can I have a cheese sandwich please? I don't like fish paste."

"I'm sorry," said the W.V.S. member, who was going round with the plate, but there isn't any more cheese."

The English woman became hysterical.

"I want cheese," she wailed, "I'm British born and I want cheese!"

We thought it tremendously funny, and it became a much used family quote.

The sandwiches were washed down by the now familiar strong tea, served in thick white cups, but now we didn't care. Everything was wonderful. No sooner was our frugal meal over, than we noticed movement in the blocks around us. We were off again.

Soon it was the turn of our section. Thankfully, we gathered up our bits and pieces, went down the steps, through an exit and out into the street. To my immense surprise, it was still daylight. Having been in artificial light for so long, we had lost all account of time. I had thought it would have been dark ages ago, but it was still early evening.

This time, double-decker buses awaited us. Mama and Baby went downstairs, but Anita and I raced up the stairs to the upper deck, and joy of joys, acquired a front seat! The journey was short, and through grimy streets. Word must have got around that the buses were full of Germans, for the streets were lined with people who shook their fists at us and jeered. Some threw stones and lumps of mud at the bus. Two women even held up a Union Jack as we passed.

"Stupid lot!" I thought, superciliously curling up my lip, "dirty, common, slummy lot!"

I felt safe in my seat at the top of the bus, looking down on them all, but deep down inside felt a small niggling fear.

Then, we were clear of the streets, and ahead lay the river and the docks. So it was true, after all. We must be going to the Isle of Man! The bus stopped, and we alighted. There was more waiting, and then at last we were walking up the gangway of a fairly large passenger ship.

Her name was 'Josephine Charlotte', and we found out later that she was Belgian. The ship was already packed with women; they were everywhere. We were lucky, mothers with babies were given bunks, so the four of us were led to a large cabin which held about a dozen bunks. We were allocated a lower one, and pushed our suitcase underneath it. While Mama settled Baby for the night, Anita and I set off to explore the ship. It was almost impossible to walk anywhere, for in every available space women were sitting or lying, there was even a couple stretched out on the bar counter!

Having satisfied our curiosity, we went back to Mama. She had acquired pillows and blankets – Baby was already fast asleep, and we arranged ourselves round about her on the bunk. How we managed to accommodate the rest of us on one small bunk was a miracle. Anita and I lay curled up end to end, and Mama propped her pillow against the wall and slept sitting up. This time I was too exhausted to lie awake; I fell asleep as soon as my head touched the pillow. Much later, I awoke to the sound and feel of throbbing engines.

"We're off!" I thought, "off to the Isle of Man!"

For a fleeting moment I felt a stab of fear as I thought of torpedoes, submarines, and mines. But I was too tired to dwell long on the subject, and pushed the thought to the back of my mind. I just couldn't be bothered with it, all I wanted to do was sleep and sleep and sleep.

When I awoke, I had no idea what time it was, having forgotten to wind up my watch. The lights in the cabin were still on, there were no portholes, so it was impossible to even guess the time of day. The ship was still moving, so wherever it was bound, we hadn't arrived yet. I arose from my cramped position, and stretched my aching back and limbs. Mama, Baby and just about everybody else, was fast asleep, but Anita opened her eyes.

"We're moving," she said, rolling off the bunk, and stretching. "Oo, I'm so stiff," she whispered, "let's go on deck and see what's happening."

We tiptoed out of the cabin, climbed numerous steps till we reached the open deck. The air was cool and tangy after the stale, stuffy cabin atmosphere. It was very early morning, but already the sun was trying to pierce a soft, misty sky. We were hot, the only ones about; other women who had had, no doubt, even less comfortable sleeping quarters than ours, were already pacing the damp decks.

"Let's see if there's any land," said Anita, running to the side and leaning over the ship's rails. I joined her. Then, for the first time, we saw the sight that was to thrill us anew the many future times we were to see it. Rising out of the pale, misty sea into a softly blue sky, we saw the outline of hills.

Already the sun, winning its battle with the mist, was caressing the land, and before long we could distinguish green fields and darker cliffs, yet the whole vision was unreal and mystical still without real substance.

"Do you think," whispered Anita, (perhaps she whispered because she thought if she spoke loudly the lovely sight would disappear) "Do you think it's the Isle of Man?"

"I think it must be," I whispered back, equally awed.

Every throb of the engines was taking us nearer, and every minute the sun grew stronger. We were still a considerable distance away, but from that magical moment the Island had captured our hearts, and we became its adoring slaves forever.

Oblivious to all that was going on around us, we hung over the rails, and watched the ship's progress. Then, reluctantly, we thought we had better go below and see what was going on down there. In our cabin all was bustle and activity. Babies were bawling and sitting on potties, adding their smells to the already stale air. Mama and Baby were sitting on the tidied up bunk, waiting for us. We told Mama what we'd seen.

"We're nearly there, it won't be long now!" cried Anita, excitedly.

"Thank goodness!" said Mama, "I ache all over. You look after Baby, while I go and get washed. Then you must go too, and for goodness sake, brush your hair!"

Anita and I looked at each other and burst out laughing, the mist had wrought havoc with whatever curls we may have had, and our hair hung down in straight damp strips.

As soon as Mama returned from her ablutions we hurried to the washroom, washed, cleaned our teeth, and with a hairbrush, tried to bring a little order into our locks.

Back in the cabin, tea was being served with bread and butter. It was a funny breakfast, but we were ready for it. Then there was nothing left to do but sit on our bunk and wait. The ship had stopped, and Anita and I were longing to go on deck and see where we had arrived, but Mama would not let us go.

"If you go up there, you may not get back here in time, and I need you to help me with Baby and the luggage," she said.

So we sat impatiently in the smelly cabin, and waited for something to happen.

I noted in my diary that there were eighteen hundred people on board the ship that night - I must have received the information from a reliable source. To transfer so many women and children from ship to dock must have been quite a feat of organisation. Who was in charge I don't know. Probably the Manx police force, with special constables as reinforcements. However, we progressed slowly, with much standing and waiting, out of the cabin, up the stairway, and finally, on to the deck and into the fresh morning air.

Eagerly I looked round. At first sight, from the old quay where the ship had moored, Douglas appeared small and ordinary: small grey houses overlooking the quayside, small shops side by side, and a fishy smell about the air. Over it all, seagulls everywhere, wheeling and screaming.

At last, our family were on the gangway, and for the first time in my life, I set foot on Manx soil. Then, we followed the long, untidy procession of people up the road beside the harbour. Quite a crowd of islanders had gathered on the pavement, and were watching us go by. It was not a friendly crowd, nor was it openly hostile. Just silent, staring people.

Fifty years later, almost to the day, on one of our numerous return visits to the Island, I smiled to see a huge banner stretched across the pier. It said in German:

WELCOME TO THE ISLE OF MAN. Put up, no doubt, for the benefit of the many German competitors in the T.T. races.

However, that day was still in the very distant future, and no banners or fanfares greeted us. We passed quite close to a group of people, and one of them spoke loudly, intending us to hear. He succeeded, for I heard him, if no one else did.

"Huh!" he said contemptuously, "look at them! And they call themselves the master race!"

I felt personally insulted. Me, a Dalheim, from an old and noble family, not of the 'master' race'. I knew I wasn't the ideal blonde and blue-eyed flower of German maidenhood, but that remark really hurt. How dare that silly, common man, I thought snootily, lump us all together with an observation like that. True, the internees were a funny looking lot on the whole, and all the jabbering in German didn't help, but we, the Dalheims, were not associated with them!

I lifted my head, adorned with its little beanie hat, higher in the air. I assumed, what I hoped was a haughty aristocratic look, and with cool condescension gazed at the 'rabble' that was watching us. No doubt, they thought, if they noticed me at all, that I either had a stiff neck or had to walk that way to stop my hat from falling off!

Then, ahead of us, we saw a large red brick edifice which proclaimed in huge letters that it was the Railway Station. The front of the procession was already passing through its Victorian portals, and before long, we too had reached it.

37. PORT ERIN

We walked through the cool booking hall in a straggling, untidy line, like sheep herded by a novice shepherd with an untrained dog. Several special constables and various men and women, with an air of authority, guarding entrances and exits, finally achieved all and sundry moving in the same direction, through the turnstiles and onto the railway platforms.

Alongside, the trains were already waiting, smaller than the mainline carriages, attached to tiny, fussy engines, raring to go. What did they care that this morning, their passengers were not to be the usual local people or holidaymakers; women and children yes, but not one bucket and spade between them!

We blinked our eyes in the bright sunlight that flashed from the highly polished brass fittings that embellished the little engines. The uncomfortable nights and the long journey behind us were forgotten. Suddenly, we felt as we always did at the start of a holiday, full of excited and happy anticipation.

Now that a crowd of us were assembled on the platform, the officials sprang into action. Mothers with smaller children, and older women, were escorted to the carriages. When our turn came, Mama pointed out that the four of us were together.

"Never mind," was the brisk rejoinder, "they're big girls, they'll just be further down the train. You get in here with the baby now, you'll see them later."

Gradually one train filled up. Chattering, gesticulating women were wedged willy-nilly into the tiny compartments. The doors were locked and one little train puffed off to its unknown destination.

Anita and I stood on the platform waiting to be directed, not daring to move, we were rooted to the ground as women milled to and fro around us.

Now, the second little train was filling up; the sunshine suddenly didn't seem so bright, nor the prospective journey ahead quite so alluring. Where was Mama? Would we ever see her again? A kindly official, no doubt noticing our worried expressions, approached us.

"Come along girls," he said, "there's room in this carriage for you. In you get!"

The small compartment seemed to be overfilled with gabbling women, Anita and I squeezed ourselves between them, sitting opposite each other. When all were settled down I saw that there were only six other people in with us. Longingly, I gazed at the coveted window seats in the four corners. What a pity, I thought, that we hadn't managed to get two of those. The door slammed shut, a railway official turned a key in the lock, there was the sound of a shrill whistle, a jerk, a shuddering, and we were off. Goodness only knew where to, but we were definitely off!

We leaned back in our seats and looked around us. The other women were talking nineteen to the dozen, in German of course, but no one took any notice of the two of us. Although the windows were open, it was stiflingly hot. I wanted to take off my coat, but was wedged in so tightly that I couldn't move. From our central seats Anita and I gazed past the others out of the windows, and watched the beautiful scenery unfold before our delighted eyes.

Once the houses were left behind, and we were out in the countryside, the views changed with a variety of landscapes and colour that filled us with joyful anticipation.

The women about us were all exchanging experiences. A blonde in a corner seat was relating to an open-mouthed audience how Churchill himself had dined at the house where she was staying. Only a couple of days ago it was, and he had assured her, so she said, that she would never be interned. Never.

We were passing through a wood, brilliantly carpeted with bluebells, their heady scent, carried on the warm air, wafted into the carriage. Anita and I exchanged rapturous glances – Oh, if only we had corner seats and could see everything more closely.

The other women did not even notice the bluebells, the sunlight filtering through the trees, and the distant tantalising glimpses of the sea. Oh, what a waste of the corner seats! There were rhododendrons in bloom, and lashings of May blossom like dollops of snow, red fuchsias bright against the blue sky. Were those primroses nestling in the banks? They were.

"Primroses!" I mouthed silently at Anita, and she beamed back. Maybe we would soon be picking them. We adored primroses.

The blonde was talking about Churchill again.

"Why doesn't she shut up," I thought crossly and looked out of the windows instead, "oh, what a wicked waste of a corner seat!"

The journey from Douglas to Port Erin, which was to be our destination, is pure joy.

Although, since this first time I have travelled the same route on countless occasions, it never loses its charm. On that late May morning, seeing it all for the very first time, it seemed as though the Island was doing its best to captivate us. It certainly did, for we have been ensnared by its delights ever since.

We saw the gorse and broom flowering mile after golden mile, its sweet, unmistakable scent filling our hot little compartment. We saw tiny lanes winding away to distant hills; there were white-washed cottages, villages, a small town. The little train chugged and chuntered at a steady pace, passing halts and small stations.

Now we were quite close to the sea again, and rattling through fields with cattle and sheep with their half-grown lambs. The other women talked incessantly, the blonde was mentioning Churchill for the third time at least. Oh, why didn't they all go away, and leave Anita and me alone to lean out of the windows and see everything properly.

There was a sudden silence around us, and I realised there was a lull in the conversation, and everyone was looking at the two of us. "I thought they were with you," said one woman.

"Oh no," said another, for all the world as though we were two pieces of luggage, "I thought they were yours!"

Six pairs of eyes gazed at us expectantly. I was already hot, and could feel myself getting hotter under their scrutiny. I resented their intrusion into my thoughts, and suddenly didn't want to be associated with these half hysterical, excitedly jabbering, German women. For a start, they spoke differently, their language was not the half German, half English family language we spoke at home. These women were not like us at all - they were real Germans! I felt very English and un-German, and had no wish to communicate with them. Why didn't they just mind their own business, and leave us alone?

While I was thinking these anti-social thoughts, Anita spoke up, "Our mother is on the other train," she explained, thus saving me the need to speak.

I looked at her gratefully. Now they would leave us alone and we could carry on enjoying the journey. The women must have sensed the hostility emanating from me, if not from Anita, for they continued their conversation and ignored us for the rest of the journey.

We had been on the train for about one hour, but now I just wanted to be reunited with Mama and Baby, to get away from these weird, irritating women! I looked at Anita and pulled a funny face. She grimaced back, and I felt a giggle coming on. I gazed intently out of the window, trying to keep a straight face.

We were drawing into a small station, the engine gave a loud, triumphant shriek and the carriages jerked to a halt. We had finally arrived at our destination.

The women around us rose from their seats and seized their belongings, their voices rising to a crescendo. One by one, the compartments were unlocked – at last it was our turn. We waited until our fellow passengers had alighted, and then Anita and I too stepped down onto the platform. A large board facing us bore the words 'Port Erin'.

The hot midday sun beat down on the hordes of women and children assembled on the platform and streaming towards the exit, while frantic officials flapped their hands and shouted instructions in loud, careful English. There was no sign of Mama and Baby.

"Where are they?" asked Anita anxiously, "why aren't they waiting for us?"

I reassured her, "they'll be somewhere here," I said more hopefully than I felt. For all I knew, their train could have had another destination.

One thing I was certain of was that Mama would see to it that before long we would all be reunited.

"We'll have to wait and see what happens," I said, my phlegmatic self taking over. I had great faith in Mama, and didn't see why I should start worrying.

Things seemed to have come to a momentary standstill. No more people were leaving the station, and women and children were sitting on the station seats, or their luggage, waiting resignedly for the next move. I think we were all exhausted and hungry, but the blue sky and warm sunshine were comforting. Surely we would soon be settled somewhere.

A ripple of movement passed through the people nearest the exit, they were gathering up their luggage and preparing to move again. This time, Anita and I were among the crowd that left the station. We crossed a small shopping street, down a short road, turned left, and across the road, to a church hall. At the end of the road we could see the sea, so unbelievably near, with green cliffs and headlands surrounding it. I felt a great lifting of my spirits. What earthly paradise was this? We were going to stay here, in this heavenly place? It was too good to be true!

There was no more time for ecstatic thoughts, for, we were now entering the gloomy portals of the church hall, and there was Mama, with Baby in her arms! We rushed up to her, now everything was going to be all right.

A kindly woman bustled up.

"There you are, dear," she said, smiling benignly, "you see, they were quite safe, and because you've had all this trouble, I'll put you in a really nice house."

Such solicitude and warmth was in her voice, we felt comforted and reassured, so we followed her out of the church hall. Our guide led us towards the sea, so blue and sparkling, then turned right and up the long seafront promenade of Port Erin.

A row of immense hotels and boarding houses faced the sea, some, painted dazzlingly white, were almost unbearable to look at in the fierce midday sun. The road seemed steep to us, as weary now and unused to hills, we toiled upwards.

Anita took Baby on her back and Mama and I carried the luggage. Our billeting officer chatted brightly to Mama, she was friendly and helpful.

"You're going to stay with Mrs Murphy," she said, "you'll like it there." For all the world as though we were just ordinary holidaymakers, and not a family of enemy aliens about to be detained at His Majesty's pleasure!

Halfway up the hill, just as I thought I could not walk another step, our guide stopped.

"There you are," she said.

Thankfully, we put down our suitcases. Anita set Erika down and held her firmly by the hand. We looked up at the house where we were to be billeted. A flight of stone steps led up to the front door of a tall boarding house. It was called 'Sunset View'. Minutes later we were being introduced to Mrs Murphy, our landlady. Introductions over, our kindly guide took leave of us, and Mrs Murphy took over.

She led us to a bedroom on the first floor, which contained a double and a single bed.

"I'll put in a cot for the baby," she told Mama. "My little boy is two now, and doesn't need it any more. As soon as you've freshened up come downstairs, we've got lunch ready. If there's anything else you need, just let me know."

She bustled about, putting out clean towels and soap. To her we were just holiday guests; she had no experience with internees. She was a little embarrassed, for we looked just like any other family coming to stay for their holidays at her house.

She left the room and closed the door. For the first time in nearly three days, we were alone as a family at last. Mama flopped on the single bed, rolling her eyes.

"I am totally finished!" she said.

Anita and I followed her example and lay down on the double bed. As for baby, she sat on the floor and loudly demanded attention.

"Oh, my goodness!" cried Mama, and dived under her bed. She emerged triumphantly with the required article!

Anita and I decided it was time to locate the smallest room, so we opened the bedroom door and peeped out. We soon realised that the layout of the house was exactly the same as at home, and our Sunset View bedroom was in the same position as ours in Sunny Bank, with the toilet half a dozen steps down. We began to feel at home.

When we returned to our room, Mama was rummaging in the suitcases for a change of clothing. We had, after all, not had a chance to change since we'd left home. Washed, changed, and feeling refreshed, we realised how hungry we were. A gong sounded from the depths of the house. Memories of holidays in English boarding houses came flooding back. The gong could only mean one thing.

"Dinner time!" yelled Anita, and made for the door.

As the four of us left our room, we were aware that the whole house was full of people. They came streaming down the stairs, women in all shapes and sizes and ages, and, of course, all talking in German, nineteen to the dozen.

We entered the large downstairs dining room, and sorted ourselves into groups around the various tables disposed about the place. I was relieved that the four of us had a table to ourselves.

Mrs Murphy stood rather awkwardly in the doorway. When the noise had subsided a little she asked for assistance in serving the meal. Two women followed her to the kitchen, and returned with plates of salad for all of us. For baby Erika and the small boy at the table next to us, there were egg sandwiches. For a while, all was silent, apart from the occasional word necessitated in passing food or condiments.

The first pangs of hunger stilled, dishes of stewed fruit and custard replaced the empty plates, and the talking started again. The women of Sunset View got down to the business of getting to know each other.

Women told of how they had been collected, where they had come from in England, from Germany, and so on. Most of them had been domestic servants in English households. Some were refugees, both Jewish and non-Jewish. Information flew backwards and forwards about the room.

There was a short pause, and someone asked Mama where she came from, and how long she'd been in England. Mama gave the details, and then played the trump card – as I knew she would!

"Thirteen years in England, ten years in our own house," she announced triumphantly.

There was a short, respectful silence. Nobody could beat that. I looked smugly at my family. Yes, we were different, we were not like all the others.

A woman at the far end of the room tapped her plate with a spoon, to gain our attention. She rose to her feet and addressed us in English – it was ungrammatical with a strong German accent. It irritated me - why didn't she speak German, instead of such bad English? She informed us that we would all help in the running of the house, the cleaning, the washing up, etc. She, herself, would do the cooking with Mrs Murphy, and would we all get together later in the evening and work out a duty rota. Her table would clear up and wash up after this meal. Tea would be served at four o'clock and an evening meal at seven o'clock, after which nobody was to leave the house.

She sat down and dismissed us with a gesture. Nobody queried this self-appointed leader, probably everyone was glad that at least someone was vaguely in charge. Obediently, we stacked our empty dishes on the table and left the dining room.

Back in the bedroom, we found the little cot already set up. Baby was becoming fretful and sleepy.

"Baby and I are going to sleep until teatime," said Mama firmly, "what about you two, aren't you tired too?"

Tired! With all Port Erin waiting to be explored, with a beach on our very doorstep – who could be tired and waste time going to bed?

"Can we go out?" we wanted to know.

"I suppose so," said Mama, "don't forget we're having tea at four o'clock."

She was already drawing the curtains. Baby was in her cot, talking quietly to herself. The whole house seemed to have settled down for a siesta. Anita and I tiptoed down the stairs. From the kitchen at the back of the house, the faint rattle of crockery was heard. There must be a mountain of washing up, I thought.

The front door stood open, and we rushed out, unable to contain ourselves any longer. We crossed the road to the grassed area on the other side and looked for the nearest way down to the beach. We were not the only ones about. All over, women and children were strolling up and down the promenade, sitting on the grass, or on the stone steps outside the hotels. It was like a popular holiday resort in high season, the only difference being that everyone was speaking German.

But, Anita and I had had enough of Germans! More than enough. In no time at all, we had spotted a zigzag path that led down to the shore. We almost flew down it, and within minutes our feet touched the soft white sands of Port Erin bay. Then we went mad. We ripped off our shoes and socks and raced to the sea.

Oh! The first delicious cold shock of our bare feet in the water! We were not German or English or anything, just two silly deliriously happy girls, splashing about in the Irish Sea.

"I wish we had our bathing suits on," I said.

"We will tomorrow," said Anita, "then we can go further in." Not being a water baby, I wasn't bothered about going further in.

"We'll get our backs brown," I said happily, flinging myself down on to the warm sand. Lying on our backs, gazing at the blue sky overhead, we discussed our amazing good luck.

"Isn't this heaps better than school?" said Anita.

"Mmm," said I, "double English on a Wednesday afternoon. Think of the poor things all swotting hard, and us just lying here."

I had a momentary vision of my classmates, bent over their books, and my empty desk. Did anyone wonder where I was? Anyway, who cared? The rest of the world seemed far away. But not all that far away. In France, there were poor souls fighting, shooting, killing, and maiming each other. I did not give it even a fleeting thought – my own selfish little, self-contained world was perfect. Yet the evacuation at Dunkirk was only four days ahead.

After a while, my stomach gurgling, reminded me that lunch had been only a light meal. Hadn't someone mentioned tea at four o'clock? I squinted down at my watch. Still plenty of time, but maybe we'd better be getting back. Our feet had dried in the sun. We slipped on our shoes and socks and made our way back to Sunset View.

The house was still wrapped in silence, we peeped into the dining room and saw the tables invitingly set for tea.

"Let's see if Mama's up," said Anita.

Mama was indeed up, and so was Baby, looking adorable in a white silky knitted dress.

"We've both had a lovely sleep," said Mama, now looking fresh and relaxed, "and we're ready for our tea."

Once again the gong sounded and we went down for afternoon tea. It was a simple meal, bread and butter, a dish of jam, and some uninteresting buns. We were famished and cleared the decks; in between mouthfuls we told Mama about the beach, the sea and the little zigzag path.

"After tea we'll go, and take Baby," said Mama, "perhaps we can find a shop that sells buckets and spades."

So, it was down to the beach again, with the two of us leading the way. A small shop on the lower promenade sold beach toys. We spent a happy hour or so building sandcastles with Baby's new bucket and spade.

"Can we take Baby for a paddle?" asked Anita.

"Not today," said Mama, "she's had enough excitement. I've been thinking, it's time we stopped calling her Baby, she's not really a baby anymore, and Erika is such a pretty name."

We agreed with her, it was a bit silly to call a twenty-month old child Baby.

It was getting on for Erika's bedtime, and happy, with sand in our toes and shoes, we climbed the hill back to our new abode. So our first day in Port Erin drew to its close.

Erika and the little boy Bobby had an early supper. Mama tucked her up in her little cot once more, and the three of us went down for our evening meal, and the meeting that followed it. Our self-appointed leader, a strong minded woman called Josie, addressed us in her broken English and read us the house rules.

There was to be a roll call every night after curfew, which for the time being, was set at nine o'clock. She then went on to talk about house duties. Mothers with small children, and children under sixteen were exempt from duties. She went on and on without interruption. I suppose at that moment the women in the house were too tired to argue or put forward their own opinions. Everyone acquiesced with everything. The sooner we could all go to bed the better. It had been an eventful day. The ructions and repercussions were to come later.

The meeting closed, the women on duty stacked the dishes and disappeared into the nether regions. The others dispersed to their various rooms, and we went to bed. We hadn't realised how tired we were. We scrambled out of our clothes into pyjamas, wrote our diaries, didn't bother with curlers, and fell asleep as soon as our heads touched the pillows.

38. SUNSET VIEW

The first sounds that penetrated my sleep-befuddled mind the next morning, were the strangest I had ever heard. A kind of high pitched crying and mewing, so, plaintive, so woeful. I lay for a while with my eyes closed, wondering what on earth was making these weird sounds.

I sat up in bed and looked round. In the dim, early morning light, I could see that Mama, Anita and Erika were still fast asleep, so it was none of them. The sounds came from outside. I crept out of my warm bed, tiptoed to the window, and drew back the curtains.

Our bedroom faced the back, and had practically no view, hemmed in at both sides, with the long grey wing of the hotel next door to the left, and our own equally grey wing to the right. The sight was grim and slightly depressing, to say the least. The strange sound was above me – I looked up and saw with disappointment a grey, rain-laden sky, and wheeling beneath it were dozens of seagulls. Their open yellow beaks were giving forth the strange cries that had woken me.

The cries of the gulls were to become a part of my life for the next few years, but I shall never forget that morning when I first heard their forlorn, plaintive crying.

The lino under my bare feet was chilly, the dull wet morning was totally uninviting, and I crawled gratefully back into my cosy bed and slept until Mama woke us at eight o'clock.

It did not take us long to adapt to our new way of life. According to my diary, the days were spent shopping and going to the beach in between the showers. Mama bought us each a pair of beach shoes, and amazingly, we even went to the cinema to see 'Treasure Island'. It must have been a matinee, for roll call always followed curfew at nine o'clock.

On the second of June the weather became settled, sunny and hot. We then spent every day on the beach, acquiring first a painful sunburn, but gradually a deep suntan.

Other women too, would lie in sheltered corners determinedly striving for the required shade of golden brown. One woman in particular always lay in the same place near the lighthouse. We nicknamed her 'the black one', as she wore a black bathing suit, and we watched fascinated, as day by day her back darkened until it was practically the same colour as her suit.

We were now venturing further afield, as yet there was no barbed wire to mark any limits and we were free to explore the whole area about us. We discovered Port St. Mary, a short walk from Port Erin, which also had its quota of internees. The shops were open to us all the time and the shopkeepers' profits must have soared with this great influx of new customers. We found a small lending library in Port Erin, and persuaded Mama to let us borrow books at about tuppence a time. I found my beloved John Buchan amongst them, and for the next few days pored over *Greenmantle*, lost to the world.

Presumably, there must have been news of the outside world, where the war was going through a critical stage. Certainly, as far as our family was concerned, we were remarkably disinterested.

Mama wondered where Papa and Eberhard were. Rumours had it that there was now a men's camp on the Island, but so far we had no definite news. No doubt we would soon receive a letter. As for Sunset View, we settled down to live amicably together.

Most of the women, we discovered, were very pleasant and friendly, and Mama always did get on well with anybody. She was usually wrapped up in her own family affairs, but was always ready to listen to problems, and offer advice. However, this was still the lull before the storm. With over twenty women sharing the same dining room, lounge, bathrooms, house duties, etc., the inevitable happened. They formed little cliques and groups, according to their age, station in life and so on.

Our family and the only other family in the house, a young woman with a two year old son, Bobby, and her seventeen year old step-daughter Zilly, were not involved with any. We were our own little self-contained units, and if there was a certain amount of friction and back chat among the others, it certainly did not concern us. While Mama and Bobby's mother took the two little ones on the beach or on the golf links, Anita and I were free to roam.

We discovered the top walk to Bradda Head, and spent many happy hours on the flower-bedecked headland. It was amazing how far we could follow the cliff paths. In those early days we must have covered miles, and it was only mealtimes having to be attended which clipped our wings.

The war, and our life in Hull receded further and further into the background – we seemed to be suspended in a dream world, bounded by the blue sky merging with an even bluer sea, as we lay or wandered hour after glorious hour on the flower-covered turf. It was a million times better than school and exams!

We soon realised why Sunset View was so named. The promenade at Port Erin faces West, and evening after evening we were treated to the most brilliant sunsets we had ever seen. Used to living in a city we had no chance of seeing the sun set in all its glory, but in Port Erin we certainly had our fill. But, even as the soft rose pink, or flaming scarlet clouds, graced the Western skies, the storm clouds were gathering over Sunset View. The peace and calm that its name implied was beginning to crack.

I think it first started with the food. The meals, which had started off fairly well prepared and cooked, began gradually to go downhill. Those of us who had private means could supplement our diet as we wished. The sideboard in the dining room began to bulge with little luxuries – marmalade, Marmite, jam and butter. There was no food rationing on the Island.

For tea, Mama would buy extra cakes from the local bakers, who had their own delicious specialities. Those who had no money were not so lucky – they had to exist solely on the food dished up.

One day, I remarked that the custard didn't taste like it used to at home.

"No wonder," said Mama, "it's made with water, and not milk."

Things really came to a head one day when the stew was burnt and Josie had tried to cover up the terrible taste with lashings of vinegar. The complaints rose to a shrieking crescendo. We listened in awe to the words bandied around the room. Josie finally gave up screaming back. She picked up her plate and rushed out of the room, crying. "I can't stand it any longer!"

She dashed into the kitchen, and we were all convinced that there, she was partaking of more tasty food than she had served us!

After two weeks of sun and sea air, Mama decided it was time to do something about my hair. She was going to treat me to my very first permanent wave. Accordingly, we went to a ladies hairdresser in the High Street, and made an appointment. The next morning after breakfast, I presented myself at the salon, feeling all kinds of a fool. I was then subjected to various forms of wet and dry tortures, the weirdest of which consisted of being strung up on wires to the electric circuit.

This was the way permanent waves were carried out in those days. I sat and suffered all these indignities at the hands of an elegant, supercilious young lady. I felt gauche and silly, but hoped the end result would be worth all the agony. "Il faut souffrir pour être belle," Mama was wont to say. Well, I was certainly suffering, both mentally and physically! Finally, the desired effect was achieved. I left the salon with a scarlet face from sitting under the hair dryer, with waves and curls clamped tightly to my scalp. I couldn't bear to look at myself. I hurried up the hill, back to the safety of our room, without anyone in the house seeing me.

Anita and Mama were waiting expectantly. They did not exactly whoop with joy, nor tell me how beautiful I looked. "You look different," said Anita, disapprovingly.

"It looks better than it did," said Mama firmly, "and don't worry, it will look more natural in time."

The gong sounded for lunch, and I steeled myself to go down to the dining room. I need not have worried; no one seemed to notice my new image, or at least they were all too polite to comment.

Mama was right as usual, within a day or two my hair was more or less back to normal. I just didn't need to put in curlers at night, a fact which made Anita green with envy, as she struggled with her curlers as usual.

On June 15th, I wrote in my diary, "Germans got Paris! Swastika on Eiffel Tower – fancy!"

It must have been the understatement of the year!

On the 17th June (no doubt I felt I ought to record a little History for posterity) my diary read, "France surrendered to Germany. Went to see *The Wizard of Oz*, was lovely. Gorgeous."

In the meantime, we had heard from Papa and Eberhard. They were in a camp in Douglas, and they hoped that soon a meeting would be arranged.

Now a rumour flew around the camp like wildfire. We were going to be sent to Canada! The prospect filled us with delight. What an adventure this was turning out to be!

Mama was more practical – she wrote at once to Miss Ellis, asking her to send on all our winter clothes. Mama knew that Canada had very cold winters.

The really hot days were over for a while, and a wind sprang up, which blew for several days, cooling down the temperature; thus the first camp fashion was born. To save their hair-dos, the women began putting on their scarves turban-wise! Port Erin acquired an Eastern look. But silk scarves were no match for the strong Manx winds as they tended to blow off, slip, or generally come adrift. So the women decided that stronger measures must be taken.

The answer was wool. The wool shops were inundated with buyers, as everyone began to crochet or knit long scarves. Mama copied a design someone else in the house had made, and crocheted a beautiful scarf in 'devil's knots'. Anita and I looked on enviously as she wound this creation about her head.

"You can knit yourselves one apiece," said Mama, "I know a nice easy pattern, that looks very effective;"

We rushed her to the wool shop and purchased two ounces of yellow wool and some knitting needles. We couldn't wait to get started. The pattern wasn't as easy as we thought, as our knitting skills were still at the knit one, purl one, drop half-a-dozen stage. The first few rows were full of mistakes, with either too many or too few stitches.

"Never mind," said Mama, "that bit will be tucked in, and no one will see it."

We persevered, and finally mastered the pattern, and knitted like fury, on the beach, in the lounge, anywhere we happened to be. Only the end of the ball of wool halted our zealous efforts. The scarves were completed, and apart from the first few rows, looked very nice.

The wind by now had abated, but did we care? Not a bit! Carefully we wound the precious handiwork round our heads, cunningly arranged the knot at the front, tucked in the ends, and set off to parade ourselves before the admiring public. I don't suppose anyone bothered to give us a second glance, but we felt very much à la mode!

About this time, my halcyon days of 'dolce far niente' were somewhat nipped in the bud. For it was decided, I don't know by whom, (I suspect Josie had had enough of seeing me idling my days away) that Zilly and I should also take part in the running of the house. So we were informed that it was now our job to polish the brass door-knobs in the house and occasionally help with drying the pots.

Accordingly I arose early, very unwillingly, the next morning, washing and dressing with a lot of unnecessary fuss and noise. I didn't see why the other three should lie smugly sleeping in their beds while I had to get up at the crack of dawn! With ill-grace, I clumped down the stairs to the kitchen, and armed with cloth and polish, climbed to the top floor to begin my task.

The house was still wrapped in slumber, and furiously, I rattled the knobs loudly as I rubbed them until they gleamed. I gradually worked my way downstairs. In all there must have been at least two dozen knobs, as every door was the proud possessor of one. By the time I had finished the house was stirring.

As I ate my breakfast, with an air of martyrdom, several women informed me that my fierce rattling of the knobs had woken them, and in future would I please be more quiet. The ingratitude! The next time it was my duty to do the knobs, I did them quietly, but less thoroughly.

"That," I thought, "will show them!"

After breakfast, I trailed into the kitchen to give a hand with the drying-up. There seemed to be a thousand plates, I toiled on.

Suddenly Josie yelled at me, "Shtop dat! You vont to drive me crazy?"

I looked at her coldly, "stop what?" I asked.

"Every time you pick up a plate, you bang it like dis," shouted Josie, and banged a plate on the draining board so hard it was a wonder it didn't shatter.

I didn't realise I was doing it. I haughtily picked up another plate, and swear I didn't do it on purpose, but I automatically banged it on the board, as I had done before.

"You heard vot I said!" shrilled Josie, her eyes glittering malevolently.

Hastily I picked up another plate and dried it without the banging bit, and the rest of the work was finished without incident. Poor Josie, she must have hated me for my supercilious condescension.

That night I wrote peevishly in my diary.

"Had to get up in morning at seven and polish knobs, and help with drying-up. Silly idea."

On the 4th July I wrote – "Nothing much doing. Arandora Star carrying internees sunk."

For me that was simply a news item, but as it turned out for many of the women interned with us, it was to be a most tragic event. Every day there were crowds of women around the office in town, demanding, begging and pleading for more information. There was little anyone could tell them at the time. Those frantic with worry about their loved ones, husbands, sons or fiancés had to wait several aching weeks before the appalling truth trickled out.

The ship, carrying only civilian internees and their escorts, had been torpedoed. In the darkness, the panic had been terrible; the decks had been surrounded by barbed wire, and many had perished needlessly. The lucky ones clinging to wreckage had been picked up, some after many hours in the sea, and taken to Australia. All this we heard much later.

For us in Port Erin, the glorious summer went on and on. We practically lived out of doors. We had not a care in the world. We regularly wrote and received letters from Papa and Eberhard. Our little family, at least, was safe.

The war in Europe had reached a temporary lull, but the war in Sunset View was certainly hotting up! Under an outwardly calm surface, trouble was seething and bubbling, often erupting in short, sharp outbursts among the women. Used to a home life of utter harmony and tranquillity, Anita and I found these outbursts fascinating, and listened gleefully as women screeched and quarrelled bitterly with each other.

One evening the Commandant called, and told us all that we were to be sent to Australia! She did not give a specific date, but hinted it would be quite soon. Anita and I were delighted. Mama, more practical, sent Mrs Ellis a telegram.

"Send all summer clothes."

Poor Miss Ellis! She had just packed the winter woollies. She immediately filled a large trunk with part winter and part summer clothes, sent if off, and hoped for the best. As it turned out, the sinking of the Arandora Star had made the Government think twice about shipping internees abroad, and we all stayed exactly where we were.

The tension at Sunset View was now unbearable. Mama refused to take sides. She told us she was too good to mix in with the other women's quarrels. We spent our days on the beach and only saw the others at mealtimes.

I hadn't bothered to write much about the real war in my diary, but I certainly recorded the house war!

"J. was real mad." "M. slapped K."

"Uproar in whole house. Commandant coming," I wrote on 11th May.

Then, one morning, Mama was called to the office. She went down wondering what it was about. There she was shown a letter I had written to Papa and Eberhard, gleefully describing in detail the goings on in our house. The office didn't think this letter ought to be sent. It might cause alarm and worry in the men's camp. So it was destroyed. When Mama told me, I was furious. How dare anyone tell me what to write and what not to write!

There was now open rebellion in the house. One side had chosen their own house speaker, a quiet, cultured, intelligent woman. She was now our representative at meetings. Yet the rows went on, and women stormed to the office, demanding to be re-housed. This was when it was announced that the Commandant was coming, and would we all be present in the dining room at a certain time.

We waited impatiently, until we saw the Commandant coming up the house steps, walk through the open front doorway, past the dining room and straight through to the kitchen, to see Mrs Murphy. After about half an hour, we heard the kitchen door open – now she would be coming to see us. But no, she walked straight through the house and out again, without even a backward glance. The meeting broke up in disorder and disgust.

However, the outcome of it all was that the next day the billeting officer called. She listened to complaints, asked who wanted to leave and who wanted to stay, and left, saying she would let us know. The result was that it was decided that everyone would leave. No doubt the office thought the ladies of Sunset View would be better dispersed among the other hotels.

So every day, two or three left for a new billet. Then it was our turn. We were told that we were going to Bradda Glen, a holiday camp further up the hill. We were to go and ask for the Manager, who would take charge of us.

We packed our bits and pieces. Mrs Murphy had lent us a push-chair for Erika, she said we could keep it as long as necessary. She saw us to the door, she had no quarrel with us. As Mama said good-bye, Mrs Murphy told her we were always welcome, any time the war was over. I remember her last words.

"Just get the ship at Liverpool."

So the Germans left Sunset View, and Mosleyites, commonly known as the 18B's, went to live there, and as far as I know, peace reigned once more.

39. BRADDA GLEN

When I was a typical self-centred teenager, I used to wonder why the women in the camp could not just sit back and enjoy all that life had to offer. What more could they want? They had no cares, no work apart from a little house duty, everything paid for, food, clothing, a roof over their heads, and beautiful scenery to boot.

Now, with the wisdom of mature years, I look back and see things in a totally different light. In those days I was a mere child, used to the restrictions and rules of family and school life. It was quite normal to have limits and curfews imposed. In fact, if anything, we had more freedom in Port Erin than at home, especially in those first weeks when there was no school. For most of the other women, plucked from homes, jobs, husbands and in many cases children, it must have been a harrowing time of uncertainty and worry. Many, no doubt, had menfolk fighting in the war. What comfort to them was the beautiful scenery then? Their lives bounded by the limits of the camp, the censored letters, the petty house rules, the curfew. Small wonder that tempers frayed and hysteria was never far from the surface.

I ask myself, could I go through a spell of internment now? I think not. To walk out of the house for an unspecified number of years, and what would become of our numerous, much loved dogs and cats? I shudder to think of their fate – who would care for them indefinitely? The awful answer is I know what most people do when a pet's life clashes with their plans, when their existence had become a nuisance or a chore. They are 'put to sleep', an expression which to my animal-loving mind, is simply another term for 'murdered'.

But, before I digress into a lecture on man's inhumanity and cruelty to the creatures that share our planet, let us return to the Summer of 1940, and the little family trudging with bag and baggage, up Port Erin hill to Bradda Glen.

For us, one phase in our internment was over, and another even more delightful one was about to begin. Bradda Glen was, as yet, an unknown quantity. Many times we had passed the stone archway bearing the words – 'Bradda Glen. Private. Residents only'. Being law abiding girls we had heeded the warning and had only looked longingly at the path that led invitingly through the woods, for Bradda Glen was a camp within a camp. In those days it was still a holiday camp, and most of the headland belonged to it, and was therefore private property. Now, we actually walked under the stone portal, we were actually to be residents of this select community.

The little path wound slightly downhill, its aspect changing round every bend. The onion smell of the chervil was stronger here than anywhere else. We walked through a tunnel of bushes, over a rustic bridge, had a glimpse down to the sea, and on under tall pine trees in which rooks were cawing noisily. A new sound, which, in future, was always to remind me of Bradda Glen.

The path ended in well-kept lawns, bordered by a fuchsia hedge and a row of palm trees. Ahead of us lay the most beautiful house I had ever seen. A low building with a thatched roof and every diamond-paned window sparkling in the sun. We caught our breath. What sort of fantasy world had we entered!

"Wait here," said Mama, and she disappeared into the open doorway of the magical house. Originally, this had been the holiday home of some rich man on the mainland, and had been the only building in the Glen. It must have broken the family's heart to sell it, but at least Bradda Glen could now be enjoyed by more people. For Bradda Glen, to my mind, is unique and one of the most beautiful spots on this earth.

As we waited for Mama, I gazed around. As usual women were everywhere, sitting on the grass, walking about and going in and out of the charming house. Soon we too would join them, and be as familiar with our new surroundings. Mama returned with the Manager, a large cheerful man. He led us up a path that went through the woods behind the house, and showed us our new abode. This was one of a pair of brick built, two-room cottages, originally part of the servants quarters. They were plain and ordinary, but shaded and protected by the tall trees round about. They appeared to me as something directly out of Grimm's Fairy Tales.

The Manager stopped before the second of the cottages. Over its maroon front door someone had painted the words 'The Nook'. He opened the door, and showed us into the room on the right.

"There you are," he said, "I'll leave you to settle in. Lunch will be in the dining room at one o'clock. You'll hear the bell."

He left us, and once again we took stock of our new home.

The room was quite large. It contained three single beds, a cot, wardrobe, chest of drawers, and a wash hand basin. There were two windows, one facing south over the kitchen roof, and one north into the woods. We loved it, it was like having our very own cottage.

We sorted out our meagre possessions and stowed them into the chest and wardrobe, decided who was to have which bed, and wondered where on earth the toilet was! It turned out to be situated down the path, round a corner behind a trellis fence. We were rather alarmed at the prospect of going there on a dark night, but Mama pointed out that the room was well provided with chamber pots for emergencies!

The loud clanging of a bell stopped all further exploration, and the four of us set out to find the dining room. We followed the other women who came streaming from all directions, and entered an enormous dining room, long and low, built on to the back of the house. Inside were rows and rows of tables, and what seemed like hundreds of wooden chairs.

The kind Manager was looking out for us, and showed us to our table. There were already two women seated at one end and we arranged ourselves at the other. The chatter and clatter in the room was unbelievable. The tables I noticed were covered with sheets, not tablecloths. The food, compared to Sunset View, was excellent. We tucked into it, while Mama fed Erika and acquainted herself with the others at the table.

Lunch over, Mama and Erika returned to The Nook for their daily siesta, and Anita and I set off to explore Bradda Glen. Where to start? We decided to go back to the main lounge, which we hadn't had time to examine properly before lunch. Compared to the dining room, it was gloomy; a large room divided into an upper and lower part.

Light filtered in through the small lead-paned windows, but did not penetrate far. It was not too dark, however, for me to see an enormous bookcase near the door, and, joy of joys, it was crammed with books. I rushed over to examine it and to my delight saw that it was unlocked, so presumably the books were available to any reader.

The books were all of the same vintage, late Victorian or Edwardian – there were novels, adventures, melodramas, romances by authors like H.G. Wells, Stanley J. Weyman, A. Hope, Max Pemberton and so on. I couldn't wait to get my hands on them. How could I possibly read them all?

"Oh, come on!" cried Anita impatiently, "you can read when it's raining, do let's get out."

So, reluctantly, I dragged myself away and we continued on our journey of discovery. Among the trees near the main house lay a long, low wooden building, 'The Ladies Hostel'. It has long since gone, and a children's playground is in its place.

Nowadays, we sit idly swinging on the little swings, reminiscing happily, "Do you remember this," "Do you remember that?"

That August afternoon of 1940 the sun was warm and the green grass invitingly soft. Some women had brought out blankets or deck chairs and were relaxing, reading or chatting quietly together, but the two of us had no time to sit!

We strolled on in the direction of Bradda Head. We passed tennis courts, and behind them a two-storied balconied building, which was called 'Sea View'. Now the path led us through a small wood, and nestling in clearings were a number of white painted, two-roomed chalets. They looked enchanting and we wished we had been allocated one of these. Behind them lay two long white frame houses, the 'Dormy Houses', originally built for men only. One path led up to them, but the other went down in front, and here was one of the most unusual features of Bradda Glen.

Before our amazed eyes, lay a long red tunnel. The Dormy houses were built on a small plateau, the path edge of which was planted with fuchsia bushes, and another fuchsia hedge bordered the other side of the path. Thus, the two rows of fuchsia bushes met in a brilliant crimson arch above our heads. It was to become a favourite walk of ours, and we called it 'Red Path'.

We skipped happily towards the end of it, and here the path divided again. We took the upper branch, which led us to a rustic bridge under tall pine trees. Over the bridge and out of the trees, the whole beauty of Bradda Head lay before us. Purple heather, yellow gorse and soft green bracken covered every inch. The air was full of scent and bees buzzed everywhere; sky and sea merged in various shades of summer blue. Even now, although I have seen it countless times, I still catch my breath at the sheer beauty of it all.

We wandered on till we reached the soft turf near the end of the path. We were not inclined to climb up Milner's Tower. We had done it often from the top road, besides, it was too hot. We flung ourselves on to the turf and just lay there letting our thoughts drift. A profound truth occurred to me.

"If we weren't German," I said, "we wouldn't be here."

"I'm glad we're German," said Anita, "aren't you?"

"Wouldn't be anything else," I agreed.

We were completely happy with our lot and wouldn't have changed places with even the two Princesses at that moment.

Shortly after we had arrived at Bradda Glen, we were told that there was to be a meeting with the men from the camps in Douglas. This was to be held at the Ballaqueeny Hotel in Port St. Mary. There was tremendous excitement as we joined all the eligible women and children who were to walk the short distance between the resorts. Elderly women were taken by train.

The Ballaqueeny was an enormous hotel at the end of St Mary's Promenade. It had a spacious ballroom, and into this we all trooped. There seemed to be hundreds of women and children eagerly awaiting husbands and fathers. Then a cheer rose.

Someone had spotted the long line of men internees turning into the Promenade, well-guarded by their escorts. They had arrived by train.

As they streamed into the great room, anxiously looking round for a familiar face, the men were pounced on by their loved ones, and taken off to quiet corners. The four of us soon spotted Papa; he was alone, this meeting was for husbands only. We found a corner for ourselves, all of us talking at once. It was a happy little reunion, pity Eberhard wasn't there, but it could not be helped.

The meeting itself was badly organised – far too many people, even for such a large ballroom, and many were still searching. After an hour or so, whistles were blown, and the men reluctantly had to collect at the exit. Alas for one young couple, they had just managed to find each other in the melee, and were embracing in a corner behind the grand piano.

Our Commandant strode up. "Come along!" she ordered peremptorily, "off you go!"

The young husband tried to explain, "We have only just met," he said in broken English.

His little wife was in tears, "Just another minute," she pleaded.

The Commandant (it was rumoured that she had once been a prison warder) was adamant.

"Out!" she commanded, and began to prod and beat them with her stick. There was really no need for that; they were not criminals, simply Germans, and judging by appearances, Jewish refugees to boot. All of us who witnessed this nasty little incident stood in shocked silence, but some of the men had seen what was going on too. There were cries of "Shame!" and some began to boo. It could have developed into an ugly situation, and the Commandant realised it.

She said grudgingly, "Five minutes then," and left the scene.

The men once more were marshalled to the exits, and after a short while left the hotel in an orderly fashion. We watched their progress down the promenade, waving from the windows until they were out of sight.

It was a warm sunny day, and we decided to return to Port Erin by the 'top' road. We had always done the 'low' road before, so it would make a change. The top road was a longer way, but well worthwhile. It led past old farms, fields and cottages. The views were wide, and the roads bordered by those lovely walls that are half stone, half turf, and covered with cushions of minute rock plants, abloom in pink, yellow and white.

It was as we neared Port Erin that we saw a tiny, empty cottage, its thatch untidy, its gardens overgrown, the name on its gate 'Rose Cottage'. We stood entranced. We tried the little gate, it opened, and we ventured down the short path to peer through the miniature dusty windows. We wished it was ours, and made plans. We would tidy it up and live in it.

"Buy it!" we begged Mama.

"I'd love to," said Mama, "let's sell Sunny Bank and all live here." It was only make believe and highly improbable, but at that moment we became addicted to cottages. Every empty cottage we saw immediately became a target for our imagination – we'd restore them, plant trees, roses, put in latticed windows, build porches, knock down a wall here, build another one there.

A fascinating occupation, and it didn't cost a penny! The best part being, that there was no need to worry about damp courses, leaking roofs, sinking walls, falling ceilings and all the other hazards that come with tumbledown cottages. This we have since found out! However, that day, the possibility of our ever owning our own little cottage was remote, but nonetheless a dream was born.

So the summer went on its happy, sunny way. Every day for us was filled with interest and action. There were other girls and boys of our own age in Bradda Glen, and we spent a lot of time together. There was a large room known as the recreation room, and here we would meet most evenings and talk, tease and generally fool around.

Our neighbour in 'The Nook', a woman called Bertha, was a kindly, talkative old soul, but she had a bad affliction. She was tormented by a terrible deep-seated, rasping cough. It used to trouble her at night, and if one awoke during the night one could hear this terrible coughing, going on and on. Poor woman, it can't have been very pleasant for her either. Mama asked her if she was taking anything to relieve this cough, but she said resignedly that there was nothing that would help. The prospect of being kept awake for endless nights stirred Mama into action, so she went to the Manager to ask if there was a possibility of us obtaining other rooms. The four of us in such a small room was not really convenient, she said. It would be better if we could be in two rooms. The Manager said that he would see what he could do. People were being released daily, and surely something could soon be arranged.

It was not long afterwards that Mama was told that we could move out of The Nook. Mama and Erika were to have a room in Sea View, and we two girls would have a room in the Ladies Hostel. This was indeed good news. The Sea View rooms with their balconies and wash hand basins were greatly coveted by all. Having settled Mama and Erika, we went off to take possession of our new room in the Ladies Hostel. Our room was right at the end, with a view deep into the woods. It was, therefore, always dark and gloomy inside, no glimmer of sunshine ever penetrated the tall dark firs, but we loved it.

The rooms in the Ladies Hostel lay on either side of an endless corridor, the floor, walls and doors all in dark wood. The floor was polished daily and gleamed softly.

When one walked or ran down it, it creaked and squeaked intriguingly. To this day, the smell of beeswax reminds me of the long, dark corridor of the Ladies Hostel.

The great advantage now was that our toilets and bathrooms were under the same roof. Our room was simply furnished – twin beds, chest of drawers, and a small hanging cupboard. Our bits and pieces were soon stowed away. We picked some flowers and arranged them in a tooth glass on the dressing table. It began to look home-like.

Mama was delighted with her room in Sea View, which certainly had a lovely view, facing south, and on fine days had the maximum of sunshine.

Not living on top of the other women as we had done in Sunset View, we found the atmosphere in Bradda Glen relaxed and contented. The women internees got on well with the Manager who was easy going and popular. After the evening meal he would give out any announcements and always ended by saying in German, "Sie können gehen, bitte."

Then the women would, with one accord, scrape back their chairs with a tremendous crashing noise and leave the room. We soon became accustomed to this ear splitting sound, but the first time Erika heard it, she screamed with fright!

The two women who shared our table immediately acquired nicknames. One we called simply "Oppo," because she sat opposite Anita and me. Oppo had a permanently disapproving expression on her face and was a born pessimist. The other woman we called "Imprison."

She had come from Ireland and had spent the first few weeks of her internment in a women's prison over there, which had, apparently, been nothing short of a luxury hotel compared to Bradda Glen. Every sentence began with "Imprison" as she compared the two places.

"Imprison," they had damask tablecloths, "Imprison," they drank from china cups, "Imprison," they had this and they had that.

It became one of those family jokes that thrive on repetition and exaggeration.

"Imprison," Mama would say, as she swept the bare floor in her little room, "we had sheepskin rugs."

"Imprison," Anita giggled, getting into bed, "we had sheets of pure silk."

"Imprison," I whispered daringly to Anita at teatime, as we tucked into our bread and jam, "we had chocolate cake every day for tea!"

The jam at Bradda Glen always tasted rather strange. Oppo wouldn't touch it. Her face would become even more disapproving as she declared it tasted of carbolic. As she came from that part of Germany where the 'c' is pronounced as a 'g', it sounded like 'garbole'. To this day we still call carbolic, garbole.

In the meantime, the authorities had decided it was time to restrict the movement of internees. We first noticed it when Anita and I went up the steep little path behind the Bay Hotel that led up to the Darragh. Mama and Erika were on the beach, but we two had decided to go for a walk. At the top of the path stood a man whose arm proclaimed 'Special Constable'.

"Where are you going?" he asked us.

"For a walk," I said, "up there."

Our obviously Yorkshire accents must have puzzled him.

"Where have you come from?" he asked.

"Down there," said Anita vaguely, and pointed to Port Erin.

"Are you German?" he asked.

"No, English," answered Anita truthfully – she was, after all, British-born and could say this with impunity. I kept quiet. The constable wasn't giving in so easily.

"Are you internees?" he asked.

"Not really," said Anita, but she realised we were beaten, "our mother is."

"Then you can't go past here," said the man.

"Why not?" asked Anita, determined to have the last word.

"Because you can't." His tone was final.

We trailed back to the beach, cross and a little deflated. We weren't used to being told where to go and not to go.

So the barbed wire fences began to surround the camp. We still had so much freedom and so many walks left that we were hardly aware of it. Nor did it bother us. Why should it? We didn't want to get out, we wanted to stay exactly where we were.

The shining silver threads of barbed wire that were strung around the camp like a spiders web protected us from the hostile outside world. A world where there was a war going on, where Germans at that time were not very popular. We felt safe and best of all, secure in our little world, there was no school. This state of bliss was shortly to end.

40. CAMP SCHOOL

Wherever there are children or young people of school age, there are sure to be adults concerned about their academic education. Thus, it was in the camp too. While we youngsters were enjoying a carefree, apparently never ending summer holiday, there were women worrying about our lack of schooling.

They decided that it was time to channel the children, who were aimlessly running wild on the beaches of Port Erin and Port St Mary, into some sort of school system. I don't know the details, but I would think that these women met together and then approached the camp officer with their suggestion. The office wholeheartedly agreed. Something should definitely be done about the children.

They found a Manx woman teacher who was willing to be in charge of the project, and wheels began to turn. Rooms suitable for schooling were allocated and teachers were recruited from the internees themselves. This proved to be no problem, for there were plenty of intelligent, educated women to draw on, who were glad to share their expertise and knowledge, and teach any subjects required.

First to be netted were the little ones, the under fives. Two kindergartens were set up, one in the club house on the Rowany golf course at Port Erin, and the other at Cowley's Cafe in Port St Mary. They were open all day, but such was the demand that the children attended either mornings or afternoons.

Then it was the turn of the next age group. A classroom was set up in the small lounge at the Bradda Private Hotel in Port Erin, and another one behind the Strand Café in the village.

I was in the Bradda Glen lounge choosing a book from its extensive library, when I saw Mama deep in conversation with an earnest little woman. She was telling Mama all about the proposed schooling, and Mama, as always very keen on things like that, gave her her full attention. Mama called me over and told me all about the plans. The little woman added her piece.

"Of course," she said, "this school is for children up to the age of fourteen only. Officially you are over school age, but we're going to start an adolescent class soon," and off she went in search of other victims.

I was not in the least worried about there being arrangements for the older boys and girls, but noting her grim efficiency didn't hold out much hope of dodging the column for long.

"Well," said Mama, "what do you think? It's a good idea, isn't it? After all, you haven't been to school since May, it's high time something was done about it."

"I suppose so," I said, unenthusiastically, and gloomily set off in search of Anita, to tell her the ill-tidings.

Anita was more optimistic; most of the children in Bradda Glen were nearer her age than mine.

"It might be fun," she said philosophically.

Anita and the other boys and girls started their schooling the following Monday morning.

"It's ever so funny," she reported on her return, "not like school at all, and the boys are real cheeky to the teacher."

School was morning only at first, so left plenty of time to follow our own pursuits in the afternoons.

I had predicted correctly – not long after the younger ones had started their classes I was waylaid by the earnest little woman.

"Good news!" she beamed at me, "the adolescent class has started at the Strand Café school, so at last you can go. You can start tomorrow!"

She beetled off, apparently unconcerned by my total lack of enthusiasm.

The Strand Café school catered for the children who lived at the lower end of Port Erin. The actual café itself still

259

flourished under the patronage of the internees. It was especially popular with the Viennese women, who said the coffee there was the best in Port Erin.

Accordingly, I set off the following day, armed with a new notebook and pencil, curious to see the set-up. Arriving down at the café I followed some girls about my own age into the door behind the café.

"Is this the school?" I asked unnecessarily, for judging by the number of children about, it obviously was.

"Yes," said one of the girls, "we came yesterday, come in with us."

They led the way into a room in which redundant café tables and chairs had been arranged in two rows facing the fireplace. A blackboard was perched precariously on the mantelpiece. It was a far cry from Newland High School – more like playing at schools, I thought. However, as I had to grudgingly admit, this very difference made it quite enjoyable.

We had a variety of subjects which included shorthand, German literature and French. The first time I read aloud from the French book the other girls fell about, laughing hysterically. Even the teacher smiled.

"What terrible French they must have taught at your English school," she remarked, "we'll have to do something about your pronunciation. No French person would ever understand you."

She was absolutely right, of course. Our French lessons at Newland were mostly written, and we had little opportunity to speak. If they laughed at my French, at least they didn't laugh at me in the English lessons, when I smugly knew I was the best. My essays were always being held up as perfect examples, and many times read out by the teacher. A fact which I would proudly record in my diary.

German literature, on the other hand, was way above my head, and I kept a very low profile as the teacher and the other girls earnestly discussed the great works of Schiller and Goethe.

Meanwhile, the autumn had set in and we were experiencing some cold weather accompanied by the strong Manx winds. It became obvious that Bradda Glen had been planned with only summer visitors in mind. There was an open coal fire in the lounge, but that was the only visible form of heating. If there was any heating in the chalets or bungalows we certainly didn't feel any.

At least we were warm at school, but Mama complained bitterly about the cold in her Sea View room. Erika, who now called herself Addy as she couldn't get her tongue round her name, had been to kindergarten a few times but didn't like it. At two years old, she was really a bit too young, Mama thought.

It became too cold for us to play outdoors after school, and we spent a lot of time in the big recreation room with the boys and girls of Bradda Glen.

The women of Bradda Glen put on a production of 'The Merry Widow'. We watched every rehearsal and every performance, sitting on cushions on the front row.' We thought it was the most beautiful thing we had ever seen.

Poor Mama was not having such a good time. Not liking to leave Addy alone in Sea View on the dark, blowy autumn nights, she would retire with her at bedtime, sewing or reading by the dim single bulb that lit the room. She began to get restless.

"This place is all very well in the summer," she said, "but this time of year it's no good. I hardly dare leave the room at night when the wind is strong, it nearly pulls the door out of my hand and wakes Addy, who hates the wind anyway."

This was quite true. Addy had a loathing of the wind, and when out in her pushchair had to be swathed in a blanket like a small mummy, with only her little face peeping out. Even then she would scream "Wind! wind!" and demand to be taken indoors again.

"It won't do," said Mama firmly, "I want to live in a proper house, with stairs, bedrooms, bathrooms and lavatories all under one roof."

We protested, we loved Bradda Glen, we didn't want to leave. Mama ignored our objections and went to the office. The office was very sympathetic. Of course, they agreed, Bradda Glen was no place for small children in this weather, and they gave Mama the choice of two houses to view.

We accompanied Mama to the first one - 'Manchester House' on Bradda West Road. The landlady showed us the room. It was an attic bedroom for four. There was lino on the floor, and it felt even chillier than the rooms at Bradda Glen, which by comparison were almost cosy.

"Not for us," said Mama, once we were outside again, "it's even further away from Port Erin than Bradda Glen." She consulted her slip of paper, "Let's look at the next one, Blair Atholl on the Promenade in Port St Mary."

It was a fine day, so we walked to Port St Mary, with Addy in her pushchair so that we could move faster. We easily found Blair Atholl and Mama rang the doorbell. From that first moment the landlady, Mrs Hislop, was kind and friendly, thus reflecting the whole atmosphere of the house. She smiled pleasantly at the four of us.

"Come upstairs and see the room," she said, "I'm afraid it's right at the top of the house, but it's a nice big room."

It was – it faced the back with a view over to Fleshwick Bay and the hills. It contained a double and a single bed, and a small iron cot. There was lino on the floor certainly, but beside the beds were thick sheepskin rugs. The bedspreads were multicoloured seersucker cotton. It looked cosy and homely.

"Yes," said Mama happily, "this is nice, we'll take it," for all the world as though she was choosing holiday accommodation

Mrs Hislop then showed us the lounge on the lower floor. The view through the large window overlooking the bay was stupendous. Several women were in the lounge and smiled at us and passed the time of day. They seemed friendly and sociable. The dining room was on the floor below, all in all it seemed to be just right for us.

"Thank you for showing us your house," said Mama to Mrs Hislop as we left. "I'm looking forward to moving in."

We took the top road back to Port Erin, Mama enthusing all the way about our new billet.

"Heavenly," she said, "shops just round the corner, toilet, bathroom and sitting room just down a flight of stairs and dining room below that. I can't wait to move in!"

41. BLAIR ATHOLL

We moved into Blair Atholl on the 16th of November, and our first impression proved to be absolutely true. It was indeed a cosy and happy place. We soon stowed away our bits and pieces in our pleasant, spacious room, then went down for lunch and to acquaint ourselves with the other residents.

There were not many, for it was a much smaller house than Sunset View. At our table were two young women, one of whom had a girl, Margot, who was six months younger than Addy. At the other table in the window was a loud bossy woman from Cologne, a volatile Austrian from Graz, and an elegant girl, also Austrian. The third table in the room was occupied by a mother with two daughters; Dolly, who was Anita's age and Gertrude, who was slightly younger than me. Seated with them was a lively young Jewess and two rather serious women, one of whom, Marianne, was the house leader.

Introductions and potted life histories over, we settled down to enjoy an excellent lunch. We soon found out that apart from being the soul of kindness, Mrs Hislop was also a wonderful cook, and her steamed syrup sponges were sheer poetry. The first Sunday morning of our stay we had tinned grapefruit, a rare delicacy that merited a mention in my diary! The even more amazing fact was that tinned grapefruit was served *every* Sunday breakfast, despite being practically unobtainable during wartime. There must have been a vast quantity stored in the cellars of Blair Atholl.

We quickly adapted to life in our new home. Mama had been right, of course. It was lonely to have everything under one roof, and a safe cosy feeling as one lay in bed and heard the soothing murmur of voices in the lounge below, as the wind howled and sighed about the house outside.

264

Anita and I now both went to the camp schools in Port St Mary. The Port Erin adolescent class had dwindled to only two pupils, as more and more women were released. When I informed the teacher in charge that I too would be leaving, as we were moving to Port St Mary, she beamed at me.

"But that's wonderful!" she trilled happily, "there's a good school at Port St Mary and far more boys and girls of your own age!"

She gave me further relevant details. Accordingly, a couple of days after our arrival in Port St Mary, I set off to find the school, which was located over a shop on the corner of the Promenade. After the long walk from Bradda Glen to the Strand school, which had become very bleak and tedious in the chilly autumn weather, this short walk from Blair Atholl was much more to my liking.

I entered the side door of the building and went upstairs in search of the head teacher, as I was told. All the doors were closed and there was no indication as to which was the head's room. I selected a door at random, opened it and looked in. A woman busy writing at a table looked at me enquiringly. "Yes?" she said.

"I'm looking for the head," I told her, "I'm going to come to school here." She pointed to the door opposite. "That's her room," she said, "she's not in at the moment, go in and sit down, she won't be long."

I went into the room she had indicated. It was small and quite bare, apart from a table, a couple of chairs and some books on a shelf. I selected a chair, settled down and waited, and waited, and waited. I became restless – walked about the room, looked out of the window, peered at the books. I sat down again.

"What a waste of a morning," I thought crossly, "if she's not here in one minute I'm off!"

Suddenly, the door flew open, and in bounced the most extraordinary woman. She was clad in brown from head to foot, brown swirling skirt, brown hand-knitted jumper, brown stockings, flat brown sandals. She had a thatch of snowy white hair and her eyes were brilliantly blue in a face still deeply tanned from the Manx summer. Her name, I found out later, was Minna Specht. She leapt across the room towards me. She stopped in front of me, cupped my face in her hands, her eyes blazing into mine.

"Ah!" she breathed, "you have suffered, yes?"

It was such an unusual greeting, I drew back surprised.

"Suffered," I said, thinking she meant I suffered waiting for her so long, "Oh no, I haven't really."

That was not what she meant at all. She sensed my withdrawal.

"You are not a refugee?" she asked, removing her hands from my face.

'No," I said shortly, feeling slightly embarrassed.

Her sympathetic manner dropped from her like a cloak. She became briskly efficient. She took down details of my age, schooling background and so on. With every answer I gave her she realised that here was a girl on whom her sympathy would be entirely wasted.

The cross examination over, she rose.

"Come with me," she said, "I will take you to your class."

I followed her across the landing, she flung open a door, there were about a dozen boys and girls seated at tables.

Minna introduced me. "Here is a new pupil, Rosemarie Dalheim," and off she marched leaving me with the teacher in charge.

"We are doing trigonometry," the teacher informed me, she was little more than a girl herself. "Please sit over there, near the window."

I settled down next to a girl who gave me a brief smile of greeting and the lesson continued. We had done trigonometry at Newland, but I had not really understood it.

I relaxed in my seat and gazed out of the window at the life in the street, internees mingling with Manx residents, talking, shopping or going about their business. It was a lot more interesting than trigonometry.

The Manx winter had really settled in now and we soon found out that Blair Atholl, too, was no match for the strong winds. On stormy days the windows rattled and shook. The rain found gaps and had to be kept out with towels and cloths. The fire in the lounge was only lit after lunch, and with so many women jostling for a warm place, we young ones had little hope of getting near the source of heat.

Beside one side of the fireplace there stood a high-backed cane chair, more suited to a conservatory than a lounge. This seat was, by her own orders, reserved for the woman from Cologne. No one dared dispute that, she was after all forty-eight years old and therefore the oldest woman in the house! We called her 'Eule' (Owl) behind her back, because it was similar to her surname, and the chair we called the 'Owl's Nest'. Sometimes, when we knew she was out, we would daringly sit in the Nest, but would leave it immediately we knew she was on her way. One of the other women would defy her too; this was the Austrian from Graz. We called her 'Dusty'. She would sit in the chair whenever it was vacant, but even she left as soon as the Owl's heavy tread was heard on the stair.

One day, however, she either didn't hear Owl come into the room, or she was in a particularly defiant mood. Owl entered the room and saw the Nest occupied by Dusty, who was unconcernedly sewing, her pins, scissors and other bits and pieces spread out on the broad arms of the chair. Owl stood speechless for a moment, then she cleared her throat loudly. Dusty calmly went on sewing. Owl's foot tapped ominously; Dusty deliberately chose another thread from her sewing box, while the rest of us sat with baited breath and waited for Vesuvius to erupt. We were not disappointed; Owl marched to the back of the Nest, with one swift movement tipped the huge chair forward. Taken unawares, Dusty, her sewing box, pins, needles and everything, lay in a heap under the chair, and we listened fascinated to the screaming curses that emanated from the wreckage.

Owl righted the chair and settled herself smugly into its broad seat. She reached up to the mantelpiece for her book, found the place where she had left off reading, and calmly continued with the story. Totally absorbed in it and totally ignoring Dusty, whose screams had turned to sobs as she sat among the debris of her sewing and tried to pick up her scattered bits and pieces. It was all rather sad and not really funny. Anita and I helped to pick up the pins, and I didn't even want to giggle.

Owl and Dusty's occasional skirmishes livened up our days. I remember a terrible row over a missing ginger bun that Dusty had earmarked for herself. It seems an utterly trivial reason for a fight now, but in those days ginger buns loomed large in importance, being quite a rarity!

On the whole the women of Blair Atholl were a peaceable lot and the atmosphere harmonious. Every evening we had 'Schweigestunde', (the silent hour) between eight and nine o'clock, so that women who liked to read could do so in peace. At nine o'clock sharp Marianne the house leader, and her satellite Martha would descend to the Hislop's kitchen, to listen to the news on the wireless. On their return Marianne would read out all the latest developments in the world to us from her special little 'news' notebook. We would all listen solemnly.

One day, Churchill was to broadcast an important message to the Nation and Marianne fussily told everyone that she was going down specially to listen to it, and would tell us all about it. Mama put her foot down.

"It's not that important, surely," she said, "it's always the same irrelevant stuff."

Marianne, struck dumb for a moment, gave Mama a horrified glance. Recovering her speech, she drew herself up reproachfully.

"Irrelevant?" she said with disbelief, "irrelevant, when the Prime Minister of England speaks, that you call irrelevant?"

"Well," said Mama defiantly, "it doesn't change anything, does it?"

There was no answer to that, and an outraged Marianne marched off, clutching her little notebook. When she returned she repeated Churchill's speech practically verbatim, with many disapproving glances at Mama, who kept quiet and listened politely.

Apart from reading, the main evening occupation among the women of Blair Atholl was knitting. Even Anita and I joined in, our skills improving the more we knitted – doll's clothes, gloves and socks progressed to jumpers and cardigans, all the more treasured because we'd made them ourselves. Anita and I got on well with our contemporaries, Dolly and Gertrude, also avid knitters, and the four of us would sit together comparing wool, patterns and stitches, gossiping like a group of little old ladies!

Addy and Margot played happily in Margot's playpen under our watchful eyes, leaving their mothers free to do as they wished. The playpen was such a novelty for Addy, who had never had one, that she would beg to play in it, even when Margot was out!

Christmas was drawing ever nearer, our first Christmas in the camp. The first day of December 1940 was also the first Sunday in Advent. A special service for internees was held in one of the Port St Mary churches, and we all went, every seat was taken.

We began to feel Christmassy. Back in Blair Atholl the little knitting bees met in the usual corner.

"What are you giving your mother for Christmas?" asked Dolly.

"Gertrude and I are giving Mutti gloves, we're going to knit one each."

Anita and I pondered awhile.

"We'll make gloves too", I decided not to be outdone, "and we'll knit a pixie hood and scarf to match."

The next day, armed with money from Mama, we went to the local wool shop. We bought dusty pink and pale blue wool and set to work, furiously knitting away in secret corners, out of Mama's sight.

Such industry was rewarded, in no time at all the presents were finished and safely hidden away. We were ready for our next project.

"What are we going to do about the others' presents?" asked Anita.

"We're going to make toys in the handwork lessons at school," I said "I'll make something for Addy, and I know what I'm making for you, but it's a surprise."

"How about Papa and Eberhard?" asked Anita.

They were more of a problem, Mama said she was knitting them some gloves, so that was out. Eventually we settled on little writing wallets covered in wallpaper, after all, they would be useful if nothing else.

At school I started making a toy dwarf for Addy, with bits and pieces garnered from the kindergarten bit box, in which we were allowed to rummage. For his beard I used sheeps' wool gathered from the hedges. I worked on it at school and in the evenings when Addy was in bed. For Anita, I made a wool holder from cardboard covered in material, having got the idea out of an old fashioned book, '*The Little Girls' Sewing Book*'. It was described in the book as 'the ideal present for Grandmother'!

On December 12th all the camp schools closed following an outbreak of scarlet fever in Port Erin. It suited us fine, deep as we were in our Christmas preparations.

Gaily we helped to decorate the lounge with paper chains and baubles that the Hislop's had provided. How festive it all looked.

Somewhere outside our enclosed little world the war was still going on, as Marianne and her news notebook would remind us, and occasionally the air raid warning would sound. Then we would all go and sit in the Hislop's cosy kitchen until the all clear went. There we would sit in the semi-dark, a candle flickering on the table and Mr Hislop would stoke up the fire in the old fashioned range to get a good blaze going to boil the kettle so that there would be cups of tea all round.

A funny world indeed, Germans probably dropping bombs on English people somewhere on the other side of the Irish Sea, while on the Isle of Man, a kindly Manx couple was keeping 'the enemy' warm and comfortable.

So, in spite of war, internment family separation and being far from home, for us the build-up towards Christmas was nearly as exciting as in those, now seemingly, far-off pre-war days. Then came 24th December, our first Christmas Eve away from home. It turned out to be a day to remember.

Exactly as at home, the lounge was out of bounds. The two young women at our table were in charge, "Any presents can be wrapped and left outside the door;" they informed us at breakfast.

Excitedly, Anita and I rushed into our chilly bedroom and parcelled our gifts in pretty wrapping paper - we were too engrossed to feel the cold. Mama had bought small gifts for Margot and the other women, inexpensive little combs in cases, pocket mirrors and handkerchiefs, which when wrapped had hand-painted labels tied on. They looked festive and pretty. We carried our quite considerable pile downstairs and placed them outside the lounge door. Was I imagining it, or was that really the sweet scent of pine tree coming from behind the closed door?

In the early afternoon there was a special meeting with the men from Douglas at the Ballaqueeny as usual. There was a festive air about the place, as we sat at long tables and tea was served. Mama had bought special cream cakes for us. We handed over our wrapped presents for Papa and Eberhard with strict instructions that they were not to be unwrapped until they were back in Douglas.

Returning to Blair Atholl we waited impatiently for tea, for after that the celebrations would commence. At tea time a lovely surprise awaited us in the dining room. The electric lights had been switched off and each table was illuminated by two candles arranged in a double strand of tinsel which sparkled prettily in the candlelight. A simple decoration, but so effective.

The food tasted exceptionally good. After the meal Kathe and Edith at our table announced that all was ready upstairs, but would we please wait in our rooms until we heard the bell. Full of happy anticipation we went up to our room and in no time at all the bell tinkled and we ran downstairs into the lounge.

What a sight met our eyes! There, in the window, stood a small real fir tree fully decorated and with seemingly dozens of candles illuminating it, and the whole room. The scent of the fir tree combined with that of the candles was just like at home. It really was Christmas at last.

Margot and Addy, both staying up late especially, squealed with delight then stood entranced, the candles reflected in their wondering eyes. They both could probably not remember last Christmas. One of the women, in red dressing gown, red cap and lashings of cotton wool about her face, came into the room announcing in gruff tones that 'here comes the Weihnachtsmann'. The two little ones gazed at her with some apprehension, which was soon dispelled as she handed them a chocolate. She then proceeded to the tree and with much wit and laughter handed out the parcels to all and sundry. There was something for everyone, even Owl and Dusty, the hatchet buried for Christmas had given each other small peace offerings. We sang all our favourite German Christmas songs and carols. Mr and Mrs Hislop and their little boy Johnny were brought up to receive the gifts we had for them.

It was all so happy and cordial, proving once again that people are people wherever they are, and not nationalities. The candles guttered out one by one, the little ones were put to bed and another treat awaited us in the shape of a hot spicy fruit tea punch and little home-made cakes to round off the evening. We left our presents under the tree and sleepily went to our beds. All in all, I thought contentedly, it's been a lovely Christmas, nearly like home. What the other women's thoughts were I didn't know; on the surface they had all seemed happy and smiling.

Looking back, I should imagine those smiles hid aching hearts. The two young women who had so gaily organised our celebrations both had loved ones, husband and fiancé in Australia. They had been on the ill-fated Arandora Star, but fortunately rescued and taken to the other side of the world. The only contact they had with them was infrequent letters, and later one wrote that Christmas Day had been very hot and the men in their camp had made a Christmas tree out of a broomstick!

Christmas Day for us was memorable too. We all discovered small gifts from the Hislop's hanging on our tree. Mama had a powder compact, Anita and I each a pocket mirror with a picture of Port St Mary on the back, and Addy had two hankies with pictures of dogs and cats. Then came a fantastic Christmas dinner with all the trimmings, goose and Christmas pudding.

In the afternoon all internees were invited to a party in Ballaqueeny and again there was lots to eat. Food seems to have been the top priority in my life at that time, for my diary is full of references to it! Tea at Blair Atholl was by candlelight again, and, wonder of wonders, there was a trifle with real cream and sherry on every table.

We were particularly well-cared for by the Hislops on the meagre allowance they received for us, and compared with some of the other houses we really seemed to be the favoured ones.

So the year of Our Lord 1940 drew to its close. It had been an enormously eventful year for our family. What would 1941 bring? Peace to the world? Freedom for us? If others speculated and wondered about the New Year, Anita and I most certainly did not. We were far more concerned about whether or not we would get Mama's birthday present finished in time for the 1st of January.

42. ENEMY ALIEN!

New Year's Eve, for us in Blair Atholl, was celebrated with much fun and laughter. After a candlelit tea there were party games in the lounge, everyone joining in. Once again, there was plenty of hot fruit punch to drink. I suspect that Mr Hislop must have laced it with something stronger than lemonade, for by the time we drank our toast to the New Year we were quite hilarious. We also wished each other a happy New Year, with much clinking of tea cups. Then everybody wished Mama a happy birthday. She hadn't had such a birthday eve celebration for years, and vowed she would never forget it. Finally, we all went off to bed. Anita wrote in her diary that she 'got drunk'.

Mama's birthday dawned grey and cold, with an icy wind that brought snow later in the day. After breakfast we wrapped Mama's present in a piece of pretty paper left over from Christmas and presented it to her in the bedroom. We had between us knitted her a pair of navy blue knickers, with an air force blue trim. Owl had given us the idea; she had knitted herself a pair and proudly paraded them for all to see. She would pass the pattern to anyone interested she said, and could highly recommend them. So Anita and I had asked her advice on the mysteries of shaping, gussets, and so on. Owl was pleased to help us, for under her rather forbidding exterior there beat quite a kindly heart.

Mama was delighted with her new undergarments and as it was such a cold day she donned them at once and paraded before us. We eyed them critically and approved. They stretched down almost to the knee looking warm and cosy, but screamingly funny.

"This style," Mama informed us, "is known as equestrian!"

We shrieked with laughter, they really were a comical sight.

"I'd rather be warm and look funny," said Mama, pulling on her slacks, "than have a cold bottom. Thank you both, they're lovely. Are you going to knit yourselves some now?"

"Never!" we screamed in chorus.

That day for dinner we had goose and wine, candles on the table again, and everyone in a festive mood. Mama had wound a strand of tinsel in her hair. How lucky she is, I thought, to have her birthday on New Year's Day.

In the afternoon a note arrived for me; I was to present myself the following morning at 10 am at the camp office. Wondering what it was all about I went there after breakfast, and was handed a form to fill in. I was told that as I was now sixteen years old I was officially registered as an 'enemy alien'. I was also to have my photo taken, so was to go on the 17th January to a photographer in Port Erin.

I set off alone on the appointed day. It had snowed the day before, but now the sun was shining as I walked along my favourite top road, marvelling at the winter wonderland. Coming into Port Erin I saw a remarkable sight. Over the sea could be seen quite clearly the snow-covered Mountains of Mourne. With the sun shining on them, every shadowy valley and brilliant peak showed up. But I couldn't enjoy looking at them just yet.

I found the photographer and presented the piece of paper I had been given. The photographer was dour and taciturn. He arranged me on a wooden chair which stood before a white sheet. Then he handed me a row of numbers to hold in front of my chest. He did nothing to put me at my ease or to make me smile. I felt an utter fool and wished I was miles away. The camera clicked, and there I was, held forever in a hideous photograph – my expression sullen, eyes shadowed, mouth grimly set. This charming picture was to adorn my alien's registration document.

It is a miracle I wasn't deported there and then as a highly undesirable alien and shipped back via some neutral country, to the bosom of my reluctant, fiercely resisting Fatherland!

However, it was over and done with, and I was out again in the crisp air. The sky seemed bluer than before, the snow whiter, and I could gaze at the lovely Mountains of Mourne to my heart's content. I took the lower road back to Port St Mary, and seeing the fields so pristine and unsullied decided to cut across them, instead of going all the way round by Four Roads. The snow was dazzling and totally unmarked, I was the sole person about, my tracks were the only ones. No house overlooked the fields, and the relief of the photo ordeal being behind me, and the sheer joy of the snow and the beauty around me went to my head. I started running around in circles making huge foot print patterns. I flung myself on my back and, swirling my arms and legs around, made eagle shapes in the snow, as we had learned to do in the soft white sand beside the Baltic Sea, ages ago. The snow was a shambles by the time I had finished. An observer from the air would have thought an ant had gone berserk. It was no ant, it was only enemy alien number 928,265 gone temporarily, but completely mad!

The weather after Christmas had become colder and colder. Our sheepskin rugs now lay on top of us and we slept under them as cosily as Eskimos in their igloos. The lounge never seemed to get warm – these days, once the fire had established itself, it was replenished only with a kind of coal dust called 'slack' which produced little, if any, heat.

To cap it all, every evening at nine o'clock sharp, Owl would heave herself out of her chair, go to her bedroom and return with a pile of blankets and a brick. The brick she would push into the heart of the fire into what little glow remained. The blankets were heaped in a great pile in the hearth, where Owl would constantly turn them to ensure that every square inch was warmed.

Between the other women it was referred to as the 'Wollberg", the wool mountain, and it effectively blocked out any vestige of heat that might still have emanated from the fire. One of the women once dared to remonstrate with Owl over this practice.

"It's cold enough in this room without your blankets covering up the heat," she said, "surely they can't be that cold? What if we all wanted to warm our blankets by the fire?"

There was a slight shocked silence at such boldness, but Owl kept calm.

She fixed the speaker with a baleful glance, and said icily, "When you have rheumatism as badly as I have, and know the agony of getting into a cold bed, then I will discuss the matter with you. Until then, you don't know what you're talking about."

There was nothing anyone could reply to that. Owl's bedding took longer to air that night, and when she was finally satisfied that it was warm enough she rose with exaggerated stiffness, deftly removed the brick with a poker and wrapped it in brown paper. Then, with much groaning and sighing gathered the Wollberg to her ample bosom, in a small martyred voice wished everybody goodnight and left the room.

Our life had settled down to a comfortable routine. Anita and I went regularly to school on weekdays, and there were weekends and occasional afternoons off for shopping and going on long walks. Only when the Manx winds were especially strong were the schools closed. Then the heavy storm doors of Blair Atholl would be firmly shut and if for any reason one had to venture out, the back door was used.

We had our regular meetings with the men, either at the Villa Marina, Douglas, when the train journeys were an added delight, or at the Ballaqueeny. Tea was always provided, but we bought our own cakes.

All good things come to an end, even the Manx winter, although it took its time. The sheepskin rugs went back to their rightful place, on the floor. The days lengthened and became perceptibly warmer, and with the spring came the first crop of rumours. There was going to be a family camp. It was going to be in Peel or Ramsey or Onchan. It was the prime topic of conversation at the Ballaqueeny meetings.

"Wouldn't it be nice," said Mama wistfully, "if we could get a little house, just for the six of us."

We made plans of what we would do in our little house for six! All the time we now heard of women being released. The first to go from Blair Atholl was Martha. We were all up early to wave her off. Her going left a vacancy for a news listener with Marianne, who announced that evening that this highly-coveted privilege was on offer, and who would like to accompany her? She stood back and waited for the rush. There were no takers.

"I would have thought," she said huffily, "there would have been more interest, in a house full of intelligent women." Dolly and Gertrude's mother rose with a false air of eager anticipation. "I'll go," she said, "I just didn't want to push myself forward in case someone else wanted to go."

No one was taken in, we knew she only offered herself so as not to hurt Marianne's feelings. She was a kind gentle soul. Satisfied Marianne led her victim downstairs to the hallowed radio. Dolly and Gertrude's mother did her best by trying to show the same interest in the news that Marianne did, but her heart was not in it. She was not always around, she was busy elsewhere, she was having an early night, she was in the middle of a complicated knitting pattern. Finally, Marianne got the message and went down alone accompanied only by her little notebook. Everybody was quite relieved at the outcome, and no more was said about a second pair of ears at the news bulletin.

The spring also brought, less pleasant things than bluebells and primroses. The air raid warnings went almost every night as German planes began their relentless bombings of Liverpool. We no longer went down to the Hislop's kitchen. We lay cosily in our beds waiting for the all clear to go. Sometimes we were asleep long before, and sometimes it was the all clear that woke us. The poor people of Liverpool were not quite so lucky. Some nights the raids were so heavy that even Blair Atholl shook.

Dolly, Gertrude and their mother were the next to be released – we were up at six, waving a towel out of the back bedroom window, as the little train chugged past the field behind the house, while Owl yodelled at the top of her voice.

There were no new women billeted in Blair Atholl, for now it had been officially decided that Port St Mary would become the family camp, and Port Erin would have the remaining women.

Easter Sunday fell on the 13th April that year. School had broken up the week before and we were on holiday. Every day we saw women leaving for their new billets in Port Erin, and we waited to see what would happen to us. Marianne was released, no one bothered with the news anymore, for there was far more excitement taking place around us. Mama heard from the office that we four would be moving to Port Erin too. We were not scheduled for the mixed camp yet, we were to go back to Bradda Glen.

Anita and I couldn't believe our luck, even Mama was quite pleased. Bradda Glen in summer was the ideal place, and summer was just around the corner. We packed up some of our things, borrowed Johnny Hislop's old pram, and took the first load to Bradda Glen. The Manager received us kindly.

"Welcome back!" he greeted us cordially, "put your things in this little room behind the office as I can't give you any rooms yet. So many women are leaving and moving around that I don't know what I've got for you till they're all settled. By the time you come to stay we'll be all sorted out." We walked back in a state of pure joy.

"Perhaps," said Anita, "we'll get one of those little cottages in the woods, all to ourselves."

"Keep your fingers crossed," said I, and we did, all the way to Port St Mary. But crossing our fingers didn't help, for the very next day Mama was summoned to the office and told we were to stay in Blair Atholl. Our family was to be in, the

279

mixed camp after all! Back we went to Bradda Glen to retrieve our bits and pieces.

We were the only ones left in Blair Atholl now, and Mrs Hislop told Mama that she could choose whichever rooms we wanted. So Mama chose the big front bedroom for herself, Papa and Addy, Anita and I would have our old room to ourselves, while Eberhard would have Owl's little single room. We spent a happy day arranging our things.

Mr and Mrs Hislop moved our big dining table into the bay window.

"Might as well have the best place in the room, seeing you've been here the longest," said Mr Hislop.

For a whole week we were the only guests at Blair Atholl, and we loved it.

Soon, our comings and goings into Port Erin and Port St Mary village were to be restricted, for only the houses and hotels on St Mary's Promenade were to be used for the mixed camp. New barbed wire fences were being put up behind the back lane. Already a barrier had been erected across the end of the promenade with a little guard room, as yet unmanned. Until the men arrived we were still free to come and go as we wished

It was 2nd May, and I decided I would make the most of these last days of freedom, and wandered off down the main street of Port St Mary. It was already warm for the time of year. Sea and sky almost merged in a pale hazy blue. A midday stillness had descended over the village; nobody was about, I was the only one, or so it seemed. I leaned on a wall, gazing out over the harbour – it was so still even the seagulls were quiet. Far away, above the big bay beyond Gansey, a small plane droned indolently. I idly watched its progress.

Then suddenly, my heart missed a beat. The little plane, so happily buzzing along in the summer sky did a sudden nose-dive into the sea. All that was visible now was its tail sticking up out of the calm sea. I stood, shocked and horrified. Perhaps I hadn't seen it properly, perhaps it was just my imagination. But no, there was the rear end, definitely sticking out, and as I looked around, the village street was still deserted.

Nobody had noticed it but me, or so I thought. What should I do? Go to the Police Station just up the road, or what? I stood, undecided. I thought of the young airmen trapped in the cockpit, probably struggling to get out. I felt very cold and shivery and totally helpless. The beauty of the day, the peace that had surrounded me a few minutes ago were gone. All I wanted to do was go back to Blair Atholl. Feeling sick at heart, and angry with myself for doing absolutely nothing at all about it, I hurried back.

Before I had reached Blair Atholl however, a siren wailed, and a short time later I saw the lifeboat take off, speeding across the still waters to the stricken plane.

"Too late, too late," I thought sadly, "but thank goodness."

Obviously people who lived round the bay had seen the accident too, and raised the alarm. Feeling reassured, I went in search of my family to tell them what I had seen.

The horror of it all remained with me for a long time. To think that life could end so quickly, on a beautiful summer's day. It wasn't even an air battle, just a little routine training flight.

Later, they brought the remains of the plane on to Port St Mary's beach. The battered nose end, with its controls still visible, lay in a corner under the lower promenade wall, with a Special Constable on guard until it was removed. We leaned over the wall, and gazed at it with ghoulish interest.

Two men, we heard, had died in it. Two poor souls, I thought, struggling uselessly with all those levers and dials, trying to get the plane back in the air again, then, drowning, trapped in that tiny space. Later, a trawler brought in the wings lashed across its bows, and deposited them on the beach. A couple of lorries removed the wreckage at low tide, and for us the summer went on.

That brief episode was the nearest I ever got to the real horror of war, yet it was totally unconnected with any warlike activities.

43. "WHO SHOULD WIN THE WAR"

Every day now, women with children, bag and baggage were moving from Port Erin into their new quarters in Port St Mary. We waited expectantly to see who would be joining us in Blair Atholl.

They finally arrived on the 7th May. There were only five. First to come was a lively, rosy-cheeked young woman. Later, a mother with a 15 year old daughter, Elisabeth, arrived.

We were just sitting down to lunch when there was a commotion at the front door and Mrs Hislop ushered in a mother and a four-year old child, Ingrid. We all got to know each other over lunch. They were all very friendly and amenable.

The following day, Mrs Hislop embarked on a vigorous spring clean of the whole house. Even I was roped in as we dusted, swept, polished, cleaned the silver and scoured the bathroom fittings. I think we all enjoyed it, the young rosy-cheeked girl, Margarete, had a ready wit, and kept us all entertained with her comments. At last the house, shining and sparkling, was ready and waiting for the men.

The men from Ramsey camp had arrived on the 8th May. We had heard a great cheering and left our cleaning to see what was going on outside. What was going on, was a long line of men with luggage, flanked by escorts in uniform, converging on the barrier at the village end of the promenade.

Word spread like wildfire. "The Ramsey men are here!" and out of the houses streamed the women and children whose men had been in the Ramsey camp. There was much laughing, shouting and screaming of the children, as the men's escorts stood by rather helplessly. But order was soon restored as newly reunited families, clutching each other happily, disappeared into the various houses and hotels on the promenade.

We, in Blair Atholl, had to wait until the 12th of May before the Douglas and Onchan camps sent their men to the mixed camp. Thus it came about, exactly a year to the day that they were taken from us in Hull, Papa and Eberhard were returned to the bosom of their family.

With the arrival also of the other three men, Blair Atholl was full once more. But what a change from a house full of women! No more bickering over ginger buns, the Owl's nest, or the Wollberg. No more Schweigestunde and no more nine o'clock news visits.

There was quite a party-like atmosphere in the lounge in the evenings, as the men swapped stories about the life in their camps. Margarete's husband had, like her, a lively sense of humour, and Elisabeth's father, who had been a lawyer in Berlin, had a dry, witty way of expressing himself.

The mixed camp now had its own Commandant, Mr Cuthbert. He was a mild, kindly gentleman, who became very popular with the internees. A totally different kettle of fish from the formidable Dame Joanna.

Mr Cuthbert himself called to see me one day. I went shyly downstairs to see what this august personage could possibly want with me. He told me that as I was now sixteen I was due to go before a tribunal and would I please call at the office later in the day and fill in some forms. The office was in the house next door, so I did as requested and was informed that the tribunal was fixed for the 20th May. It would be in Douglas and Mama could accompany me. I rushed back upstairs, two at a time, to tell the others the news.

The evening before the great day I put my curlers in with more care than usual. A good impression was essential, I thought, after all one didn't have a tribunal every day. Anita watched me screwing the metal contraptions into my soaking wet hair.

"What will they do with you?" she asked.

"Do?" I replied airily, "nothing – Mama says they just ask you some questions, that's all."

"What sort of questions?" Anita wanted to know.

"Oh, things like where you were born and so on."

" Why can't they ask you those here in the Office? Why go all the way to Douglas?" insisted Anita.

"I don't know, but everyone has to go before a tribunal when they're over sixteen and an enemy alien."

"Will I have one when I'm sixteen?" persisted Anita.

"No, you're British-born."

I finished my ministrations to my hair and peered anxiously at my face in the mirror. Was that a spot about to appear on my chin? Surely not! Not just in time for my tribunal. I rubbed the offending place angrily.

"Are you getting a spot?" asked Anita with sisterly concern, she never suffered with the hateful things.

"I hope not," I said, getting into bed, "goodnight, we have to be up early."

"Put some spit on it," suggested Anita kindly, "it might go away in the night."

I knew it wouldn't, but I rubbed spit on it just in case.

The next morning Mama woke me, bright and early.

"It's a beautiful day," she said, "and it's going to be warm, so wear your pink and blue summer dress, and take a cardigan."

I got out of bed unwillingly, now that the day had arrived at last I wasn't so eager anymore. On my pillow lay a metal curler. Oh no! I looked at it in dismay, that meant one strand of uncurled hair. Today of all days.

Mama put her head round the door. "Hurry up," she said, "Mrs Hislop's got our breakfast ready," and off she went downstairs.

I put on my dress which looked fresh and pretty, combed out my hair and tried to arrange the lank, straight tress under the curly ones. The spot, luckily, didn't seem to be developing at all. I pinched my cheeks to make them pinker, and practised a few smiles. Anita stirred under the bedclothes, and mumbled something.

"I'm off now," I said, but she was already asleep again.

"Lucky thing," I thought, and trailed down to the dining room.

Like the last meal of a condemned man, there was bacon and egg for breakfast, an unheard of treat. I ate it with relish and had just finished when there was a knocking at the front door. Mrs Hislop appeared in the dining room with a tall policeman.

"I'm here to take you to the station," he told Mama, "we have to leave now to catch the train."

I picked up my cardigan and Mama and I set off with our escort. We walked through the barrier and down the road to the station, the policeman and Mama making desultory conversation about the weather. The little train came puffing along and stopped. The policeman put Mama and me into a compartment by ourselves.

"You'll be met at Douglas," he said, and went back to Port St Mary and his usual duties.

The journey to Douglas was always a delight, a rare treat. This early morning with the sun already shining brightly, was no exception. We sat in our respective corners, gazing out at the ever-changing scenery, thinking our own thoughts.

"What will it be like?" I wondered.

The journey seemed shorter than usual and all too soon we arrived at Douglas. We alighted from the train and with the other passengers went through the ticket barrier, where another policeman awaited us. He accompanied us through the streets of Douglas. People glanced at us as we passed – at least I thought they did. I felt important.

We reached a large building and went inside. Our escort took us into a waiting room and left us. As we sat there on the polished seats in the empty room I could feel my courage sinking into my shoes. I didn't feel important any more, I felt gauche and silly.

"Will you come in with me?" I whispered to Mama.

"Yes, of course," she said. I felt more cheerful at that.

After what seemed like hours, the door opened and our escort returned.

"This way please," he said and led us to another room.

I forced my shaking legs to carry me, and clutched at Mama's arm.

"It's all right," she whispered, "it will only take a few minutes."

The room we were ushered into was panelled in dark wood; it was probably some sort of council chamber. Three elderly men sat in a row behind a desk facing us, one of them wearing full uniform. I ventured a feeble smile which was ignored. I could feel myself blushing at this rebuff. No need to have pinched my cheeks, I would be as red as a beetroot in a minute.

Mama and I settled on two hard wooden chairs opposite the awesome trio! The policeman took up his position behind us at the door. Complete silence reigned. I could hear my heart thumping loudly in my ears, my mouth felt dry, and my face burned as with a fever. I gazed stonily at the floor, there was a rustle of paper, and a voice spoke.

"You are Rosemarie Dalheim?" it boomed into the silence.

I looked up and licked my lips to reply.

"Yes!" squeaked a tiny shrill voice. It must have been mine, I had never heard anything so silly. I wanted to giggle, but was too frightened even to do that. The booming voice, which emanated from the middle gentleman, went on.

"You are interned with your parents, are you not?"

The little voice squeaked assent.

"If you were released without your parents would you have anywhere to go?"

"No," I said briefly, and not quite so squeakily, my confidence returning, it wasn't so awful after all.

"Are you still at school?" asked one of the others.

I was getting bolder, my blushing had subsided and I felt more at ease.

"Yes," I replied in a more normal voice.

It would soon be over, and we could go back to Port St Mary. Then the uniformed gentleman spoke for the first time.

"Who do you want to win the war?" he barked.

It was a ridiculous question for a man of his rank to ask a terrified sixteen year old schoolgirl. In fact, looking back, the whole tribunal was like a scene in a comic opera.

One would have thought that three grown men would have better things to do during a war.

I stared at him in consternation, this question, so unexpected, so unprepared for, took my breath away. I had never really thought about it, it was too complicated, too complex. It was all a question of divided loyalties - my true answer would probably have been both, which was impossible. At that moment I wanted more than anything in the world for Germany to be victorious, just to spite the man who had asked this stupid thing. It seemed as though the whole universe held its breath as it waited for my answer!

I crossed my fingers surreptitiously. Into the awful silence the silly, squeaky voice piped treacherously, "England!"

I felt as if I had betrayed everybody, family, ancestors, the whole German nation.

"I don't mean it!" I screamed silently at them all, "you know I don't, but what else could I say?"

The uniformed gentleman had, however, not finished with me. His second question was even more devastating than his first.

"Why?" he snapped.

Up to now, all my answers had been monosyllabic, but this question required a little more. With a detached kind of horror, I heard the little voice go burbling on, perjuring my soul with every word it uttered.

"Well, I've always lived in England, all my life nearly." My throat seemed to close up, I made a sort of clicking sound, then the reedy little pipe prattled relentlessly on.

"I mean, I don't really know Germany well, I've not really lived there you know, I've always lived in England, nearly all my life, you see."

It was like a record with the needle stuck.

"I only know Germany from holidays, really."

I could feel my chin beginning to quiver strangely and my teeth starting to chatter. I clamped my mouth shut, and thought "I can't say any more, I can't." But the three wise monkeys sitting there seemed to have lost interest in me. I doubt if they even heard my ramblings. They were probably thinking of their lunch. They whispered together and gathered up their papers.

The spokesman cleared his throat, and announced, "Interned until further review," or words to that effect.

I was past hearing or caring. It was all over, and two minutes later we were out in the bright sunshine among the shoppers in the Douglas streets. As we walked to the railway station with our escort a few paces behind us, Mama made bright normal conversation, which I barely heard. I was thinking of all the silly things I'd said, and of all the brilliant and clever things I should have said. Suddenly, I just wished we could go back home to Sunny Bank and lead a normal life, where wars were just things that dear old Tinny rambled on about, while we sat in our desks at Newland and giggled and nudged each other, far more interested in her eccentric ways than any boring old wars.

Back on the train I stared gloomily out of the window still brooding over what I had said, in my mind's eye seeing generations of past Dalheims and Schmidts rise facelessly out of graves, shocked by my betrayal. I saw battalions of German soldiers, young and handsome in their grey-green uniforms, stare at me accusingly. Would they ever forgive me?

"I had to say it," I cried silently to them, "what else could I say?" Still they hung about. "If I'd said Germany I might have been shot!" I added dramatically, which I didn't believe myself, but the ghosts seemed appeased, and faded away.

I settled back in my seat to enjoy the passing Manx countryside. It was past lunchtime I noted, looking at my watch. I felt enormously hungry and hoped Mrs Hislop had saved us enough food, with a bit of luck it might even be syrup sponge day.

As Mama and I sat down to our belated lunch, the rest of the family crowded, round for the news.

"What was it like?" asked Anita.

"All right," I replied nonchalantly.

"What sort of things did they ask you then?"

"A lot of silly things, like who should win the war!" said Mama, putting the whole affair into its right perspective.

"What did you say to that?" asked Anita.

"I hope you said England," said Papa, "otherwise things could get awkward."

"Of course I did," I said, tucking into the pudding, which joy of joys was syrup sponge, "I daren't say anything else."

"Did they believe you?" wondered Anita.

"I suppose so," said I.

"Anyway," said Mama, "it doesn't make the slightest difference what you said. The main thing is you're still interned and we're all together in Port St Mary."

I looked round at my family clustered about me, and out of the window to the green cliffs and blue sea beyond. Mama was right as usual – family and being together was all that really mattered, and what nicer place could there be than Port St Mary on a sunny May afternoon?

"Can we take Addy down to Gansey?" I asked.

"Yes, as soon as she wakes up," said Mama, taking the dishes into the kitchen.

Later, as we sat on the sun-warmed rocks at Gansey beach, Anita and Addy picked up the little yellow shells and made pictures with them, but I still ruminated over the mornings events.

"If Germany did win the war, we'd be all right anyway," I said to Anita's back. She didn't even bother to turn round.

"Why?" she asked.

"Because we're German, of course," I replied.

Anita arranged a pile of shells into a flower shape.

"I'm not," she reminded me, "I'm British-born!"

"You're both," I said, "you can choose, you and Addy, you can be just what you want. It depends.

"Depends on what?" asked Anita.

"On who wins the war," said I.

Anita lost all interest in tribunals and wars.

"Addy," she said, "can you find me some more shells in this orangey colour?"

The two of them searched among the rocks. I leaned back against the sea wall and gave the problem one more thought.

"If Germany wins," I muttered vengefully, "I'll have a list, that's what I'll have, a list of people to get even with. Top of the list will be those three daft men."

Feeling that I had satisfactorily settled the score between me and my interrogators, I jumped up and joined in the search for the pretty shells. Life was good again, and carefree, and happiness was looking for orangey shells in the warm rock pools at Gansey.

But, waking in the middle of that night, a thought struck me, a thought so terrible that I sat up in bed in a panic. One of those men had been writing down everything I said, I was sure of that. If Germany won the war, and that damning piece of evidence was found I would certainly not be 'all right'. I huddled under the bedclothes.

"It would be better for me," I thought traitorously, "if England won," and on this treacherous note of self-preservation, I fell asleep. I was definitely not the martyr type!

44. "PEOPLE SHOULDN'T DIE IN THE SUMMER"

My tribunal was behind me, the long summer stretched ahead, and I could now concentrate on more important things in life, like clothes. I contemplated the meagre contents of my wardrobe, all two of them. There was my 'tribunal' dress, which was one of Mama's altered to fit me, and my blue and white Newland dress, roomily cut to allow for girlish growth, which would probably fit forever! But I had outgrown all other things, and they were now waiting for Anita to grow into them. Mama, I decided, would have to do something about it, and Mama said that she would think about it. Her problem was soon solved, for an acquaintance from the house next door offered to sell Mama some of her teenage daughter's outgrown clothes.

Mama jumped at the chance. "Anneliese's mother," she told me, "is going to bring round some of Anneliese's clothes for you to try on later, and if they fit we can buy them."

Anneliese, in my opinion, wore lovely clothes, so I was pleased at the prospect too.

The next day Mama met me on the stairs as I came in after a walk.

"The clothes have come," she said, "they're all in your bedroom."

"What are they like?" I asked Mama, following her in happy anticipation.

"Some are quite nice," said Mama, "you'll see."

I certainly did see! The minute I entered the bedroom and saw the clothes spread out on the two beds! Everything seemed to be in a hideous sage green of different shades. I stopped, horrified.

"It's all green, not even a pretty green," I said disappointedly, "don't buy any of them!"

"Anneliese went to a boarding school where the uniform was this green," explained Mama, "but not everything is green – look."

On closer inspection, there were indeed one or two things I liked. A very pretty multi-coloured summer dress, a lilac cardigan with gold buttons, a tartan skirt and a white short-sleeved jumper. These were all I wanted, even though the skirt was too big and slightly baggy.

Mama had other ideas. "Not the cardigan," she said firmly, "lilac is for old ladies," and to my everlasting regret, she put it aside.

"These green clothes are not really all that bad," Mama went on, holding them up. First a ghastly green wool dress, with short sleeves which fitted well, but the colour did nothing for my complexion.

"It will be nice and warm with a cardigan," said Mama, "and I'll buy some pretty buttons to brighten it up."

The next dress was even worse. It was a hideous spinach green in a sort of ribbed crepe, which also had short sleeves. It totally drained me of any colour. The front opening gaped unbecomingly, and there seemed to be no form of fastening.

"You can fasten it with a brooch," said Mama, "there's that pretty rose one."

She rummaged in a drawer and brought out a little pink glass rose that she had bought for about sixpence. She pinned up the offending neck. "Lovely," she said standing back admiringly.

It was anything but lovely!

All that now remained was a straight skirt with a kick pleat at the back, with a blazer to match. The school crest had been removed from the top pocket and it showed a darker shade of the quite horrible bilious green of the outfit. ,

"Not that!" I pleaded, "I'll never, ever wear it."

There was a knock on the door, Anneliese's mother stood there, beaming. "Well," she said, "are they suitable?"

Mama picked up the green suit and the lilac cardigan.

"I'll have all the things except these," she said, "how much?"

"Give me ten shillings."

Mama handed over the money, and Anneliese's mother picked up the rejects and went towards the door. Then she hesitated – she wasn't going to be lumbered with the green suit either. She put it back on the bed.

"We'll put that in with the others," she said with false generosity, "it's pure wool, and will be good for the winter."

She left, clutching the lilac cardigan.

"Why," I thought crossly, "didn't she put that in too?" I couldn't win. "I shan't ever wear that green thing," I said defiantly.

"We'll see," said Mama, hanging my new acquisitions into the wardrobe, "it would look nice with the white jumper."

As it turned out, I did wear the skirt, reluctantly, and it didn't look too bad worn with the white jumper. The blazer I wore about twice, and then Mama realised it was a hopeless case, and gave it away later to some poor deserving wretch in the women's camp.

Life in the mixed camp proceeded happily and peacefully. It was really like a family holiday without an end. The housework, shared among the women, was no great burden. The men did the washing up, and Elisabeth, Eberhard and I peeled mountains of potatoes every evening. The rest of the time was all our own. We had shopping expeditions into the village twice weekly, and everybody went. We did not buy that much, we mostly went for the change of scenery. Our purchases consisted mainly of little luxuries, chocolates, cream cakes and most important, cigars for Papa. Papa always said that as long as he had his cigars, he was happy anywhere!

Once a week there were cinema visits to Port Erin, and we rarely missed one. In the camp, much to my delight, a new library opened, and I must have been its best customer. Apart from English books there were German ones too, and these I read with as much enjoyment as the others, for by now my German was greatly improved.

Addy too was well provided for, there was a lovely selection of delightful English and German books for the little ones.

Then the field behind the Ballaqueeny was turned into allotments for the men, and Papa, who loved gardening, was one of the first to acquire one. We helped him dig and prepare the ground, sowed lettuce, radishes, carrots and peas and looked forward to a summer of home-grown vegetables. We even had a little rockery and a patch of colourful flowers. Many a hot, sunny afternoon would we spend sitting on the small 'lawn' in our allotment having a makeshift picnic of lemonade and biscuits. Sitting there in the sunshine with the beautiful scenery all about us, it was hard to believe that there was a war going on, not all that far away. How lucky we were! We heard rumours of air raids over Hull, but did not know the extent of the damage. Yet that summer Hull suffered terribly and many lives were lost. Miraculously, our house had only the windows blown in, but these were boarded up immediately by the authorities and no further damage occurred. So, while the citizens of Hull were being subjected to all sorts of horrors, we – the enemy – had not a care in the world.

Very hot days were spent on the beach and in the sea, for the usually temperamental Manx summer was remarkably good that year.

Our spiritual needs, too, were well catered for. The Jewish community, who all lived in the Ballaqueeny because of their special diet, had their Synagogue in the Town Hall. The Catholics and Protestants had visiting priests and preachers, and services held either in Cowley's Café or in the 'Newlyn' which also housed the doctors' and dentists' surgeries. The services were all held in English and I enjoyed singing all my favourite hymns from Newland. They were far more rousing than the dirges we sang at the German church at home!

To my great delight, the Hislops acquired a black puppy, Jock, and they said we could take him out whenever we wanted to. No puppy ever had more walks than Jock did. I took him out two or three times every day, and pretended he was my very own.

Then my wings were clipped once again, for it was decided that I should continue my studies at Port Erin camp school. So two days a week, an escort of a rather grumpy retired police inspector, marched a small handful of teacher and pupils along the top road to Port Erin. It was mornings only, therefore quite bearable, and I loved the walks there and back, but I didn't really benefit much academically. However, school broke up at the end of July, and we were promised our own Port St Mary school in September.

We in Blair Atholl were all so happy; we integrated well and must have been one of the most harmonious houses in the whole camp. Little did we know that tragedy was soon to strike, and in the most unexpected place.

I came down to breakfast one morning in August, and Margarete was not in her usual place.

"Tummy upset," her husband was telling the others, "I'll take her some porridge." Everyone gave him their favourite remedies – peppermint or camomile tea, no food for a day, just liquids, and so on.

"She'll be all right after a day in bed," said her husband, taking up her porridge.

But she wasn't all right, and the camp doctor, an internee, was called. She thought it might be bladder trouble, and prescribed something or other. Nothing seemed to help, however, and it was decided to take her to hospital in Douglas for observation.

Her husband carried her downstairs and into a waiting car. Her usual rosy face was drawn and pale, but she managed a smile and a wave to us all as we stood on the steps and wished her well. We never saw her again. It turned out that she had a burst appendix which caused peritonitis, and all attempts to save her life failed.

Ingrid's mother, Eberhard and I were sitting on the steps outside the house when the Commandant came up to tell us the sad news. We received it with the usual disbelief at unexpected death.

"It can't be true!" cried Ingrid's mother, "she's too young to die!" and she rushed into the house weeping.

The Commandant stood for a moment, struggling to keep his own emotions under control. "He was with her when she died," he said, as though that was any comfort, and walked through to the back of the house to tell the Hislops.

Eberhard and I sat mutely on the sun-warmed steps, each thinking our own thoughts. I felt numb and cold in spite of the warm afternoon, trying to come to terms with the terrible news. The sky and the sea were as brilliantly blue as before, the sunshine as bright. From the beach below echoed the sounds of laughter and children at play. It was a lovely day. "People shouldn't die in the summer," I thought sadly, "it isn't fair." The days that followed were hushed and silent. The young widower spent most of his time with the Hislops, but when we did see him his face was set and stony, as though carved in marble.

Margarete was buried in the cemetery at Four Roads. The hearse was followed on foot by mourners. It seemed as though half the camp had turned out to pay their last respects.

Later, Mrs Hislop washed Margarete's clothes. Her gaily coloured summer dresses hung on the line in the back garden, the Manx wind billowing out their shape as once her young form had done. I saw them from my bedroom window, and the sight saddened me.

I thought again, "People shouldn't die in the summer, it just isn't fair."

Life slowly returned to normal in Blair Atholl. The young widower, instead of being sent back to the men's camp, was allowed to stay. It was probably felt that he had suffered enough, and to uproot him again would have been downright cruel!

45. THE MATRICULATION EXAMINATION

The promised school did not materialise in September. Perhaps the mixed camp lacked the driving force of a Minna Specht! However, a kindergarten was opened in Cowley's Café, as there seemed to be no lack of under school-age children. We could see them setting off on their little walks, two by two, holding hands. They were in the charge of a middle-aged, rather formidable lady. Mama said that Addy could give it a try after Christmas. She had her third birthday at the end of September, and was now old enough.

If there was no school, there was a variety of classes to attend. There were handicraft lessons twice a week, which I went to regularly, and made all sorts of toys, bags, pin cushions, etc., with the colourful felt and American cloth provided. I got on very well with the teacher and made several extra items for her, which she sold and gave me the money. Riches! It was only sixpence or a shilling at a time, but the first money I had ever 'earned'. There was also an art class. I went twice, but it was not my sort of art, and what's more, I didn't like the teacher, who was very supercilious of my efforts!

Then we had country dancing. This was attended by people of all ages, and as the woman in charge was jolly and outgoing, we had great fun.

By now, Anita and I had nicknames for all the residents in our house, picked after much deliberation, so that if mentioned no one would relate to themselves. Ingrid's parents we called 'Panna and Manna', Elisabeth's father was 'Oak Tree' and her mother was 'Moke'. The young widower we called 'Kalk'.

Addy caused the two of us great embarrassment once when she shouted, "Oak Tree, Oak Tree," as that gentleman entered the room. Oak Tree was very fond of Addy, they would go off together to the library to choose story books. He beamed at her, "What, my child?" he asked kindly.

Anita and I tried in vain to distract Addy.

"Oak Tree!" she shouted again, with a cheeky look at us. "Du bist Oak Tree!"

"Ja, ja," he said, patting her curly head, and Anita and I gave a sigh of relief as Addy stopped shouting and took her latest book for Oak Tree to read.

It wasn't until October 27th, five days before my seventeenth birthday, that some sort of school started in rooms in Cowley's Café. There was an odd collection of teachers, both men and women. In my class there was an assortment of pupils of all ages, which included Anita, who by now was nearly fourteen, and counted as an 'adolescent'.

School was held every morning, but after a week or two the numbers had dwindled in our class. At seventeen, I thought I was really too old to be going to school. That sort of thing was all right for 'swots'. I wondered if, like some of the others, I could opt out. The office however, had great plans for me. One day the teacher who was vaguely in charge, said she wanted to see me after school. Wondering what she wanted, I waited. She told me that the office had decided that I should be allowed to take the Matriculation exam, and gave me some forms to fill in and sign. We discussed subjects and she said the office would provide the necessary books.

Mama and Papa were delighted when I told them. To this day I am amazed that there was such determination by the office to continue the education of such a reluctant, not even brilliant or dedicated scholar as I was! There was even more to come. A small study was provided, with a fire laid every day, where I could pursue my studies in warmth and quiet. I loved my little room, and went every day, reading my set books, sitting close to the fire, toasting my toes. I still wonder why I had such preferential treatment. I was not even 'British-born'!

It was not surprising that I enjoyed my cosy room so much, for, by now the autumn had slipped imperceptibly into winter. Our second winter on the Island. The lovely days of summer were a mere memory. We had forgotten how chilly the winters could be. We were better provided for this year. We wore our 'relief slacks', a free item of clothing issued to every woman who wanted it. These slacks were made in a heavy woollen material and were really beautifully warm. Worn with our hand-knitted jumpers in oiled Manx wool, they kept the icy winds at bay. Mama, Anita and I wore them on weekdays, but on Sundays we donned skirts, and shivered! The sheepskin rugs went back on the beds, and bed-socks in a variety of pastel shades and patterns appeared on our knitting needles to be given as Christmas presents, or to grace our own chilly feet. By now I had made so many gifts in my handicraft classes that I had a boxful under my bed, there was something for everyone, and I looked forward to bestowing them.

As usual, once school broke up we were busy putting the finishing touches to our Christmas presents, sitting in our cold bedroom and demanding that nobody came in without first knocking at the door. I also decided to make a little Christmas tree, just for our family. It was a pretty little concoction of cardboard circles covered with green paper and glitter, decorated with tiny birthday cake candles. Simple enough and extremely effective later, when the candles were lit.

We had the usual school party, with food and presents – this time I received a hand-woven scarf. Once again, Anita and I helped to decorate the lounge with last years' paper chains, but this year we decorated the tree too. Once again, there were candles and tinsel on the dining tables on Christmas Eve. Then we all went up to our own rooms for our family celebrations.

In the big, cold front bedroom I lit the candles on my little tree. It was a tiny source of light and warmth as we passed round our presents to each other. Addy shouting in delight at the dolly she had specially ordered from Father Christmas, and many other things besides. It was, indeed, a far cry from our warm elegant room in Sunny Bank, but we didn't care, for we were together, and it was Christmas and nothing else mattered.

The family celebrations over, we all met in the lounge. The candles on the tree were lit, a fire burned cheerily in the grate, the Hislops joined us, and more presents were handed out. We sang German and English carols and songs, then played party games, and feasted on biscuits and ginger wine.

So ended our third wartime Christmas Eve, and our second in the internment camp. It was a time of much fun and laughter; a time of simple treats and home-made gifts; a time to look back on with great nostalgia. Fifty years later, the real meaning of Christmas seems to have disappeared under the rush, greed and commercialism of the festive season.

On Christmas morning there was a special church service, then we returned to one of Mrs Hislop's Christmas dinners, with crackers, candles and all the extra trimmings that made it memorable. That year my present from the Hislops had been a powder compact, and in honour of the occasion I had powdered my nose, feeling very grown up and sophisticated.

The week between Christmas and the New Year I spent conscientiously reading and re-reading the set books for my exams. I would rather have curled up with a library book, but I realised that the exams were only three weeks away. I had made up my mind that I would pass, come what may, and for the first time in my life took my studies seriously.

New Year's Eve was much the same as before, with new candles lighting up the tree. We played party games and toasted the New Year, 1942, with home-made punch. Everybody wished everybody else a Happy New Year.

Moke said, "Let's hope it's better than the last one, and we'll all be free this time next year."

I pondered her words, and reviewed the past year. All in all, it had been a lovely year, for our family at least. As for being free next year – yes – but only if the war was over by then. Until that day, I was perfectly happy where I was.

Once the New Year celebrations were over my revision went into 'overdrive' to say the least. Never did any one pupil have so much cosseting and tutoring. An English teacher came to my study every morning and went over my English Literature books with me. Mama coached me in German grammar and French. Eberhard concentrated on my maths (always my weakest subject) and I was even given special leave to go out after curfew to visit a teacher who also revised French with me.

The two weekends before the great event I had my breakfasts in bed, and then, because it was the warmest place in the house, stayed in bed, well wrapped up, to continue my reading. A princess could not have had better treatment. In fact, in those three weeks before the exam I worked harder than in all the five years at Newland High!

The great day, Tuesday 13th January, dawned. Wearing my navy, orange and yellow Newland jumper for luck, armed with my freshly-filled fountain pen, and good wishes of everyone in the house, I hurried to my beloved little study to take the first exam, English Language. The invigilator, a woman from the office, was already there, and the fire blazed brightly in the hearth. In the room were two tables neatly set with clean blotters, stacks of lined paper, ink bottles and so on.

"There's a young man coming to take the exam too," said the invigilator, "which table would you like?"

I chose the one nearer the window and wondered who on earth the 'young man' was. He came clattering up the stairs a minute later, a gangling ungainly youth, sweating profusely, with red nose, spots and lanky hair. I was unimpressed. I thought they must have dug him up from the women's camp.

"Now we're all settled," said the invigilator, cosily, handing out our papers, "shall we get started, any questions?"

There were none, so she put an alarm clock on the mantelpiece, consulted it, and said, "Start now!"

She then settled herself in a comfortable chair by the fire and got out her knitting. We turned to our papers and read them through. I loved English and finding the questions to my liking, I began to write, totally absorbed.

Things were not going so smoothly at the next table. There was much sighing and shuffling of feet and rustling of paper, until finally the boy's hand shot up.

"Please," he asked the invigilator, "may I smoke?"

"I don't mind," said the invigilator, "but we must ask the other candidate first." She asked.

The 'other candidate' looked down her snooty little nose, "No," she said firmly, "I don't like smoke," and went on smugly with her writing.

Poor lad! He didn't stand a chance with me, who had been raised on impeccably handsome film stars like Clark Gable and Ronald Colman, who swooned over Errol Flynn, David Niven and Douglas Fairbanks Jr., and other such matinee idols. If he had even remotely resembled one of these gorgeous creatures I would have fallen over backwards to oblige him. He could have chain-smoked all around me! As it was, I resented his very presence, for I wanted to be the only internee taking the Matriculation exam, and I didn't want anyone sharing the limelight! I had no pangs of conscience on denying him his harmless little request then, but now, years later, I feel ashamed at my mean attitude, and wish I had been kinder. Halfway through the exam, coffee and biscuits were brought for all three of us and partaken of with great relish. It must have fortified the young man for he became more settled after that.

As for me, I finished my paper well before time, and with smug satisfaction leisurely read it through before sitting back, folding my arms, and gazing nonchalantly out of the window. I noted, gleefully, that my despised young companion was still struggling to finish before the invigilator said, "Time's up, put your pens down."

We handed in our papers and I went down the road to Blair Atholl and my lunch. The boy fished a packet of squashed sandwiches and his cigarettes out of his jacket pockets. He did not even glance at me as I went past him. Returning after lunch for the first part of the Maths exam, I noticed the window was wide open to dispel any smoke that might offend my delicate nostrils!

This time I was not quite so smart and quick as I struggled with what was my worst subject. My young companion however, never paused in his work, jotting down figures and calculations with speed and precision. It could have been worse, I told myself, as once again, we handed in our papers.

The following day we had Geometry and French. The Geometry theorems were unbelievably elementary and I felt I had done well. The French exam in the afternoon was not too bad. When it was over I breathed a sigh of relief, only two more to go and I would be free.

On Thursday it was German Language and English Literature. As my German was as fluent as my English I completed the paper in no time at all, and this year I was the only candidate. I imagine the boy must have had different subjects which he took at a later date. The invigilator and I were not alone however, for a puppy had followed her in. She asked me if I objected to its presence, which of course I didn't. It played and gambolled about us all afternoon. The atmosphere in the room with the crackling fire, the knitting invigilator in her armchair and the playful puppy was most relaxing, a far cry from Newland exams, with the awful silence and the eagle-eyed, watching teachers. If the surroundings were so different from Newland, the relief when the last exam was over, was exactly the same. It felt as though a weight had been lifted off me as I came out into the cold, fresh Manx air.

"Finished!" I thought rapturously, "no more swotting, no more set books. Now I can read and read and read exactly what I want!"

The camp library was still open. I skipped in, to come out armed with half-a-dozen books, and hurried back to Blair Atholl.

46. TANTE ROSEMARIE

There was not to be as much time for reading as I had imagined after all. For a start, I still went to school most mornings for a variety of unusual lessons: Shorthand, Spanish, German Literature, in which we studied Goethe's Faust, and a strange subject called 'Kunsthistorik', the History of Art, which I neither understood nor was interested in. At least it gave the man who taught it a small extra income, for teachers were paid five shillings a week.

Elisabeth and I had now been 'promoted' to cleaning the stairs, and we beavered away with brushes, dustpans and dusters, on alternate days, except Sundays, which we had off.

On really cold days we spent a lot of time in our beds, reading or knitting! The lounge did not really warm up until the afternoon, and was not the ideal place to sit and read, unless draped in blankets. The lounge fire was Oak Tree's special chosen task, and he would spend ages raking, riddling and husbanding every tiny scrap of cinder to augment the meagre daily coal allowance.

By the afternoon and evening the lounge would be warm enough for us to discard our blankets – all of us except Oak Tree, who really felt the cold. He habitually wore two blankets, one round his waist, the other over his shoulders. Moke knitted him a balaclava helmet to keep his neck and ears warm, and a pair of fingerless gloves so that he could still play his beloved patience. For Oak Tree was a dedicated patience player, his speciality being a double patience that covered half the table. His spare frame shrouded in blankets, his feet cosy in a foot muff, he would sit hour after hour engrossed in the game. Patiences that worked out were always left in neat rows and piles when he went down for meals, whereas a failed patience was scooped into an untidy heap and abandoned as Oak Tree walked away, muttering, "Schlecht gemischt!"

We soon picked up the rules of the game and became addicted players too, pouncing on the coveted packs of cards whenever Oak Tree was otherwise occupied.

Kalk tried to start a bridge four with Papa, Oak Tree and Eberhard. Half the evening he would spend telling the others how they should have played their hands. Once he cried out in exasperation, "This is not a Bridge club! It's a sleep club!" but he struggled on for a while before giving it up as a bad job.

Apart from the weekly visits to the Port Erin cinema there were showings of silent films in one of the large rooms in Cowley's Café. These were accompanied by a gifted pianist, and we never missed one.

Occasionally there were opportunities to meet friends or relations in Port Erin. The meetings were held in the huge semicircular room of Collinson's Café, with its stupendous view of Spaldrick Bay and Bradda Head. Tea was always served, and we provided our own cakes or biscuits, as we chatted away with camp friends, catching up with their news.

Weather permitting, there was a weekly ramble out of the camp confines – we would walk down lovely lanes and footpaths, seeing even more of the southern part of the Island. Anita and I never missed a walk if we could help it. Not only did we enjoy the variety of new places visited, another attraction was the handsome young Special Constable who was one of our regular escorts. He always brought up the rear of the column of walkers, so Anita and I would lag behind the others, which meant he was always on hand to help us over stiles or stepping stones. This would be accompanied by much clutching and girlish shrieks and giggles, totally unnecessary, as we were perfectly able to jump the streams or climb the stiles without assistance. Once, this Adonis gave us each a toffee – Ambrosia could not have tasted better!

Anita had been having piano lessons from a fellow internee in the mixed camp. Being more musically gifted than I, she had, in a few months, reached the stage it had taken me two years struggling to achieve. There was an old piano in the dining room, and in the piano stool we discovered a book of easy duets. Many happy hours we spent tinkling away, and when it became too much for our fellow inmates to bear we would take ourselves off to Cowley's Café and use the piano there, when the kindergarten was not in session.

Addy had started kindergarten after Christmas, and enjoyed going. One of the helpers there was short-tongued, and Addy would amuse us all by singing "Thing a thong of thixpence" and "Little Mith Muffet that on a Tuffet". No amount of teasing or corrections on our part could persuade her to change it. That, as far as she was concerned, was the right way to sing it!

Apart from all these occupations and entertainments we also had to fit in letter writing. Every internee was allocated two letter forms per week. These were made of a strange shiny paper, presumably to reject invisible ink, and our family having four fully-fledged internees between us collected eight forms from the office every Monday morning. They cost us not a penny to send to anywhere in the world. We wrote 'Internee Mail – Postage Free' across the top and did not waste a single one.

We wrote to Tante Hanny and Tante Agnes in Berlin, to Mane and Leo in Hannover, and friends back in Hull. We received letters back from Germany via a neutral country and all had been opened by censor. There was a large sticker on, to remind us. Not that we could have written anything that would have changed the course of the war. We wrote about things dear to our hearts, the little everyday happenings, the cute things Addy said and did, the flowers we found on our walks, about Jock and the funny little tail-less Manx cats.

In return, we regularly received the news from Berlin and Hannover, which all sounded so normal and peaceful. Tante

Hanny had had a birthday party, Tante Agnes had baked a special cake, there had been ten guests and Konrad had played their favourite tunes on his recorder. They thought about us and drank a toast to us, and a speedy reunion.

Mane's letters were always a pleasure to receive. She had an entertaining way of writing, and everything that happened to her seemed to be hilariously funny. Leo's letters were more serious, they were my very favourite ones. I had never met him, yet we seemed to be on the same wavelength. In a roundabout way, he informed us that he had been called up again, although he was then forty-two years old. He was sent all over the country, training young recruits, and sometimes Mane joined him. They sent us photographs of a holiday they had had in the Alps at Innsbruck, where they planned to buy a house and settle after the war. We would all go and stay there and have wonderful times together. Plans, plans, only plans, but there is no limit to dreams, and at least Leo had his dreams. Sadly, like millions of others, he was to die in Russia. But that was still way ahead, and in the meantime I wrote to my favourite uncle ,and looked forward to meeting him some day. Parcels also winged their way over from Germany – toys and picture books for Addy, embroideries for Mama, Anita and me, and once even a large smoked sausage from Berlin. This delicacy was eked out for days, thinly cut and thoroughly enjoyed! Friends from Hull occasionally sent parcels too, especially one old dear who knitted pretty dresses for Addy and enclosed small treats for the rest of us.

Anita once received a parcel all to herself which was from some relief organisation- who instigated it we never knew. It was full of pretty clothes and included a small note saying that if she knew of any other child in the camp who would like a clothing parcel, to send their name. "Not", the note went on, "Nazi children. We don't send parcels to Nazi children."

I remember thinking, "How silly, children aren't Nazis, they're just children." Which of course, was quite true.

The 'A' category internees received lush parcels from the German Government, but we, the 'B's and 'C's had to be content with the occasional Red Cross parcels. These contained tinned chocolate, rosehip sweets and frugal little paper games and painting books. Still, they were parcels, and always welcome.

On the 4th March, I received an official looking letter. Upon opening it I gave a shout of delight- I had passed my exams! After receiving congratulations from everyone in Blair Atholl, I hurried round to the office to give them my good news.

The staff there congratulated me and I walked on air for the rest of the day. For, in my heart of hearts, I had not expected to pass. I was even more delighted when I heard later that my young companion had failed his exams. "Serve him right!" I thought nastily. I was not a particularly nice girl in those days and I couldn't bear to think of anyone else sharing my limelight, although this limelight was purely imaginary. I doubt if my passing the exams caused even the slightest ripple in the camp. Still, I was the first to have taken and passed the exam in the camp, whether there were ever anymore I don't know.

March 4th was also the day that the first baby was born in the mixed camp – a boy, and his mother was my French teacher. That certainly caused quite a ripple!

The Manx winter was drawing to its usual reluctant close, and after three days of snow in March, the weather gradually began to improve. The winds were not so bone-chilling and wild, the sun's rays became stronger and warmer, and in sheltered places one could sit without a coat. Indoors, Oak Tree shed his balaclava and one blanket.

Papa was sent to London for another tribunal, and was gone for two weeks. I hoped and hoped we wouldn't be released, but Papa was always sending in applications. Why does he bother, I thought? Why can't we just stay here, where it's so lovely? I need not have worried, for Papa's application was turned down yet again. After all, there were still plenty of 'C's left, before they would start on the 'B's.

Easter was at the beginning of April that year. We painted hard-boiled eggs for Addy and Ingrid and had church services on Good Friday and Easter Sunday. School had broken up some days before and there would be no more school for me. It was official -I looked forward to a life of leisure.

I had finally got hold of '*Gone with the Wind*', having had to wait until all the adults in the house had read it. I had waited impatiently as it passed from hand to hand. Were there ever such slow readers in this world, I thought! But at last it was my turn, and the world about me disappeared as I became absorbed in the compelling tale of Scarlett O'Hara. I finished it in record time, then was sorry I had read it so quickly, so started to read it all over again. There was no one to pass it on to except Elisabeth, and she didn't seem to care all that much.

Having finally, reluctantly put aside *Gone with the Wind*, I consoled myself with the thought that there were still hundreds of books in the library, and a whole glorious summer ahead to sit in quiet corners to read.

One lovely morning, at the end of April, I took Addy to the kindergarten planning to call at the library on the way back, then find a sheltered corner of the promenade or Gansey Rock to read my new book. It was not meant to be! On arriving at the kindergarten, I found a harassed woman in charge, coping single-handedly with about twenty excited tiny tots. I knew most of them, and some of them rushed at me, tugging at my hands and clothing, asking me to play with them.

Obligingly, I joined in for a while, finally prising myself loose and heading for the door. But the kindergarten teacher had other ideas. She waylaid me, a gleam in her eyes.

"Why don't you stay and help me?" she asked, "my helper was released last week, and the office hasn't sent me a replacement yet."

The children clustered round. "Please stay, please!" they begged. I liked little children, and my resolve weakened. I could always read in the afternoon, and so I capitulated.

"All right," I said graciously, "I'll just go home and tell them I'm staying." I ran back to Blair Atholl in search of Mama. It was her day for washing! I found her in the Hislop's outhouse, enveloped in clouds of steam, surrounded by all the paraphernalia of wash day. The steaming copper, the zinc tub, the scrubbing board and the cake of green soap.

"Good," she said, "you're just in time to hang out the washing."

She handed me a bowl of wrung-out laundry. As I pegged it out on the line in the Hislop's small garden I told her about the kindergarten. She thought it was a very good idea.

"It's time you did something useful," she said, "better than just sitting about reading."

I didn't really agree with her, but didn't bother to argue, for Mama was, in my opinion, still old-fashioned, and thought that girls should always be doing something useful.

I walked back to the kindergarten, and in doing so took the first steps in my future career!

The morning passed quickly and pleasantly. I was still little more than a child myself and had always enjoyed playing with Addy. The session over, the teacher asked if I would like to come again the following day – maybe if the office agreed, I could stay permanently. I couldn't very well say no, she was a formidable lady, and I was quite in awe of her.

When I arrived the next morning the teacher informed me that she had been to the office, and they were quite willing for me to be their new helper. Would I go and see the man in charge of schools, Mr Cole, later that day if I decided to take the job? I didn't really have much choice in the matter; people were always telling me what to do, I was used to it!

Mama and Papa were delighted when I told them my news, it was quite an honour to be chosen, they said. After all, there were dozens of women in the camp who would have been glad of a nice little job like that. I sought out Mr Cole at the office and told him that I would like to help at the kindergarten. I was surprised and delighted when he told me that I would be paid five shillings a week, and I could collect my wages every Friday afternoon. Five shillings a week! I had never heard of such riches. That would be one whole pound a month. Oh the things I could buy with all that money!

On the 1st May I became officially employed. Addy and I set off together. It was a beautiful day, and in honour of the occasion I wore my brand new hand-knitted white jumper. It was a pretty lacy garment with puffed sleeves and a drawstring neck. I felt good in it. I felt even better as we went through the entrance to the kindergarten. We passed close by the little control hut at the end of the prom, which contained a couple of Special Constables. As I went past they whistled at me! I couldn't believe it was me they meant and I blushed and hurried on, but it made my day. For the first time in my life I felt beautiful and desirable, like Scarlett O'Hara and all the heroines in books and films. Surrounded by a rosy glow, I entered the kindergarten back to reality!

The kindergarten was part of a large complex known as Cowley's Café. This consisted of two halls, a shop and two rooms over it. The upstairs and the shop which overlooked Port St Mary's main street were used as school rooms; the larger of the two halls was used for socials, silent film shows, country dancing and other entertainments. The smaller hall which opened onto the garden was used for the kindergarten, and this room also doubled up as the Lutheran Church on Sundays. Then, a table covered with a grey army blanket, supporting a simple wooden cross and two wooden 'barley sugar' candlesticks, borrowed from the mantelpiece of some boarding house, became the altar.

Addy and I walked straight through to the garden where the early arrivals were already playing. A small group had found something on the path, and, their heads close together, formed a circle of brunette, blonde and flaxen hair. A mixed bunch of children, Jew, Gentile, German and British-born, united in wonder and entranced by what they were observing. A charming scene with the bright summer flowers, the blue sky and sparkling sea as a backdrop.

One of the children saw me, and, anxious to share the enormous pleasure with me, called out in a shrill little voice,

"Guck mal, Tante Rosemarie! Ein Marienkäfer!" Tante Rosemarie obligingly went over to admire with them one of God's tiniest, prettiest creatures, a ladybird. I didn't really approve of being called Tante – it made me feel about fifty! However, it was the custom in the kindergarten. The woman in charge was Tante Herta and far more worthy of the title than I was, and in my opinion, really far too old to be prancing about in childish ring games the way she did! For all that, she ran the kindergarten with authority and efficiency in spite of very limited resources. A modern day kindergarten or Nursery teacher would have been horrified at the equipment our kindergarten possessed. There was a large rocking horse, several small chairs, a few dolls and cradles, a doll's pram, some pull-along trains and cars, a couple of colourful beach balls and a few well-worn picture books. The garden boasted a sand-pit with a few buckets and spades.

The rest of the entertainment was up to us. We played endless ring games in German and English, and told stories in both languages. Although the main language was German most of the children were bilingual, and if they weren't no one bothered to translate, which they accepted. Some of the German rhymes had actually been translated by some enterprising soul and both versions were always sung. Tante Herta's English was, in my opinion, quite comical, and the rendering of some of the English versions always made me want to giggle. She would trill "Vee open now ze duffcott vide," and the little ones would mimic her perfectly.

In spite of the lack of costly toys and games the children were completely happy. They shared, and waited patiently for their turn with the pram or the rocking horse. We acquired old baking tins and wooden spoons for the sand-pit, and the cakes and pies we made were as good as any made with more conventional equipment. We had our imagination, and that is all that is ever needed to keep children happy. We played outside whenever the weather was fine. We found shiny-backed beetles, watched butterflies, birds, and listened to buzzing bees. We made daisy chains, and searched for pretty or unusual stones or shells in the gravel paths, with which to decorate our sand-pies and castles.

There were few arguments, tears or tantrums. If only the grown-ups of this world would live together as tolerably and amicably as little children, what a pleasant place it would be.

47. THE BRADDA PRIVATE

The summer was now in full swing, the weather was mainly warm and sunny. Anita and I spent most afternoons on the beach, with daring little excursions into the sea on really hot days. Curfew was now extended, so in the long evenings we went out walking after tea, or to the allotments to water the now flourishing plants. Sometimes we would go round to the back lane to watch the Italians playing bowls. There were not many Italians in the camp – four or five families at the most. They had their own house and did not mix much with the rest of us. We liked to watch them at their game of bowls and listened fascinated as they argued amongst themselves in their volatile language, sounding as though they were ready to cut each other's throats, but remarkably always ending with jovial shouts of laughter.

Anita, now fourteen, was in the top class in the Cowley's Café school and had only two classmates, Rita and Hannelore. They had hilarious times. They were made prefects, and sometimes put in charge of the younger children. This consisted mainly of a strong arm wielding a ruler! Once, one of the camp teachers for some reason or other had offended them, so when he came to take the lesson he was confronted by three grim-faced girls, arms folded, lips pressed together, eyes glaring straight ahead, totally ignoring him. When he finally gave in and stormed out, they collapsed in giggles.

They ran away from one young teacher who, heavily pregnant, chased them down the rows calling "Girls, girls! Ze lesson, vee haf ze lesson, come back!" but they pretended to be out of earshot.

They were not so bold with their P.E. teacher, an ex-army instructor who drilled them on the beach with military discipline and precision. He also tried to teach them to swim, tying a rope round their waists and dragging them along, into the sea. Anita was convinced he was determined to drown them, and who could blame him! Maybe some of the other teachers had dropped a few hints. A gentle Manx woman took them for English and they read poetry outside among the wild flowers. A German with an over-enthusiastic use of lavender hair oil read Shakespeare with them. It put Anita off lavender hair oil for life, but luckily it didn't put her off Shakespeare.

Eberhard too, had a job. He had joined the group that went on archaeological digs with Dr Bersu, a professor from Leipzig. They were finding all sorts of interesting remains.

I remember one day they found a bracelet, or part of one. "Thousands of years old," said Eberhard, "prehistoric no doubt."

I remember being surprised that they wore bracelets in 'those days'. It sounded so civilised and normal.

Eberhard's wages were three shillings and sixpence a week, but I'm sure he worked harder at his digging than I did at the kindergarten.

On Sunday afternoons Anita and I liked to sit at the back of the allotment field. Here, the barbed wire came right down to the Gansey/Port St Mary road. We watched out for the passing cars carrying Manx families on their weekend jaunts. They were few and far between, but we would wave frantically at each one, they, the free ones and we, the caged. Yet I would not have changed places with them for all the tea in China!

So, the summer seemed set in its pleasant, easy-going pattern, with nothing to alter its course, but behind the scenes changes were already taking place. Gradually all those in Category 'C' had been released. The huge Ballaqueeny Hotel, which housed the Jewish internees because of their special dietary needs, was now only half full.

"When all the 'C's have gone, they'll start on the 'B's," prophesised Papa.

"Hope they don't," I said, "I wish we were 'A's."

"I don't," said Papa, "they'll repatriate all the 'A's before the end of the war. How would you like that?"

I mulled that one over. In the past two years I had become more German than ever before in my life. I thought romantically of my 'Heimat', my Fatherland. The beautiful countryside, the imposing cities, the elegant parks, the cake shops. Then I had a sudden vision of Sunny Bank, the back garden with its apple trees and little summerhouse in dear, ordinary Hull, and I knew where my heart really belonged.

"'B' is the best thing to be," I said with conviction.

Rumours began to circulate the camp late in July. We were definitely going to be moved, as yet nobody knew where. At any rate, somebody had it on good authority that our landladies had been told we would all be gone by the end of the summer.

Mrs Hislop said she knew nothing about it, but we'd all find out soon enough if there were to be any changes.

We did. On August 8th the office announced that we were all going back to Port Erin in two weeks time – further details would be given out later. We were in a state of happy anticipation. Port Erin! But where in Port Erin? As it turned out, the mixed camp was to be behind the women's camp on Bradda and on August 13th we received official notification of our new billets. Our family was going to the Bradda Private Hotel.

In my diary that night I wrote "Yippee!" for we knew the hotel well. It was the big one that overlooked Bradda Glen.

We started to pack; it was amazing to find how much we had accumulated over the last two years. We crammed it into suitcases, bags, boxes, and tied labels, for the luggage would go up on lorries, and we would walk.

The kindergarten closed on August 14th and Tante Herta and I packed up the few bits and pieces worth saving. They were going to the Port Erin kindergarten. Then Tante Herta formally shook hands with me, thanked me for my help and wished me well for the future. I felt very grown up, but I regretted losing my job and the five shillings a week that went with it. However, it was nice to be a lady of leisure again, and I hurried back to Blair Atholl to help with the clearing up.

We finally moved on August 18th, at three in the afternoon. In warm sunshine we walked the short distance between the two villages. In Port Erin the women had turned out in force to wave us on our way, and we saw many familiar faces, making it feel good to be back.

Nothing had changed – the promenade was as steep as ever as we toiled up to our new abode, which lay halfway up Bradda. There it was. The great cream-painted imposing pile of the Bradda Private Hotel.

"Gosh!" I thought, "it will be just like living in a castle!"

What had started out as quite an ordinary, if large, double-fronted boarding house, now had so many extra wings and bits and pieces added, it really did look like a castle, especially the tessellated trim on the top bay windows.

Inside it was just as impressive. To the left of the entrance lay a vast ballroom with shiny parquet floor, small platform and grand piano. The landlord was seated at a table in here, allocating rooms. We joined the queue and soon emerged with our room numbers, and then climbed the broad staircase in search of them.

Mama, Papa and Addy had a much-coveted bay windowed front bedroom on the first floor. Eberhard had a small single room tucked into a corner at the back, and Anita and I had a delightful twin-bedded room at the side, with views over Bradda Glen to the sea and the Calf of Man. We were ecstatic. It was like starting a holiday.

Without waiting for the rest of the family who were busily sorting through the bags and suitcases piled up outside the hotel, Anita and I raced off to our beloved Bradda Glen. It was just as it had always been, as though we had never left. We ran around looking at our old rooms from the outside, for already the new residents, the Ballaqueeny people, were taking over.

"We can come here every day now," said Anita happily, "no need to even live here."

We went back for the evening meal and to seek out the dining room. This was another great room crammed with tables of various sizes, and people already seated at most of them. We had a large round table close to the fireplace, which was to prove very comforting in the cold days ahead.

In all, there were about sixty internees in the hotel, including several small children of Addy's age, and the noise and chatter that first evening was rather daunting. Among the many unfamiliar faces only Kalk had come from Blair Atholl. However, we soon had everybody sorted out, and quickly settled in. The funny thing was that the hotel was always referred to as the 'Bradda Private' and not just plain 'Bradda'.

We had been in Port Erin only a week, when all the allotment holders were allowed to return to Port St Mary, to harvest any crop that might be ready. Accordingly, our entire family joined the crowd gathered at the barrier, which now stretched across the road at Collinson's Café. Anything for a trip out, we thought, even though the few radishes, carrots and lettuces could have been collected by one person! It was nice to be back in Port St Mary, even though we only went straight to the allotment field and back. A few days later we went again and then no more, for the field opposite the Bradda Private had been divided into plots, and Papa had already started digging round the edges of his.

We could now go into Port Erin village on Monday and Wednesday afternoons, mainly for shopping, but we went anyway and enjoyed being back in familiar streets, or on the beach, We met folk we knew from the women's camp, all in all, it was a very relaxed atmosphere. As long as we were back in time for the evening meal it didn't seem to matter where we went. We still went to the Port Erin cinema once a week and joined in the women's entertainments, held in the great circular room of Collinson's Café. There were Austrian and Bavarian evenings, as well as plays, cabaret and dancing.

The ballroom at the Bradda Private was our favourite daytime place, for there were lovely sitting corners in all the bays, and it was the ideal place for Addy and the other little ones to play. There was also a smaller lounge which had been earmarked for a quiet reading room, with a selection of newspapers and magazines, neatly arranged on a large central table. I think each family paid about a penny a week towards it, maybe even less, for a woman's magazine cost only two pence and newspapers one penny apiece. The only sounds to be heard in this room were the rustlings of paper. A man was in charge of it and made absolutely sure that no magazine or paper was sneaked out. If ever he was not around the door was firmly locked.

Apart from these two public rooms there was only the dining room, and here most people would remain after the evening meal had been cleared. Mama always said that English people sat round their fireplaces and Germans sat around tables, as they weren't used to open fires! This was quite true, everybody had their occupations – knitting, embroidering or gossiping for the women; cards, chess and so on for the men. One table played Chinese Chequers every evening and sometimes, joy of joys, asked Anita and me to join them. There was an elderly Salvation Army man who used to play chess with his friend, and when his friend preferred to read taught me the game. I enjoyed playing with him as he usually let me win, which gave me an inflated opinion of myself as a chess player. Playing with others later I soon found out that I was not all that good!

There were talks and lectures to listen to, some of them very interesting, others way above my head. We also had whist drives and beetle drives with small prizes for winners - in fact, never a dull moment. We had our own beach at Spaldrick Bay in the mixed camp, but as very few people used it, Anita and I mostly had it to ourselves.

Port Erin's kindergarten was held in the Rowany Golf Club house, just outside our barrier, and every day a young woman would wait at the gate for any children of the mixed camp who wished to attend. I had taken Addy down to the gate on several occasions and waved her off as she and her small companions trotted up the hill to the kindergarten. Then one afternoon I had a surprise, for the woman in charge of schools came up to Bradda Private especially to see me. She asked if I would like to work in the kindergarten again. I was enjoying my days of leisure, but I also missed my five shillings a week, which had been mounting up to a goodly little sum in a cocoa tin! So I agreed to go. She told me that as one of the girls was leaving there would be a vacancy, so would I report there on the 17th September. The men at the barrier had been informed and I could go through with the children. Mama and Papa were impressed.

"They really must think you're good, if they've chosen you from all these other women," said Mama proudly, and even I felt flattered.

More likely, the real reason for my being chosen was that I was amenable, spoke English without a guttural accent, and was 'B' category, therefore middle of the road. I duly joined the little flock waiting to go through the barrier on the appointed day, and set off up the hill to the little club house. It was a totally different set-up to the Port St Mary kindergarten. There were three rooms, a large one, a smaller one for the younger children, and a little room upstairs for books and storytelling. The whole place was furnished with children in mind, plenty of small tables and chairs, bright pictures on the walls and cupboards crammed with toys and games. Many of the wooden puzzles and other equipment had been hand-made and painted in bright colours. The whole place had been set up with much loving care and thought.

The children, boys and girls alike, wore pinafores in printed cotton and each had their own named and pictured peg in the cloakroom. The woman in charge was a kindly soul named Maria. She had her own system for running the kindergarten, and we all worked well together. Here the main language spoken was English, and though we still sang

German nursery rhymes, the children were spoken to only in English. Maria's English was atrocious, but she gamely soldiered on – the children didn't notice anyway, they just spoke a mixture of anything, and we all understood each other!

This kindergarten was also open in the afternoons so we would all go home for lunch and turn up again for the afternoon session. I thought I should have been paid double for the extra time, but still received only my five shillings weekly.

We had a large part of the golf course at our disposal and on fine days would go for many a pleasant walk.

With my wages coming in regularly once more, my cocoa tin of money was filling up nicely. I decided to save up for some new clothes. From the 'relief' we had our free slacks and shoes. We knitted jumpers, cardigans and skirts. Mama had knitted a pretty winter dress for Anita and suggested I do the same for myself, but I couldn't be bothered to get started, and besides it would take months before it was ready.

"When I've saved enough," I decided luxuriously, "I'll buy myself a really pretty dress."

I had already inspected the meagre collection in the Port Erin shops and found it wanting, but the same shops also sold materials and there were plenty of dressmakers in the women's camp who would no doubt be glad to earn a few shillings making a dress for me. I began to dream of colours, materials and styles. As usual, however, I was to have no choice in the matter.

I came home from the kindergarten one day, to find Mama reading a letter from her friend, the pork butcher's wife, in Hull. She read out various bits of news and then "P.S. Lucy is sending you a parcel of clothes, hope you find them useful for yourself or Rosemarie."

I received the information without enthusiasm, I had no more illusions about other people's cast-offs.

"Lucy," said Mama, "is the most elegant daughter, and always buys her clothes in exclusive shops."

I wasn't impressed, after all Lucy was at least thirty, I was only seventeen. I wasn't interested in elegance. "Perhaps," I thought hopefully, "they'll all fit Mama and not me." Mama dashed my hopes immediately, "Lucy is more your size than mine," she said, "I can't wait for that parcel."

The parcel arrived in due course. Mama brought it into our bedroom and eagerly removed string and paper. The contents were few, and soon unpacked. There was a man's suit, in an impractical pale grey stripe.

"That will do for Eberhard," said Mama, "he's grown out of his best suit. I'll take it to him later."

I had seen what was left and was sunk in gloomy disappointment. There was an almond green wool suit and a winter dress in dark bluey-green.

"You can have them both," I said, not too hopefully, for Mama was already holding them up and exclaiming with false delight.

"What a beautiful suit, and so clean. Why it's hardly been worn, try it on."

I did so, and hated it. The skirt had a couple of pleats back and front and looked like a sugar bag on me. The jacket would have been quite nice if it hadn't had the most awful huge, curved reveres.

"Very fashionable," said Mama, "you look really grown up in that, and the jacket will also go with your tartan skirt. You'll look like Lady Soandso, on her country estate."

"Lady Soandso," I thought bleakly, "wouldn't be seen dead in a thing like that!"

Mama was holding up the dress. "Try this on now," she said.

The only redeeming feature about the dress was its colour and the material, a kind of fancy woollen weave. I reluctantly slipped it over my head, and pulled it over my hips, then gazed in horror at the awful apparition I saw in the mirror. Lucy must have been a lot slimmer than me when she wore that dress, for it fitted me like a second skin, and bulged where I bulged with my puppy fat. The sleeves were unbecoming 'leg of mutton', tight at the wrist then ballooning from elbow to shoulder, but the most horrific of all was the neckline. A deep V, which plunged alarmingly low, too low for my sense of modesty.

"I can't wear it," I said shocked, "not with that neckline."

"Of course you can," said Mama, "those necklines are worn with modesty vests, get one of your lace hankies."

I took one out of the drawer, and Mama deftly arranged it.

"There," she said, "just a couple of tiny safety pins and it's done."

I was aghast, a modesty vest! That was what old women wore, like Tusky and other equally ancient teachers. I removed it hastily.

"It looks awful," I said, "anyone can see it's just a hanky."

"Well then tuck a scarf in," said Mama, "that blue and purple one will match nicely."

Sighing, I found my scarf, and tucked it round my neck. Now, there are women who are adept at arranging scarves around necks, a flick here, a knot there, a strategically placed clip or brooch and hey presto! A result of casual elegance, of studied nonchalance and an arrangement firmly anchored. Then there are the others who, struggle as they may with knots and brooches, never achieve the desired effect. I was destined to be one of these unfortunate souls and my first attempt at scarf arrangement was an utter failure. It was simply a scarf bundled round my neck - no amount of pulling and tucking in could alter the fact.

Anita came in. "You look muffled," she said with sisterly honesty, "and your bottom and stomach stick out!"

"It's scratchy," I said, determined to be awkward.

"Now it's not as bad as that," said Mama unconvincingly, "it looks nice and cosy and you can wear it on Sundays. Wait a minute, I have just the thing for it," and she hurried off.

I pulled out the scarf in despair, and then Mama came back waving a large bunch of artificial violets. "There you are!" she said, and stuck them firmly down my unresisting, non-existent cleavage.

Actually I did wear the dress on Sundays and special occasions, and always with the violets tucked in, held in place by a hidden safety pin. I think now how remarkable it was for Mama to have packed the violets in the first place. She must have been the only internee who thought that artificial violets were an essential and indispensable necessity for camp life.

Mama gathered up the grey suit and hurried off to bestow it on a presumably more grateful Eberhard, and Anita went with her. Left alone, I stood in front of the mirror and studied my full length view, which was totally depressing. Out of the shortish tight skirt stuck two sturdy bare legs, ending in thick hand knitted socks and sensible shoes. I removed the violets and struggled out of the dress. I pulled on my slacks and jumper.

"There," I thought, "that's more normal." Then I flung myself on to my bed and indulged in a little daydreaming.

At seventeen, I already had my own ideas about the clothes I would really like to wear: soft wool dresses in pretty shades, with high necks, softly gathered sleeves and swirly skirts; tartan kilts, gaily swinging in a myriad of tiny pleats; pretty summer cottons with puff sleeves, sweetheart necklines and flouncy skirts. In books, heroines always 'flounced' out of rooms. I looked at the offending dress bundled on to a chair. How could anyone ever flounce in that thing? It was hopeless. How much longer was I going to have to wear clothes I didn't like? Would the war ever end? If it did and I wasn't ancient by then and wearing modesty vests by then as a matter of course, what clothes I would wear!

My imagination drifted off into the realms of sprigged muslin, dimity, dotted Swiss, organza, all the delightful materials one read about. I saw myself floating, slim and beautiful in an exquisite gown, through a chandeliered ballroom, where handsome men fell worshipping at my feet. Anita burst into the room, shattering my dreams.

"Why are you lying down, are you ill?" she asked, "I'm going down to Spaldrick, coming?"

With a sigh, I got off the bed, pushed dress and suit into the wardrobe and soon forgot all about them as we raced down the steps to Spaldrick Bay. Slacks, jumper and sensible shoes were just right here. A floating dimity gown would have looked silly and impede my progress, by catching on the bramble briars!

48. THIRD CHRISTMAS

The summer was gradually, lingeringly drawing to its close. The bracken was changing colour and once again there were blackberries to be picked in Bradda Glen. They were a welcome supplement to the rather predictable meals at the Bradda Private. Although the food was mainly cooked by internees, it lacked the personal touch and came nowhere near the high standards of Mrs Hislop's cuisine. Steamed syrup sponges were a mere memory, as was the Sunday morning grapefruit. However, there was one consolation; a small pantry with two gas rings, which was available for the internees to cook little extras. There was a gas meter that took sixpences, but every tea time it tended to become overcrowded with women loudly arguing as to whose turn it was and whose sixpence was in the slot. Finally, the house leader made a rota for those women who wished to use it, and all had their own day and time. When it was Mama's turn we usually had pancakes, fried eggs or our favourite 'Kartoffel Puffer' – she also made a concoction of fried onions and apples in a pan of lard, which, when cold and set was absolutely delicious, spread thickly on slices of bread.

House duties shared out among so many residents were few and far between, so instead of cleaning the stairs daily my turn came round once a fortnight, as again, there was a rota. I also took my turn at serving meals.

Anita was now attending the Port Erin school. No longer was it in the Strand Café, but in a house further up the hill. She did the long walk from one side of the bay to the other four times a day, but as there was quite a crowd of boys and girls going together, it was no hardship. Anita and other Lutheran children of her age group also attended Confirmation classes on Saturdays. These had started in Port St Mary and continued in Port Erin, and were held in the school house by our resident Lutheran Pastor, who also lived in the Bradda Private. Judging by Anita's accounts of the lessons they were no more reverent than mine had been.

For a start the class would hide in corners and cupboards before the lesson, and had the pastor tramping up and down the stairs searching for them and calling out, "Where are you? I know you're here! Come out!"

When he was out of sight they would silently come from their hiding places, and sit waiting for him, innocently angelic.

The pastor, however, was their match, and would look at his watch and say, "As we are ten minutes late starting, we will have to go on ten minutes longer, won't we?" in spite of the protests of the cheekier ones that he was the late one who had kept them waiting.

One boy, Anita said, refused to speak German, so had to have everything explained in English, and learned the English version of the Catechism, but the pastor soldiered on. He was a stubborn, determined man.

Addy's birthday at the end of September was marked by a simple, touching ceremony at the kindergarten. On a table, lit by four pink candles, stood a miniature set of hand-made table and chairs. Seated on the tiny chairs were two small dolls made of pipe-cleaners and tissue paper. I had never seen anything so sweet and simple, I shall never forget Addy's small round face, rosy in the candle glow, gazing in delight at her pretty little gift. We all sang 'Happy Birthday' then Addy's favourite song, 'Kommt ein Vogel geflogen'. A song I always thought most poignant when it came to the last line, 'Denn ich kann Dich nicht begleiten weil ich hier bleiben muss'. (I can't come with you, I must stay here.) Sung lustily by small internees I always thought it very apt!

My birthday, one month after Addy's, was my eighteenth and I was beginning to feel old. The day before, Mama had treated me to another perm. Not such an ordeal this time, as I knew what to expect and the girl who attended me was a friendly little chatterbox. But I still went through those terrible first days, feeling hideously conspicuous, waiting for the style to 'drop', after which I felt more normal. I felt even better when Mama told me that one of the women had remarked to her that I was 'Bildhübsch' – pretty as a picture in my new hairdo. It made my day. Teenagers in those days were not often told they were beautiful or clever or whatever good qualities they had; people were better at pointing out their faults and shortcomings.

With two birthdays out of the way, Anita and I could concentrate on Christmas, which was not so far off now. We had already bought a black doll for Addy, which was hidden on the top of our wardrobe, away from her prying little eyes. I was knitting a doll's outfit and Anita was making a pull-along cart in her woodwork lessons, and a set of red and white gingham pillows and covers to go with it. So Addy was well seen to; it was the others who were causing problems. However, as a wage earner, I decided generously, we would buy their presents for them. We would have fun going round the shops, and even though the Port Erin shops had a limited selection of goods we eventually found suitable gifts for all the family.

For Anita, I was secretly making a tapestry bag in which to carry her school books, and she too was busy on some secret project for me. We also designed and painted our own Christmas cards and gift tags, and any spare minute I had was spent stitching up toy stuffed cats, which the staff were making as presents for the kindergarten children. Our bedroom resembled Santa's workshop.

The Manx winter was now making itself felt. It was really too cold in the bedroom to be painting and sewing for any length of time, as our fingers and toes reminded us, but it was our third winter on the Island, and we were becoming hardened to it.

Christmas at the Bradda Private promised to be a splendid affair. Half a dozen men and women had appointed themselves as organisers of the festivities, and a few days before the celebrations the ballroom was declared out of bounds. Army blankets draped over its glass doors allowed not even a glimpse of the preparations within. The kindergarten had already had its end of term party, and parents had been invited to join in the fun, in playing simple party games. For the finale, the children made a pretty tableau of the Holy Family surrounded by angels, whilst the grown-ups sang 'Silent Night'. Addy, in a white nightie and tinsel in her hair, was one of the angels. Maria had lit a host of candles and they were the only source of light inside,' as outside was already darkening. Again it was a moving and touching little ceremony which I shall never forget. This always came to mind in later years when I would wind tinsel round the heads of my small pupils as I prepared them for the Nativity play. The party over, every child was presented with a toy cat wrapped in tissue paper, and reminded on no account to open them until Christmas Eve. Then it was a scramble to get back to our hotels and boarding houses up and down the hill, before curfew.

On Christmas Eve, our evening meal was served earlier than usual. Presents for the children of the house had already been collected and well labelled, to be placed under the tree. Anita and I were very proud of Addy's little black doll, sitting in her red and green painted cart, amongst the gingham cushions.

Tea over, we were told to wait in the dining room until we heard the gong. The little ones were, by now, wide-eyed with excitement and could hardly contain themselves. Tantrums were very much in the offing. Just in time the gong sounded, and we all moved as one body towards the ballroom.

"Children first!" boomed a voice, and there appeared a white-whiskered, red-robed figure - Santa Claus himself. He flung open the double doors – what brilliance met our eyes! The organisers had excelled themselves. An enormous tree glittered in one corner of the ballroom, all around tables decorated with greenery and candles, and a fire burned brightly in the fireplace. A pianist provided a background of Christmassy music, softly played.

"Come along children," said Father Christmas, leading the way, "you come and sit round the tree," and an awe-struck little band followed him to the giant tree. The rest of us dispersed ourselves around the tables, as the children were already gazing at the array of presents under the tree.

"If you want any of these lovely toys, you must first sing to me," said the benign saint in the red robe.

The pianist struck some chords and the children lustily sang the songs they knew so well. Then the labelled toys were handed round. It had been requested that there should be only one gift per child, and when they had been presented, among much teasing and banter from Father Christmas, the children ran to their families to show their spoils. There followed more singing and reading of stories and poems relating to the festive season. The candles glittered and sparkled on the tree, and the tables, the singing and music were so beautiful that I wanted it to go on forever, but the candles guttered to the end of their short life span and went out one by one. The electric lights were switched on, then those who wished, dispersed to their own rooms for private celebrations.

In Mama and Papa's room, my little cardboard tree from the previous year had been assembled and refurbished with new candles and glitter. We handed out our presents to each other, and everything was just what everyone had wanted. How simple our gifts were, how modest our wishes, how lovely it all was – yet there was a war on, but how little it affected us.

The tree remained in the ballroom until Twelfth Night. On New Year's Eve there was much jollity at the Bradda Private, with music and dancing and the New Year toasted in the usual tea-based spicy hot drink.

A talented resident of the Bradda Private had written witty poems, each concerning a family in the hotel. He read them out and we fell about laughing as he found just the right words and situations to suit each family. At midnight we shook hands all round and wished each other a Happy New Year. As usual people wondered where we'd all be next New Year. I didn't really care. The only reality for me now was life in the camp, and as long as there was still a war on I was quite happy to stay there.

49. RELEASE

As usual, no one took much notice of what I wanted, least of all the Home Office. Daily one heard of people being released. The 'C's were nearly all gone – soon, inevitably it would be the turn of the 'B's. I pushed the thought to the back of my mind, and there it stayed. No point in worrying about the far-distant future, there was enough going on in the present.

At the kindergarten, Maria was released in February, and we had a little party with chocolate cake to celebrate. At the end of it she wished everyone well, kissed the children, and handed me a key.

"You will be in charge now," she informed me, "you have been here longer than any of the other girls. YOU will have to come a little earlier to unlock, don't forget!" She went off, waving to us all. She looked very happy.

So began my short spell as a 'head teacher', using the term very loosely indeed. There wasn't much extra to do except unlock and lock up after each session, for we all knew exactly what we were doing, and continued in this vein. This state of affairs lasted less than a month. One morning someone from the office brought along Maria's replacement. She was a tall, slim, dark haired, confident woman. She was introduced to us all. Her name was Erika. Introductions over, the official left, and Erika turned to look at the children, who with typical curiosity, had gathered round. Erika seated herself on a small table and smiled down at them all. "Well," she said, "what shall we sing?"

I think the children were as surprised as I was, for there was a brief stunned silence before suggestions began flowing in.

Up to now, in both kindergartens, the children had always been told what to do, what to sing, what to play, and so on, now they were actually being asked to make a choice. It was then I realised that here was a professionally trained woman, and not just a well-meaning child minder.

Under Erika's influence the kindergarten subtly changed. Not only were the children consulted as to the day's programme but also the helpers, and I discovered that there was so much more to running a kindergarten than just keeping the children clean, happy and occupied.

Nature takes no notice of wars and other interruptions and continues in her own sweet way. This, the fourth spring of the war, was as lovely as ever. The cold winds lessened, the sunny spells were longer and warmer, the first primroses peeped shyly from sheltered banks and the gorse bushes, rarely seen without a few golden spikes, now lavishly covered themselves in a profusion of sweet-scented flowers. Soon there would be bluebells, wild garlic and pink campion in Bradda Glen. How could anyone fail to be enchanted by such an earthly paradise? If only, I thought, the Home Office would forget all about us and we could stay here forever.

Easter that year came at the end of April. For the kindergarten children we laboriously stitched together three-sided cardboard Easter eggs, decorated with flowers, chicks and bunnies. These were then filled with a variety of sweets and chocolates, and presented on the last day of term.

For ourselves, we painted hard-boiled eggs in bright colours, and I was secretly making a small picture book about Easter bunnies for Addy.

Easter Sunday on the 25th April, was a bleak, cold day with the Manx winds back in full force. No going for Easter walks that day, but the bright flowers on our dining tables reassured us that spring was really here and soon the winds would abate and the balmy days return. They did, and once again we were sunbathing in sheltered corners in Spaldrick Bay, and life continued in its pleasant, easy way.

Once a week there was a very special moment in my life. On my way to the afternoon kindergarten session I would pass a young man who came from the men's camp in

Douglas to visit his parents in the Bradda Private. He was tall, rather aloof-looking and wore a small trilby hat, which he raised every time we met. The mere fact that he acknowledged my insignificant presence sent me blushing happily on my way. Once I met him on the stairs in the Bradda Private. This time he actually spoke.

"Good day," he said. What rapture! I nearly fell down the stairs with shock and delight!

Several decades later, I heard that this young man became a well-known millionaire. Life, alas, is full of missed opportunities!

Winter had one last fling on May 10th when we woke to a snowy landscape and a raging blizzard. By the evening it had all disappeared and a few days later we were wearing summer clothes again.

The 27th May, the third anniversary of our being interned, was also Mama and Papa's engagement day and therefore celebrated with cream doughnuts – Papa's favourites. Sadly, that was the very day that Leo was killed on the Russian front, but we didn't know that until sometime later. I will always remember the very last letter we received from him. It was not written in his usual light-hearted style but deeply reflective and philosophical. He must have had a premonition that death was very near, and the little house in the mountains was not for him after all.

For me, the worry of being released had receded. After all, there were still lots of others who actually wanted to go, so they could all go first as far as I was concerned. Besides, Papa had said that even if we were released we wouldn't be allowed back in Hull as that was a 'protected area'. So really we had nowhere to go, and they couldn't just turn us out, could they? I clung to that hope.

In vain, on the 5th June I was in our bedroom writing a letter to Berlin when I heard excited voices on the stairs.

"Dalheims sind released!" cried a female voice, in the usual mixture of German and English used in the camp.

My pen poised in mid-air, I couldn't believe my ears. "It's not true, it can't be," I thought, and firmly went on with my writing.

Minutes later, Mama popped her head round the door,

"We're released!" she said excitedly, "we've just had word from the office!"

"I know," I said flatly, "I've just heard someone talking outside, anyway, we can't go, we've nowhere to go."

I don't suppose my reaction surprised Mama, after all she knew exactly what my feelings were. She noticed my letter.

"If you're writing to Germany," she said, "you can tell them the news straight away."

"I've no room left," I said shortly, signed my name, folded the letter form into three, sealed it and wrote on the front the address and Internment Mail – Postage Free. On the back I wrote the sender and 'Y' Camp, Isle of Man. How many more times could I do this, I thought sadly. Letters to and from Germany would stop, and we would be back to twelve words via the Red Cross, which took ages and were useless. Someone called across the corridor to Mama asking if the news about us was true, and Mama left me for more receptive ears.

I gazed out at the lovely view I had taken for granted over the past year. The pine trees of Bradda Glen, beyond them the sea, sparkling in the summer sunshine, in the distance the outline of the Calf of Man. I couldn't leave it all behind, it was part of me now.

Anita came into the room, her hands full of wild flowers.

"Is it true?" she asked, "are we released?"

"Yes," I said, "Mama just told me. Horrible isn't it?"

Anita wholeheartedly agreed with me. She loved the Island as much as I did. Like me, she said,

"But we've nowhere to go. What will happen?"

"We'll have to wait and see," I said philosophically, "Mama and Papa will think of something."

The gong sounded for lunch and further speculation was abandoned. Arriving in the dining room we found quite a crowd gathered round our table, excitedly talking to Mama, Papa and Eberhard, congratulating them on their good fortune. Their beaming faces turned to Anita and me and goodwill flowed towards us.

I smiled weakly, after all, they meant well – how could they guess my heart was broken? I felt more like crying than laughing.

"If they're so eager to go," I thought, "I'll swap with them all."

"What I'm looking forward to most of all," Mama was saying, "is my own kitchen."

Of all the reasons for release, that was the most extraordinary I had ever heard.

"But your kitchen is in Hull, and we can't go there," I said.

"There are other kitchens where I will be just as happy," said Mama, "Papa and I will think of somewhere to go, you'll see."

Anita clutched at a straw. "But the allotment," she said, "we've got all those vegetables and things. We'll have to wait till they're ready, we can't just leave them."

"Someone's already asked if they can have it after me," said Papa, "so that's all right."

"Cheek!" I thought sulkily, "we've had all the work and they eat all the things, it's not fair!"

It wasn't, but then, all's fair in love and war.

50. AUF WIEDERSEHEN

Once the Home Office had decided that our family no longer constituted a threat to the country's war effort, it wanted rid of us with almost unseemly haste.

Papa was told that we could leave as soon as we had an address to go to. Papa now had the bit between his teeth, and seemed as anxious for us to leave as was the Home Office.

An acquaintance of his from the men's camp had gone to Leeds on his release, and they still kept in touch. Papa wrote to him asking if he could recommend Leeds for our family. His reply was prompt; Leeds, he wrote, was the ideal place. There was plenty of empty property, there was work, there was good schools. Also, it was surrounded by lovely countryside and air-raids were practically non-existent. All the time he'd been there they hadn't had a single one. He could recommend the boarding house where he himself had stayed as temporary accommodation, and should he make reservations?

We all read and re-read his letter. I wasn't much bothered about the work and schools, but I liked the sound of the countryside, and no raids. Papa wrote back and told him to book us in the boarding house as soon as possible. He did, and we had our address.

"It won't be any different from now," I protested, "just living in a boarding house. Why can't we stay here?"

"We'll soon have our own place," said Papa confidently. He proved to be right, for within less than a month of our release we, and all our furniture from Hull, were settled in a charming house in the Leeds suburb of Headingley. The house had attics, cellars, gardens, and red roses round a pretty porch. Papa had bought it for a ludicrous price of six hundred and fifty pounds. "Only in England," Papa said, "can an enemy alien buy a house in wartime." In the meantime, we were busy packing our accumulated possessions into tea chests. In between, I desperately tried to savour our last days of internment on the Isle of Man. The Island seemed more beautiful than ever, the flowers so profuse, the sea so blue. I envied all the other internees, blissfully, nonchalantly going about their daily lives. The whole glorious summer ahead of them and no threat of imminent release to cloud their horizons. Oh how I envied them!

All too soon it was our last week and I had my farewell party at the kindergarten, and then came our last day. That evening, after our final, lingering walk round Bradda Glen we said goodbye to everyone in the Bradda Private and reluctantly went to bed.

The bedroom, stripped of our pictures, vases of flowers, ornaments and hand embroidered cloths, looked bleak and bare.

"Wonder where we'll be tomorrow at this time," I said gloomily to Anita, as I settled down to sleep.

"In bed somewhere in Leeds," said Anita sleepily, "goodnight."

The day of our release, the 23rd June, was as sunny as the day we had arrived on the Island over three years ago. We breakfasted in solitary state, then set off to walk to Port Erin station. Our main luggage was to be sent on and we carried only hand luggage, which included a potted geranium, a cutting from one of Mrs Hislop's, which we decided to keep as a small living memento.

The long road to the station was, at that early hour, practically devoid of people. A woman internee, sweeping the steps of one of the hotels, and noticing our luggage, waved her broom at us.

"Gute Reise! Alles Gute!" she called out.

At the station the little train, its engine puffing impatiently was already waiting. We had a carriage to ourselves. This time we were not locked in; we were now as free as the other passengers on the train. An official from the camp handed Papa our tickets for the journey, wished us well, and left without a backward glance.

The engine gave a shriek, there was a sudden jerk and we were off. From my window seat I watched the countryside rolling past. I could not take my eyes off it. I wanted to store it forever in my memory. It seemed as though the Island had again decked itself out in its best, this time to say goodbye. Every leaf, every flower, shone to polished perfection, the colours fresh and brilliant. I wished I had two sets of eyes to look out of both sides of the train at once!

The journey had never seemed so short. We were at Douglas and Mama and Papa were fussing with the luggage. We alighted and joined the people walking down to the ship. On board it was surprisingly full, but we found ourselves a corner on deck to settle in. Leaving the others, Anita and I went off to lean over the rails to watch the preparations for departure. Soon the gangway was up, the mooring chains pulled aboard, and we were off. We watched Douglas recede rapidly; soon we could no longer make out the houses and hotels. Only the shape of the hills behind was left, then soon even that was gone. There was only the sea around us and the Manx gulls crying and wheeling above us. Anita and I stood side by side at the ship's rails a long time, not moving or speaking, just looking and looking at the spot where our lovely Island had been.

It had been a fantastic interlude in our lives and we had both been the right age, young enough to have no responsibilities or cares, yet old enough to appreciate everything that had been offered. It would always be a cherished part of our lives. Indeed I had lived on the Island longer than in my native Germany.

But the best part of it all is that the Isle of Man is ours forever. We can go back whenever we want, and if that's not always possible, I can go at any time in spirit.

I can walk down the lanes and along the shores in all seasons and weather. I can see the sea-pinks against the blue sea, the primroses nestling in the banks, the scarlet fuchsias, the golden gorse, and the blue sky beyond.

Whatever time, day or night, I wish to go, the beautiful Isle of Man is always there.

Waiting for me.

51. BRITISH SUBJECT

The war was over, at last!

Apart from a feeling of great relief, nothing, for our family at least, really changed. We were settled in Leeds and for two years had led a contented life.

Anita attended Lawnswood High School and Erika went to the local Infants' School. She also had a neighbourhood friend of her own age, coincidentally called Erica Dales! I worked in a wartime nursery, earning six times the amount I had in the camp, and Eberhard had a job in a woollen mill. Papa had the garden and an allotment and Mama had a delightful kitchen where she performed culinary miracles with our weekly rations. We had a grey cat and a chinchilla rabbit.

We loved our house and garden, we liked Headingley and Leeds City centre, unbombed, with a variety of large stores and shops but a tram ride away. But it wasn't Hull. We explored the beautiful surrounding countryside by bus, bicycle and on foot, but we missed the seaside.

We even had regular church services in German. These were held in the crypt of an Anglican church in town, and conducted by a refugee Lutheran pastor. He had a faithful little flock, who turned up without fail, to every meeting.

We could have stayed in Leeds, but it wasn't home and as soon as restrictions were lifted we jubilantly made arrangements to return to Hull. So we came back to Hull and Sunny Bank and picked up the threads of our life before the war. Anita went back to Newland, Erika went to Tusky's, I 'taught' at Skidby village school, and Eberhard found a temporary job in a laboratory. Papa reclaimed his old allotment and Mama her Sunny Bank kitchen. The little cat had come with us, the rabbit had been adopted by a Headingley neighbour.

One thing only remained to be done. Naturalisation. Papa sent for application forms. I had my own, filled it in, poised to sign it and hesitated. A thought had struck me.

"I can't do it!" I said, "I don't want to be naturalised!"

"Why ever not?" asked Papa, "it won't make much difference really."

"But if there's another war, we won't be interned if we're British," I explained.

"There will never be another war with Germany," said Papa, prophetically, "the next war, if there is one, will be with Russia."

I thought it over for a moment longer. One could always marry a Russian, I supposed. The idea did not appeal to me, and with a flourish, I signed my name.

So, in due course, I became a British subject and the proud possessor of a passport which would enable me to "pass freely without let or hindrance" in 'foreign lands' Officially and on paper, at least, I was no longer a 'foreigner'.